Code Collar 2030

Race Or Be Replaced

Victor Singh

Copyright © 2025 by Victor Singh Patpatia

ISBN: 978-82-693335-3-4

Copy Permissions & Reproduction: No part of this publication may be reproduced or transmitted without prior written permission, except in the case of brief quotations embodied in critical reviews, academic papers, and certain other non-commercial uses permitted by copyright law.

Marketing & Media: Permission is hereby granted for the reproduction of short excerpts, the book cover image, and the author's biography for promotional, marketing, or journalistic purposes, provided that full credit is given to Victor Singh Patpatia and the source is cited.

Limit of Liability/Disclaimer of Warranty: The information provided in this book is for educational and entertainment purposes only. While the author and publisher have used their best efforts in preparing this book, they make no representations or warranties with respect to the accuracy or completeness of the contents of this book and specifically disclaim any implied warranties of merchantability or fitness for a particular purpose. The advice and strategies contained herein may not be suitable for your situation. You should consult with a professional where appropriate. Neither the publisher nor the author shall be liable for any loss of profit or any other commercial damages, including but not limited to special, incidental, consequential, or other damages.

Cover Design: Assish

First Edition: 2025

Contents

Foreword By Maxim Salnikov 1

Introduction 4

Chapter 1 From Gutenberg to Zettabyte 9

Chapter 2 AI Evolution 18

Chapter 3 AI Literacy ABC 41

Chapter 4 Work 75

Chapter 5 Prompt craft and Writing Smarter 100

Chapter 6 Humans are Complex and Fallible ... 116

Chapter 7 Trust 151

Chapter 8 The country with no innovators? 159

Chapter 9 Generation Z and AI 184

Chapter 10 AI Cause of Job Polarization? 203

Chapter 11 Collaborative Partnership? 224

Chapter 12 Middle Managers 237

Chapter 13 When AI Manages $1.9 trillion 253

Chapter 14 Project Leaders 275

Chapter 15 Lawyers 295

Chapter 16 Software Engineering 311

Chapter 17 Real Estate Agent 329

Chapter 18 Universal Basic Income 344

Chapter 19 Where do we Go from here? 363

Afterword by Eirik Norman Hansen 370

Acknowledgement 374

Notes 375

Foreword By Maxim Salnikov

Over the past two decades, I've worked at the intersection of software development, cloud strategy, and most recently, AI transformation. Along the way, I've observed just how our roles as knowledge workers continue to evolve.

What once seemed like an exercise in incremental digital progress now resembles a tidal wave of change forced by the rise of generative AI. That's why I found *Code Collar 2030* by Victor Singh both timely and essential.

Victor first reached out to me over LinkedIn, and we quickly bonded over our mutual interest in AI. We soon engaged in a meaningful conversation about the societal shifts we're both passionate about, namely the role of technology and how it serves people, and the process of preparing professionals to lead, not just follow.

I am so glad I did, because AI technology is so fast-paced, there is no one book which is able to adequately cover the entire field. During our conversations Victor openly accepted that it's more about how we can responsibly leverage it but in doing so we need to understand the technology for ourselves, his book intends to set the stage for the conversations we all need to have. But this work manages to successfully give us tools we need to have more informed conversations about AI, and ask better questions - about our roles, our values, and the kind of future we want to build together.

This book articulates Victor's personal and provocative arguments on what AI truly means for the future of knowledge workers.

Victor doesn't shy away from hard questions. What happens when algorithms write code? Will project leaders and middle managers be replaced by autonomous agents when matters of trust, purpose, and work identity are redefined?

His subtitle - "Race or be Replaced" - captures a sense of urgency, but I prefer to frame it like this: Adopt AI fast to lead, stay competitive, serve better - and do so responsibly. After all, humans typically understand the pattern of our mistakes while spending a lot of time convincing others that the world works in a peculiar way. We are also typically very bad at performing risk assessments in the sense that we seem to be very optimistic about technology without fully understanding its consequences. This is especially the case when we try to make any sort of prediction about complex technologies, including AI. That is exactly what this book enables you to do; leverage the power of AI for your own success. Whether you're a developer, team lead, manager, policymaker, or simply curious knowledge worker, Code Collar 2030 will equip you with critical insights and critical ethical perspectives. And that you will find his work to be both reflective as he challenges us to think not just about what AI can do, but what we should do with it. I believe many readers will find themselves reflecting more deeply on AI's role in our future because of this work, especially as we enter a new phase of digital transformation - powered by the cloud and accelerated by this kind of AI centered technology.

Maxim Salnikov
AI Apps and Developer Productivity GTM Lead
Microsoft Western Europe
Keynote Speaker, Technical Community Builder

Introduction

Code Collar 2030 picks up where my first book, *Unleashing AI* (published in June 2023) left off. In that book, I discussed artificial intelligence (AI) and explored how AI could impact various aspects of our lives—creativity, policies, emotional intelligence, relationships, and more. It was a broad introduction, touching on many topics.

In this work, I'm focusing on something more specific: the complex relationship between AI and the "knowledge worker"— defined as someone whose value lies in thinking, analyzing, and creating. AI is reshaping the way we work, and I've spent a great deal of time thinking about what that means. Analysts and reports say that by 2030, while the world will have 170 million new jobs, separately, we will lose 92 million positions. Moreover, nearly 40% of what we can do in the workforce will no longer be relevant. The bottom line - AI is changing the very nature of "work". What are we going to do when most of it is automated?

Thinkers like Joseph Schumpeter, Peter Drucker, and John Maynard Keynes have shaped my thoughts on innovation, economic transformation, and the evolving nature of work. Their insights provide a valuable lens through which we can examine the present and future of knowledge-based professions in Norway.

Technology itself is not bad. But the amount of time it traditionally takes us as a society to understand and leverage it - wisely - has led to the invention of several destructive inventions throughout history (dynamite, gunpowder, and the Internet are a few of them). Still, technology has connected the entire world, given everyone a voice, and helped people find content they love. The same can be said for social media, which was built by algorithms. Algorithms, by design, promote whatever is most emotionally engaging—which is often, unfortunately, outrage, conflict, and misinformation. Human fallibility remains one of the biggest factors contributing to the delay in adapting to new technology. AI seems to be another example of our society's tendency to make mistakes, overestimate our abilities, or underestimate the complexity of new technological tools. For two decades, I've enjoyed various roles as a knowledge worker. Now, as AI fundamentally alters every knowledge worker's role, I find myself asking: what are we, as a society, losing as we relentlessly chase progress, and are we doing so not in a quest for increased efficiency – but more leisure time?

Deciding on a title is never easy, but my mind kept coming back to **code** and **collar**. "Code" felt like a natural choice—after all, at its core, artificial intelligence is nothing more than complex strings of computer code. But why pair it with "collar"? That term immediately brought to mind the familiar concept of "white-collar" work. "Collar" suggests an active effort to limit and control. We collar dogs, we're collared by dress codes, and increasingly, we talk about 'collaring' AI—putting guardrails on its capabilities, aligning it to human values, preventing runaway systems. The phrase 'code and collar' captures both what AI is (code) and what humans desperately trying to do to it (keep it in control/collar it).

"Collar" has always been about labor classification—blue-collar (manual), white-collar professional, pink-collar service, even the newer "gold-collar" specialized knowledge workers. Pairing it with "code" suggests a new category entirely: work done by or through code itself. The terms blue-collar and white-collar, which appear to have come into use first in the U.S. as early as the 1930s are widely understood to signify two very different kinds of jobs. Shirts with blue collars were work shirts, worn in factories, garages and mills. Shirts with white collars were worn by directors and vice presidents but also by accounting clerks and salespeople. It was made popular by the American writer Upton Sinclair and sociologist C. Wright Mills published *"White Collar: The American Middle Classes."* In it, he charts the decline of the old middle class of small business owners and the rise of professions and bureaucracies.

That said, "2030" felt like a fitting year for my title. For the more observant reader, who has noticed the subtitle *"race or be replaced"*, it's blunt. It's urgent. But it's also my invitation for you to learn, experiment— and hopefully make you think more critically. The alternative – being left behind - isn't much fun.

The book discusses through three broad themes. Some chapters are fully developed arguments. Others are deliberate provocations — starting points for reflection rather than conclusions. Both have their purpose.

You are holding something that cost more than it should have. I hope it earns that cost.

Chapter 1 From Gutenberg to Zettabyte

Skip this chapter if you already know how information evolved. Come back when you wonder why AI learned to write by reading everything humanity ever wrote.

Humans never stay the same— we are hardwired to push limits, chase ideas, and build things – all stemming from our ability to utilize language to pass along and build upon all information.

Humans have always been collectors of information. Today, that information—or data—is the fuel that makes AI work. But where did it all start? Long before we even had a language to speak, we were finding ways to record the world around us. This chapter traces that journey from ancient history to the massive digital world we live in today. The chapter explains how our oldest habits built the modern brains that now make us wonder if we still are the masters of our own information, or is the AI taking over?

Gutenberg's revolution

You are holding one of the most wildly successful, non-artificial pieces of technology in human history, and you are currently skimming through words on a sheer sheet of paper which took me over 18 months to produce. And there is a slight chance that you almost did what most students do these days — asked an AI to give you the gist in three bullet points, requested a summary of the whole book, or simply had it read to you as an audiobook. But here you are. Holding paper. Which, as it turns out, was once a privilege access to information reserved for only a handful of elites and scholars.

This all changed with Johannes Gutenberg's printing press around the early 1400s, which allowed quick and efficient text production. This burst of information – first from religious texts and scientific treatises, and then onto works of literature and political pamphlets emerged as the building blocks of shared knowledge, accessible to a wider audience than ever before. Of course, not all of this information was accurate. (Thanks to the printing press, the concept of misinformation isn't a new invention. But at least it didn't spread as quickly back then!) By 1500, an estimated twelve million printed works were circulating throughout Europe.

Because of the printing press, it soon became much cheaper to share ideas. For the first time, the middle-class could afford books, unlocking huge amounts of *human* potential.

This access to information ignited a cultural and intellectual revolution. For the first time, knowledge could be widely shared among the general population, empowering people with new ideas and challenging the authority of those who had long controlled the flow of information.

The printing press also facilitated the exchange of ideas, which in turn fueled scientific breakthroughs, social change, and artistic expression. It also played a crucial role in shaping cultural and linguistic development. Increases in the circulation of printed material allowed more and more people to learn how to read, leading to a surge in literacy rates across Europe.

The printing press is proof of the transformative power of technology. It broke down barriers to knowledge, fostered intellectual growth, and fueled social change. Its lasting legacy continues to inspire innovation today, reminding us of the profound impact that new ideas and technologies can have on the world.

Extra, Extra—the newspaper is born

In the lively town of Strasbourg in 1605, a small printing shop was producing the *Relation*, the world's first regularly issued news periodical. This was not just a simple pamphlet; it was well-organized and reliable, providing frequent updates on events happening both near and far. Catering to the early readers of newspapers, who were hungry for information about distant happenings and new developments, marked the dawn of a new era. News from distant lands soon reached readers on every continent, expanding beyond the traditional boundaries of any single city.

By 1661, newspapers were established in most major European cities and had evolved into serious communication tools which shaped public opinion, informed political discussions, and even sparked revolutions. This explosion of readily available information was crucial, even if the news spread slowly.

Morse code, radio, and TV

In 1825 several letters arrived too late about Lucretia, the pregnant wife of Samuel Morse. Sadly, by the time he returned to New Haven, Connecticut, she was already dead and buried. This tragedy deeply affected Morse and is often cited as a powerful motivation behind his desire to create a system for faster communication. He worked on a device that could transmit messages over wires using electrical signals.

This was called the telegraph, and the code he developed for it, Morse Code, revolutionized long distance communication. Various services continued to use it through the late 20th century, before it was largely replaced by more advanced communication systems, namely the telephone and radio.

Morse's telegraph inspired future innovations in electrical communication. Alexander Graham Bell, a Scottish teacher of the deaf and inventor, pursued his own vision, driven by his aspirations to communicate with his deaf wife and mother. As a professor in the field of sound and speech, he improved Morse's telegraphic device to allow for the transmission of the human voice, ultimately developed what he called a "harmonic telegraph" to transmit human voices - rather than just coded signals. On March 10, 1876, Bell successfully tested his invention and famously called his assistant through the device: *"Mr. Watson—Come here—I want to see you."* This invention eventually became known as - the telephone.

Even though people in Norway used the telephone as far back as 1877, it took time for it to be used widely throughout the population. In fact, this did not happen until around the First World War. By then, Norway had one of the highest telephone use densities in the world after Denmark and Sweden, but far behind the USA (which was in a unique position).

Although many people were still communicating over the wires, 22-year-old Guglielmo Marconi still dreamed of the ability to transmit messages wirelessly. Building upon the foundational principles of the telegraph and telephone, he patented his system of wireless telegraphy, which effectively allowed for the transmission of Morse Code signals over the air. Marconi invented radio communication on June 2nd, 1896. Suddenly, the world became more aware of its connections and provided households around the world with entertainment and information. Decades later, on September 7th 1927, another dreamer—Philo Farnsworth, a farm boy with an impossible vision—brought pictures to the air in the form of television. This technology has given people around the world a new way to gather information. However, it also handed governments a new way to manipulate its citizens with that same information. Still, at its core, television (TV) was invented as a means of entertainment, while also giving people a window to the world through faster information. Television became common in Norway during the 1960s, although official, regular broadcasts did not begin until August 1960. Throughout the decade, TV spread rapidly, and most households eventually owned a television set. Before that, only a small number of TV licenses had been issued in 1960, and coverage was limited to certain regions.

The Digital World

Each technological leap in communication—oral, written, printed, and electronic—refined our global reach. With each leap, the speed and amount of transmitted information grew, and took a new form, culminating with the invention of bits and bytes available on the internet. Suddenly, people no longer need to pursue knowledge - it just came to you, instantly, from anywhere in the world.

The internet was not created overnight. Early networks were clunky and limited, used mainly by academics and scientists. The most important shift arrived in 1983 with the invention of TCP/IP as a standard protocol. It allowed different computer networks to easily communicate with one another. The internet, as we know it, was born. In 1973, scientists at Norway's NORSAR facility at Kjeller established the first international satellite connection to ARPANET, making Norway one of the first two countries (alongside the UK) to link to the network from outside the US. Twenty years later (c. 1991 - 1992), Oslonett was one of Norway's first commercial Internet Service Providers (ISPs), and became prominent by 1993. Despite being one of the very first countries to be connected to the internet, for the average person on the street it was still something new and unfamiliar. However, that would soon change as technology improved and access expanded. Despite being one of the earliest connected countries in Europe, internet development in Norway eventually slowed as other countries began to adopt and incorporate the new technology, generally speaking, internet use was initially limited to a rather narrow circle: governments, universities, and so-called tech pioneers who helped to shape its early development. But in the 1990s, the advent of domain names gave websites their familiar, friendly names, and made the internet more accessible to the general public.

In 1991, Tim Berners-Lee introduced the World Wide Web, which transformed the internet from a mere network of computers into a visually relatable and accessible cyberspace. By the late 90s, personal sites, forums, and even social networking sites such as Six Degrees and Friendster began to mushroom, and over the next two decades laid the foundation upon which the social media revolution would blossom.

With each leap forward, the internet rewired how humans interacted: emails replaced letters, chat rooms connected complete strangers from opposite sides of the world, and the rise of social media platforms, including Facebook, Twitter, Instagram and TikTok, gave people completely new ways to share their lives and ideas - sometimes with profound consequences.

Then, in the late 2000s, AI came into play. Every search, every "like", every online experience allowed for the collection of data—. AI not only processes this information but learns from it. Search engines began to predict queries before people finished typing them into the on-screen text box. Social media algorithms soon understood people's interests better than they did. As we will discuss later, the internet continued to evolve into an enormous, self-expanding database that AI continued to absorb as it refined its understanding of human behavior. This 600-year journey from Gutenberg's press to today's data surge set the stage for AI's explosion - but the technology itself (AI) has a story equally worth understanding.

Chapter 2 AI Evolution

As explained in the previous chapter, AI is the culmination of centuries of progress in communication and information sharing.
The internet, often described as the nervous system of the modern world, serves as a training ground for AI. Its vast data streams enable AI systems to learn, adapt, and grow, highlighting the relationship between humanity's drive to communicate and AI's ability to process information. This chapter covers 75 years of evolution extensively, starting from its theoretical roots to its current state of rapid advancement.

The Dream of Thinking Machines

While the Nazi regime hosted the 1936 Summer Olympics, Europe stood on the brink of war. Meanwhile, a quiet British mathematician, Alan Turing, was busy laying the groundwork for a revolution no one saw coming. The 24-year-old published a paper about an imaginary machine which, given enough time and tape, could solve any mathematical problem. His 1936 seminal paper, "*On Computable Numbers*," introduced the "Turing Machine," a theoretical device that could carry out any calculation a human would be able to complete.

Another seminal article released in 1950, "*Computing Machinery and Intelligence*," asked "Can machines think?" In this same article he also presented the famous *"Turing Test"* as a benchmark for machine intelligence.

Turing proposed building *unorganized machines* that learned like children rather than simulating an adult intellect. Similar to how a child learns through interaction and education, these machines would adapt and improve through trial and error. Turing also introduced a test that would forever change the way we think about machines and intelligence. This test, known as the Turing Test, involved a human questioner, a human respondent, and a computer acting as a human respondent.

Through written correspondence, the questioner had to determine which 'respondent' was the human. If the machine could have a conversation with a human without being detected, it therefore demonstrated human-like intelligence.

In 1956, a group of visionaries gathered at Dartmouth College under the leadership of John McCarthy. This event, known as the Dartmouth Conference, marked the birth of AI as an academic field. Their ambition was clear: to create machines that could reason, learn, and solve problems.

The Checkers-Playing Program

In 1959, Arthur Samuel, an IBM engineer, coined the term "*machine learning.*" When he published a report called *"Some Studies in Machine Learning Using the Game of Checkers"* to describe this methodology, Samuel wrote: *The studies reported here have been concerned with the programming of a digital computer to behave in a way which, if done by human beings or animals, would be described as involving the process of learning. . . We have at our command computers with adequate data handling ability and with sufficient computational speed to make use of machine-learning techniques, but our knowledge of the basic principles of these techniques is still rudimentary. Lacking such knowledge, it is necessary to specify methods of problem solution in minute and exact detail, a time-consuming and costly procedure. Programming computers to learn from experience should eventually eliminate the need for much of this detailed programming effort.*

He developed a checkers-playing program which learned from its own mistakes, consequently improving its performance over time. This was a groundbreaking demonstration of how machines could learn from experience, laying out the foundation for future AI systems.

Symbolic AI and the rise of expert systems

In the 1960s and 1970s, researchers became interested in the concept of "Symbolic AI", in which knowledge was represented through symbols and subsequently manipulated using logical rules. During this time, researchers also developed expert systems designed to replicate the decision-making processes of human experts in various professional fields, including medicine.

In 1966, Joseph Weizenbaum at MIT created ELIZA, an early AI chatbot that simulated a psychotherapist. Using simple pattern matching, ELIZA gave the illusion of understanding, paving the way for advancements in natural language processing and conversational AI. During 1966–1970, the Stanford Research Institute introduced Shakey the Robot. Shakey was one of the first robots to integrate reasoning and physical actions, maneuver, and perform tasks. This innovation set the stage for AI-driven robotics.

Building on these advancements, in 1973 Professor Ichiro Kato at Waseda University released WABOT-1, the first humanoid robot capable of holding a conversation. It featured artificial electronic eyes (cameras) for distance and direction measurement, artificial ears for recognizing spoken Japanese, and an artificial mouth to respond, allowing for basic speech recognition and communication. Its hands also mimicked human fingers with tactile sensors, allowing them to grip and transport objects. Its legs could be used for bipedal walking on flat surfaces. Although slow and limited, this was revolutionary for its time. These systems represented one of the earliest examples of robotics blending with AI to simulate humanlike interactions and movements. Additionally, although WABOT-1 showed the primitive intelligence of a 1.5-year-old child, it was the first of later robotics projects aimed at achieving human-like behavior and adaptability.

In the 1980s, another central development in AI was taking shape. Richard Sutton, a computer scientist at the University of Alberta, pioneered a new approach called temporal difference learning. This method allowed machines to learn by constantly updating their predictions about the future based on their current experiences, essentially "learning a guess from a guess." Sutton's work laid the foundation for reinforcement learning, in which agents learn through trial and error by interacting with their environment and subsequently receiving feedback in the form of rewards or penalties.

The AI Winter and the Revival of Machine Learning

The field of AI faced significant challenges due to overstated promises that failed to deliver practical results. Additionally, any early successes were limited by the difficulty of representing real-world knowledge in symbolic form, along with computational limitations of the time. This challenging period, from 1987 to 1993, was commonly referred to as *"AI Winter."* Symbolic AI and expert systems, which relied on rule-based logic, could not adapt to complex, practical problems. These systems were also expensive and required constant updates. Additionally, progress was slowed by limited computational power and inadequate storage. All of these problems contributed to the AI Winter, which was accelerated by all the hype behind AI research, along with a slowdown in development.

As AI systems underperformed, public disillusionment grew. Governments and organizations began cutting funding and shifting their focus to other technologies. This damaged AI's reputation and reduced interest in the field, leaving researchers with fewer resources to advance their work. This period of stagnation persisted until the late 1990s when the field was restored through breakthroughs in machine learning and neural networks. Machine learning really began to flourish as its practitioner integrated statistics and probability theory into their approaches. At the same time, the personal computing revolution began. Over the next decade, digital systems, sensors, the internet, and mobile phones became commonplace, and provided all sorts of data for machine learning experts to utilize while training adaptive systems.

Deep Learning

In 1997, IBM's Deep Blue made history by defeating chess champion Garry Kasparov, showcasing the raw power of AI and creating headlines worldwide. An equally important milestone was quietly taking shape in neuroscience. Researchers Wolfram Schultz, Peter Dayan, and P. Read Montague published a groundbreaking paper in *Science* titled *"A Neural Substrate of Prediction and Reward."* They essentially discovered how our brains learn. They found that dopamine neurons, which are responsible for feelings of pleasure and reward, play a key role in a process called *"prediction error."* Simply put, our brains constantly compare what we expect to happen with what actually happens. If the outcome is better than expected, dopamine neurons fire, signaling a reward and reinforcing the behavior that led to it.

This process is remarkably similar to how some AI systems learn, adapting their behavior based on feedback and rewards.

This breakthrough in neuroscience went largely unnoticed but quietly laid the foundation for future AI development. By understanding how the brain learns through the release of dopamine, scientists were able to design smarter algorithms that mimic human learning.

Around the same time, the internet and personal computers became increasingly popular, and also generating massive amounts of data.

This data proved to be the fuel for AI machine learning. Additionally, the programming language Python emerged as a powerful tool for AI research. Its simple syntax and extensive libraries made it easier for researchers and developers to create and experiment with AI algorithms. Breakthroughs in neuroscience, the data explosion, and the rise of programming languages like Python all set the stage for an AI revival.

In 2006, Geoffrey Hinton and his team at the University of Toronto reignited the field with their work on deep neural networks, demonstrating their power in tasks like image recognition and language translation. The era of deep learning had begun, and with it, a new chapter in the evolution of AI.

The 2010s marked a turning point with the emergence of deep learning, a subfield of machine learning that uses artificial neural networks with multiple layers (hence "deep") to extract higher-level features from data. It was around this period that AI really started learning from data and evolved beyond only rule-based learning. Another breakthrough, multimodal, occurred during the 2010s, when AI began utilizing images, music, videos and text, and AI Agents started processing and integrating information from multiple sources. In 2012, computer scientists Alex Krizhevsky, Ilya Sutskever, and Geoffrey Hinton at the University of Toronto managed another breakthrough with the development of AlexNet, which won the ImageNet competition using deep learning techniques. This achievement affirmed deep learning's ability to complete visual recognition tasks by giving the machine lots of examples to learn from – all thanks to the researcher Fei-Fei Li, who co-created ImageNet. She provided a massive dataset of labeled images (training data) that has been crucial for training AI systems in visual recognition. Before this evolution, deep learning, experts had to spend a significant amount of time teaching computers what to look for during a search. Deep learning allowed computers to figure things out on their own. As computers became faster and had more access to available data, deep learning programs became more efficient at a variety of tasks, including image comprehension. Deep learning basically changed how computers learn - and how they interact with their users.

Modern AI Era

AI's journey continued with Ian Goodfellow's 2014 introduction of Generative Adversarial Networks, which tasked one network to generate false data, while another attempted to identify it to ultimately create realistic images, videos, and art.

In 2016, Google DeepMind's AlphaGo made headlines by defeating world champion Go player Lee Sedol, a victory which demonstrated AI's ability to learn and excel in complex, creative games that required intuition. Go is an ancient Chinese board game that is much more complex than chess.

Google's BERT model, introduced in 2018, revolutionized natural language processing by helping machines better understand word context in sentences. This advancement led to more accurate search engines, chatbots, and voice assistants.

During the 2020s, AI started becoming more autonomous, and was able to set goals, and develop paths to attain these goals without constant human intervention.

The release of OpenAI's GPT-3 in 2020 (and its 175 billion parameters) showcased the true power of large language models. Capable of generating human-like text across various tasks, GPT-3 marked a major milestone in generative AI. November 2022 when OpenAI posted they released ChatGPT 3.5 for public. Bets were placed on how many people would actually try it within the first week. The smart money, apparently, underestimated humanity's curiosity, because over one million people signed up in seven days. For the first time in history, ordinary people — not researchers, not engineers, not people with three PhDs and a government grant — could sit down, open a browser, and have a conversation with a large language model. The model in question was GPT-3.5, and it was, to put it mildly, a lot to process. So was the waitlist.

AI played a crucial role in drug discovery in 2021, speeding up vaccine development during the COVID-19 pandemic. AI-powered tools also saw increased use in medical diagnostics and early disease detection.

In December 2021, Anthropic was founded and tasked with the primary mission of developing safe and reliable AI systems that are beneficial to humanity. The Claude Android app was later released, which expanded the reach of its AI chatbot to a broader audience. The company has received significant investments from companies such as Google and Amazon.

In 2023, AlphaDev and GNoME launched even more significant science-related AI applications which made the process of algorithmic sorting more efficient and increased the efficiency of discovering materials.

The same year, OpenAI introduced its multimodal GPT-4 to the public, which featured increased comprehension along with the ability to generate both text and images. GPT-4 effectively expanded AI's potential to process complex inputs and perform tasks like generating captions for photos. In 2023, there were 25 AI-related regulations on the books, up from just one in 2016. The following year, 2024, the total number of AI-related regulations increased by 56.3%.

AI-driven autonomous vehicles made significant strides in 2023, with companies like Tesla and Waymo pushing the boundaries of self-driving technology using deep learning, sensors, and reinforcement learning.

Google is known to not move until they were certain they wouldn't jeopardize their billion-dollar business revenue which they were getting through the ad revenues. But seeing the competition, Google was not left with any choice. On December 6, 2023,

Google launched Gemini, a new generative AI model and chatbot designed to compete with OpenAI's GPT-4. Gemini incorporated advanced natural language understanding and multimodal capabilities, processing text, images, and sounds. Following an initial integration into Google's Bard chatbot, Gemini was expected to expand across various Google services. In 2024, AI technologies like DALL • E and MidJourney continued to disrupt the art world, enabling users to create hyper-realistic artwork from text prompts. This sparked debates about the role of human creativity in AI-generated content.

On February 15, 2024, OpenAI announced Sora, a revolutionary text-to-video model capable of generating videos from text prompts. This marked a significant leap forward in generative AI technology, enabling the creation of realistic and imaginative video content from text inputs.

Weeks later, Apple announced its new Private Cloud Compute service, designed to handle more complex AI queries. This service runs on Apple Silicon servers, ensuring the same level of privacy as their consumer devices. Apple also plans to collaborate with other generative AI services, including Google Gemini.

Meanwhile, Elon Musk's X is reportedly exploring deeper integration of xAI's Grok chatbot into its social networking platform X (Twitter). This development suggests X is working to enhance Grok's capabilities and increase its presence within the app. Musk also claims that his Neuralink division had successfully implanted its first wireless brain chip into a human.

The Ballie Samsung AI companion, which was first announced in 2020, will act as a personal home assistant, autonomously driving around the home to complete various tasks.

The same year, in March 2024, three new Norwegian language models were released, built on GPT-like architectures Bloom and Mistral and published under open-source licenses. Developed by researchers at the University of Oslo in collaboration with Sigma2 and the National Library, the project is part of a national effort under the NORA AI network to build shared infrastructure for large Norwegian language models.

Two models were trained entirely from scratch on Norwegian data, while the third was adapted from an English model by the French company Mistral AI. Altogether, the models were trained on more than 30 billion Norwegian words.

On 20th January, 2025 DeepSeek, a Chinese AI company, stunned the tech world with its app, quickly becoming the most downloaded free app in the U.S., surpassing even ChatGPT. Specializing in LLMs, DeepSeek developed a powerful AI system for just $5.6 million—much cheaper than its Western competitors. This disruption triggered massive losses for AI giants like Nvidia and Microsoft, and DeepSeek's decision to make its model open source further accelerated global AI progress. The company's success also helped to intensify competition between the U.S. and China over AI leadership.

This rapid progress in AI has been fueled by massive financial investments, reflecting the growing recognition of its transformative potential. To date, 80% of the $56 billion invested in generative AI has flowed into U.S. based companies, leaving Europe and Asia to compete for the remaining 20%. A staggering $37 billion—has already been directed toward American companies building foundation models, which are the cornerstones of modern AI innovation.

High-profile players dominate this landscape. Microsoft backed OpenAI, creator of the groundbreaking ChatGPT, raised $6.6 billion, while Anthropic secured $4 billion in funding from Amazon.

Elon Musk's xAI attracted $6 billion in May 2024 to develop its own AI vision. Meanwhile, tech giants such as Google (Gemini), Meta (Llama), Microsoft (Copilot), and Musk's X (Grok AI, developed by xAI) are all locked in a fierce race to push the boundaries of LLMs.

These investments highlight the strategic importance of AI to both corporations and nations. For the U.S., the focus is clear: dominance in foundational AI technologies to secure economic and geopolitical leverage. Europe, by contrast, must grapple with its comparatively modest funding and find new ways to compete by leveraging its regulatory expertise, ethical frameworks, and niche innovation.

From Turing to AGI

Goldman Sachs assessed in their Q4 report 2025 that Artificial General Intelligence (AGI) capable of carrying out work "indistinguishable" from human output could wipe out a fourth of the world's current jobs, and nearly 50-60 percent of all knowledge professions worldwide. What happens if we innovate a form of AI that can learn, think, and adapt across a broad spectrum of activities - better than humans? The impact could be far reaching, altering not only specific jobs but the entire structure of the global workforce. If history is any guide, could we also eventually find ourselves engaged in a new "civil war", between machines and humans?

AGI refers to AI systems that can complete any intellectual task that a human can perform. While we're not there yet, progress towards something like agentic AI is more definable. This system has the capability of independently executing complex tasks. While these systems are indeed transformative, they are also fundamentally different from AGI, which represents the ability to think, reason, and adapt across all domains like humans.

I wonder how future generations will earn a living, and how their output will be measured. Perhaps universal basic income will become a reality, as in receiving compensation simply for being a member of society. Or maybe there will be programs that teach people new skills for the ever-changing job market (reskilling). Agentic AI might seem like AGI due to its autonomy and versatility, but it lacks the ability to develop what we call "general knowledge" across various professional fields within knowledge work —a hallmark of AGI.

Humans generate approximately 402.74 million terabytes of data every single day. It is estimated that a significant portion of the world's data has been created in only the last several years, facilitated by advancements in technology and the increasing digitization of our lives.

Over the span of 13 years, the global data volume has surged from 2 zettabytes in 2010 to approximately 149 zettabytes in 2024 — an astounding increase of nearly 75%. The world's three wealthiest companies, in terms of data, are Alphabet Inc. (Google), Meta (Facebook), and Amazon. These tech giants dominate not just because of their financial wealth, but because they have amassed and refined enormous datasets that power their business models. Google, for example, holds vast amounts of search data and user behavior insights, Meta controls social media data from billions of users, and Amazon collects extensive consumer purchasing and product data.

This historical overview of AI development highlights a fundamental truth about humans: technological progress is seldom the result of a singular genius but rather the product of many researchers, engineers, and thinkers working collaboratively over time.

It also reveals a recurring theme in technological history: innovations often precede their most significant applications. Many inventions find their true purpose only after being created and repeatedly refined. From Turing's early computational ideas to today's advancements in deep learning, AI's evolution reflects our growing understanding of human thought and its potential to be replicated in machines.

However, the broader information/digital revolution (computers → internet → AI) that began in the 19th century is nearing completion. As of massive investments started pouring during the late 20th century, many businesses are still struggling to grapple the full implications of this "AI race". While AI promises to revolutionize industries and solve global challenges, it's rise also raises concerns about job displacement, algorithmic bias, and the ethical dilemmas of relying on increasingly powerful machines.

Control in the complex world of AI?

As the world tries to understand all that's "new" with AI, if you read my first book, you might remember the AI Act. One year after its passing, the European Union officially implemented this global standard for ethical AI practices, effective 01 of August 2024, and required accountability and transparency from AI developers. It was the world's first comprehensive AI law, which is similar to the GDPR (related to privacy.) The new AI act directly targets the most concerning uses of artificial intelligence—prohibiting intrusive social scoring systems that diminish human complexity to numbers, shutting down unfettered bio-metric surveillance that imperil our basic freedoms, as well as criminalizing manipulative AI aimed at taking advantage of human vulnerabilities.

Most importantly, perhaps, this rule will finally bring the most advanced models in the industry under regulatory control, when it becomes active on August 2, 2025. This includes OpenAI's powerful GPT-4, Google's cutting-edge Gemini, and Anthropic's subtle Claude 3.5 —effectively putting an end to the AI Wild West, while ushering in a new era of more reflective – and cautious technological governance.

AI and the remaking of work

I believe most experts tend to underplay this technology, much like many did about the internet when it was "new." It's easy to underestimate how much an AI influenced world can change within a lifetime, and how it continues to impact the changing nature of work in the post-industrial era, reflecting a broader transformation in how society views the role of work in people's lives. Every technology has positive and negative consequences. However, when it comes to AI, the range of these consequences is extraordinarily, even as it enjoys a widely recognized and significant potential for good.

Still, it comes with significant downsides and high risks. In this latest technological evolution, we also slowly witnessed the rise of the knowledge economy in the mid-20th century, where information and technology became the primary drivers of global economic growth, which the internet made possible. As our economies became more reliant on knowledge and innovation, the traditional manufacturing-based job market began to shrink, giving way to new forms of work centered around technology and services. Historical data from SSB shows that since 1950, more than 20 percent of the Norwegian population worked in agriculture. However, by 2020, that figure dropped to less than 2 percent. For the last several years, the traditional "primary" industries (fishing, agriculture, etc.) currently account for about only 2 percent of total employment, compared to 13 percent in 1970. This is a startling statistic given the fact that farmers represent such a small percentage, yet are essentially responsible for feeding the rest of the population. This shift reflects a major transformation in the economy, where industrialization, automation, and the growth of the service sector have fundamentally changed how people work and where they find jobs. technological advancement, including those seen during the Industrial Revolution, often resulted in significant disruptions to labor markets. Entire sectors, like traditional crafts and agriculture, faced widespread job losses as machines took over tasks once performed by human hands. However, these changes also created new industries, such as railroads, textiles, and steel, which provided opportunities for employment and contributed to higher living standards for many. While this historical pattern suggests that new jobs will emerge with the rise of AI, such as new job opportunities, especially in data analytics, machine learning, and AI development, this time around a successful transition may be more elusive. Historians have warned of the potential creation of a *"useless class"*, a segment of the population rendered economically irrelevant due to AI and automation.

According to research done by Epoch in 2025, the evolution of AI is 30 times faster than anything before, and one should be concerned about a paradoxical future in which unemployment rates could soar even as businesses struggle to fill positions requiring advanced technical skills. In other words, rapid technological change has always been about humans becoming more efficient and productive, but knowing our human nature, we are still trying to grasp these complexities in order to ensure AI benefits us all. As I end this chapter, I am both worried and excited; after all, AI is human-made, and history has proven countless times that we are unpredictable and sometimes don't make the best judgments. Should we continue to let machines do our best thinking at work, or are we able to learn how to work alongside AI and use it to enhance our own creativity and solve 'unsolvable' problems? The rest of this book will cover many of the knowledge worker professions — why they are still important, and how to leverage them. In the end, I hope to provide you with a more critical understanding of it all. Hype and fear about AI obscure a simple fact- these are not magical creatures or living entities, but sophisticated tools developed by humans, with all our genius and prejudices. To map our machine-assisted future, we need to demystify the workings of the machine.

Chapter 3
AI Literacy ABC

As of December 2024, nearly 50% of Norwegian businesses had no clear strategy for implementing AI or measuring its effectiveness. Furthermore, Statistics Norway (SSB) reports that only 24% of organizations with more than ten employees are currently using AI tools. Before reading any further, it's best to understand what AI is and how it actually learns. For simplicity, in this chapter I will refer to these technologies by their acronyms – AI, MI, and their subfields, and this will be the default throughout most of this book.

What is AI?

Consulting firms and business often believe AI is represented into three boxes:
Data→Model→Value (shown below). However, it is in fact something much more complex, and its development requires tons of groundwork (prompting, fine-tuning, memory, using the tools, orchestration) before a single model is trained. We also need to be honest about the bias, hosting, security, and cost factors.

I don't blame people, since AI lacks a universally accepted definition, leading to varying interpretations. I will use a very simple definition from my previous book, *"Unleashing AI."* AI isn't like a person. Rather, it's more like a tool. AI doesn't think, feel, or understand in any human sense. It doesn't have consciousness, intentions, or desires. But it is a sophisticated technology that processes data, recognizes patterns, and generates output based on statistical probabilities.

It's more like a "very clever" tool that we humans built. Its purpose is to simulate some parts of how we think (brain). Think of it this way: we built AI to copy certain parts of how our brains work. Not the whole brain, not consciousness, not emotions, just specific thinking processes. AI takes enormous amounts of information and searches through it looking for patterns that humans might miss or take forever to find. Once it discovers these patterns, it uses them to make predictions or decisions about whatever task we've given it. It does this by looking at huge amounts of information (data) to find patterns. Then, it uses these patterns to make educated guesses or decisions to achieve a specific goal we give it. And it's always learning to get better at that one job. They're not just tools we use—they're more like digital assistants that can actually *do* things, not just *suggest* things.

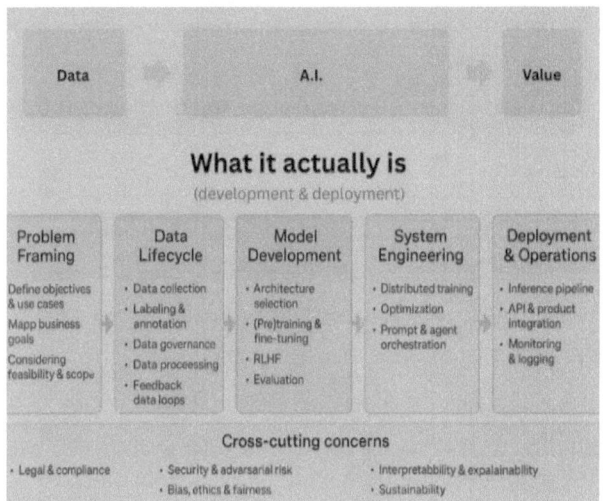

Every AI system relies on three core ingredients

1. **Data** (the raw material)
2. **Algorithms** (the processes that find patterns)
3. **Models** (the trained output we use in applications)

Data is Alpha & Omega

Despite Gutenberg's groundbreaking innovation in information distribution, the Internet has transformed access to knowledge in ways he could never have imagined. Incredibly, nearly ninety percent of all the data that currently exists on the Internet was generated between 2021 and 2023, driven by advancements in technology and the increasing digitization of our lives. In 2024, it's projected that 402.74 million terabytes of data will be created every single-day. This data continues to serve as raw material - the fundamental component of information. Think of it like this: if information used to be documented on ink and paper, now it's all collected on digital bits and pieces. Every Google search, every social media post, every online purchase creates new pieces of information which are instantly stored, analyzed, and shared across the globe through this ever-expanding sea of information—our contemporary ink and paper.

Numerical Data	Categorical Data
Time Series Data	Text

The amount of data generated annually has grown exponentially since 2010. In fact, between 2010 and

2024, global data volume surged from 2 to approximately 149 zettabytes, an astounding increase of nearly 75%. Because data is a crucial component of AI development, allowing it to predict and understand with startling accuracy, data labeling has become increasingly important. When machines learn, they work with four main types of data. *Numerical data* consists of numbers used for measurements, such as temperature, height, or price. *Text data* is made up of words and sentences, which includes emails, articles, or social media posts. *Time series data* is a sequence of numbers collected at regular intervals over a period of time and is often used to predict future trends. For example, the Norwegian Oil Fund often uses time series data to determine which stocks to invest in, all with the assistance of their AI system. Finally, *Categorical data* represents distinct groups, such as gender (female/male), species (animal/human) or health related (Healthy/infected). AI often utilizes this process to focus on a particular data set.

Algorithms

AI has two core components, data and algorithms. These algorithms dive deep into the vast ocean of digital information, sifting through countless streams, identifying patterns, making predictions, and occasionally mimicking humans with shocking effectiveness. For example, social media platforms now understand its users so well they curate feeds to their liking with alarming accuracy. AI continuously evolves and shapes your online experience—often when you don't realize it's happening.

In this manner, the internet has become a vast training ground for this new type of intelligence that learns from our digital trails. AI's role in our modern day lives not only alters how we work but also shifts the balance of power in the modern world. It begs the question - do those who control the most data also control the future?

An algorithm is a step-by-step instruction to solve a problem. So, the basics of computer science is not only how to represent any information but also how to process the information.

Models

AI needs to be "taught" with training data using models, which is the information given to an AI in order to help it learn how to perform specific tasks. Testing data is the information used to check whether an AI is reliable and accurate.

OpenAI GPT-5, Claude Sonnet 4.5, and Gemini 2.5 Pro are all known Large Language Models (LLMs). Below is the historical graph showing advancements within the field, which emerged in 2017. Since then, the capabilities of LLMs have progressed dramatically. In fact, as of 2025, various sources claim there are more than 1.000 models available to help solve various real-world tasks.

A Brief History of LLMs

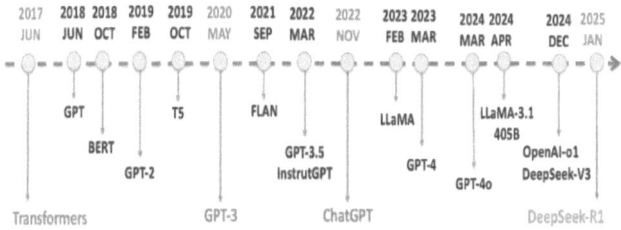

Creating datasets for training AI models/applications begins with the process of accurately labeling data. The addition of relevant labeling, specifically text tags, image annotations, and

3D object recognition, improves the efficiency of AI development.

Data which is augmented with tags provides additional context through the use of semantic algorithms. In addition to A providing an extra layer of analysis, they also ensure that the data is secure and in compliance with data privacy laws.

Large Language Models—the AI systems behind ChatGPT and similar tools—have essentially consumed the entire written internet: news articles, Wikipedia, scientific papers, novels, even social media posts. They've read more text than any ever human could in a thousand lifetimes, absorbing patterns in how we write, think, and communicate.

But reading everything isn't enough. These systems need to prove they are capable of learning. That's where testing data comes in—fresh information the AI has never seen before, used to check if it can apply its knowledge to new situations. Think of this phase as a student's final exam after years of studying.

The result? AI systems that can write poetry, debug computer code, analyze customer sentiment, and hold conversations that feel surprisingly human or even create music. All because we found a way to transform human knowledge into a language machine we can understand.

Five key capabilities of AI

There isn't one single, universally agreed upon list of exactly five "capabilities" that fully define AI. But based on my previous book, and the consensus among professionals, AI as technology seems to replicate or surpass human intelligence. According to the following five capabilities components:

1. How it learns
2. How it reasons and decides on a certain outcome
3. How it solves problems
4. How it interprets and perceives information, and
5. How it executes tasks autonomously (agents, robotics)

Each of these components play a key role in how AI systems function, by improving their ability to interact with its surroundings, humans, along with its ability to perform complex tasks. However, an AI system does not necessarily need to have all five of these components to be called AI. Different AI systems are designed for different purposes and might emphasize certain components more than others. More advanced and general-purpose AI systems will likely incorporate several or all of these components to a significant degree.

For instance, a sophisticated virtual assistant like the ones on smartphones uses Natural Language Processing (**NLP**) to understand your voice, reasoning to process your requests, problem-solving to find information or perform actions, and potentially incorporate Machine Learning to personalize its responses and learn your preferences. Some might even incorporate perception if they can process images or video.

How AI learns?

How AI learns is often associated with Machine Learning (**ML**), which is a subfield of AI that focuses on developing computer systems that can learn directly from data without following explicit pre-set instructions. AI models are typically trained using large quantities of data, which can be labeled, unlabeled, or a mix of both (with or without human intervention). This training process allows the model to learn underlying patterns and improve its predictions.

Over time, as the model is exposed to new data—or receives feedback through user interactions. It can also be refined by updating its parameters based on new information, allowing it to gradually become more accurate at making predictions. A model is then evaluated by testing it on data the model has never encountered before. Evaluating the model on unseen data helps assess its generalized ability and suitability for the intended problem. Finally, once the model is trained and evaluated, it can be deployed in real-world applications. There are many types of machine learning, including supervised learning, unsupervised learning, reinforcement learning, and deep learning (DL). Deep learning uses neural-network technology for its learning process. Think of neural networks as computer programs inspired by the brain's structure. They learn complex patterns from data by passing numbers through layers of interconnected 'neurons.' By analyzing vast amounts of examples, these connections get adjusted until the program becomes highly efficient at tasks like understanding and generating language, a capability we'll look further into in this chapter.

Generative AI is built by transformers which rely on different learning techniques to process data, primarily using supervised and unsupervised learning. While their learning approaches overlap, they help achieve different goals and have different applications. The foundation of any ML model is the dataset used to train it; the quality and quantity of data are essential for accurate predictions and performance. After the data is collected, ML model developers must choose what they want the model to do, and what information to use. After they create an architecture, parameters, which are adjustable values within the model, influence its performance. During training, the model learns from the provided data and modifies its parameters to minimize errors. Machine learning models are mainly categorized into four primary types. Supervised learning, unsupervised learning, semi-supervised learning and reinforcement learning.

Supervised Learning

ML is designed for specific tasks, meaning its learning method depends on the problem it is solving. One of the most common techniques used in ML is supervised learning, in which the system is trained on labeled data, and uses a labeled dataset to learn the relationship between input data and output labels.

For instance, Norway's banking sector uses supervised learning to detect fraud. Banks such as DNB and Nordea train AI models using historical transaction data, where fraudulent and legitimate transactions are labeled. The model learns to identify patterns in fraudulent behavior, such as unusual spending activity or transactions from foreign locations. Over time, the AI improves its accuracy in predicting fraudulent transactions before they occur. Among the many algorithms used for supervised learning, *Random Forests* are considered one of the most reliable "off-the-shelf" classification methods. They combine the results of many decision trees to deliver high accuracy, handle both categorical and numerical data, and require minimal tuning, making them ideal for practical AI applications like fraud detection

Unsupervised Learning

Most AIs learn like a diligent student, but with a teacher hovering nearby, pointing out right and wrong answers. But some AI systems work more like detectives—they're handed a pile of evidence and told to figure out the mystery on their own.

This is called unsupervised learning, and it's exactly what it sounds like: no supervision, no handholding, just raw pattern recognition at work.

That type of unsupervised learning involves training a model on a dataset without specific output labels. A practical example is Telenor's AI-driven network monitoring system, which detects anomalies in mobile network traffic. The AI identifies unusual activity, such as sudden spikes in data usage, which could indicate a cyberattack or technical fault. Since there are no predefined labels for what constitutes an "attack," the AI clusters data and flags deviations from the norm *(The most common unsupervised learning method in AI is clustering, particularly K-Means, because it's simple, efficient, and works well across many types of data.)*.

While machine learning holds promise for analysis of images on a mammogram, Cancer Registry of Norway scientists are pursuing a more ambitious frontier: detecting cancer decades before a tumor even forms. Using unsupervised learning, scientists have begun analyzing RNA signatures in blood serum for lung, breast, and colon cancers.

Unlike traditional methods that look for visible masses, this approach identifies "molecular whispers"—patterns in our biology that begin to shift and evolve up to ten years before symptoms or a diagnosis appear. The results have been particularly striking in lung cancer, confirming that the body's chemistry changes long before current diagnostic tools can "read" the danger.

Reinforcement Learning

Imagine learning to ride a bicycle without anyone explaining balance, steering, or pedaling. You'd simply hop on, fall off, get back up, and try again—each crash teaching you something new. This is exactly how Reinforcement Learning works: AI systems learn by doing, failing, and gradually getting better. The most foundational reinforcement learning algorithm is Q-Learning, though modern applications typically use more advanced methods like PPO (Proximal Policy Optimization).

Norway's Gjensidige Insurance has developed an AI-based customer service chatbot that continuously improves its responses based on user interactions. By learning from customer feedback, the chatbot refines its ability to answer questions more accurately over time. RL is unique in the sense that it does not require pre-collected data. The AI can begin with no information and interact with its environment to learn new things.

There is a possibility that a model trained for fraud detection in one bank may not perform well in another. Generative AI, on the other hand, relies on vast datasets, which can contain biases. Biases are systematic errors in judgments and decision-making that occur in the processing and interpretation of information. The root causes of those errors are often the unconscious tendency of all humans to favor or discriminate against something or someone in a way that is not objective or neutral. That bias consequently leads AI to produce biased results or reasoning. This is very similar to how our brains work. The generative models in our brain work like an internal representation of our environment, a mental model built from how we perceive our surroundings, our past experiences, our social learning, and social education, all of which allows us to predict things before they happen. Our brain collects actual sensory data, such as visual, auditory, somatosensory, and feelings, and compares all of it with the data predicted by its simulation. This is how we can identify most surprises before they happen in our surroundings.

However, humans often end up making biased decisions, which results in skewed or unfair outcomes. Similarly, generative AI models can sometimes produce outputs that are factually incorrect or nonsensical hallucinations, underscoring the need for careful human oversight. There are ethical concerns with both types of AI, including privacy, job displacement, and the potential misuse of this technology.

What if AI could not only create, but also take action based on its own results or decisions? Agentic AI can reason, plan, and act on their own to handle complex workflows with much more autonomy, while simultaneously creating high-quality output. They're like self-driving cars that navigate complex road conditions, making split-second decisions to ensure your safety. Or think of Devin AI, the AI software engineer that can design, code, and deploy entire software projects. And then there's Forethought's AI, a customer service whiz that can handle complex queries, engage in natural conversations, and take action to resolve issues quickly and efficiently. No AI may perfectly replicate human intelligence. The brain is a vastly complex organ, and fortunately, there's no true general AI yet. The possibility of such machines, however, motivates much of the AI industry.

Deep Learning

DL minimizes human intervention further. It is an advanced ML that learns datasets ranging from a small amount to petabytes using neural networks. According to Andrew Ng, Deep Learning is an advanced ML technique. Ng, one of the few world-renowned experts in this field, believes access to more data seems to produce better predictions. DL teaches computers how to perform tasks by learning from examples, as well as filtering inputs through layers in order to learn how to better predict and classify sources of information. This occurs regardless of whether DL has access to sound, video, picture, or text. Other AIs such as Convolutional Neural Networks (CNNs) - which are used in image recognition - and Recurrent Neural Networks (RNNs), which are used in sequential data like speech and text processing. Lastly, we have transformers, and I am not talking about Hasbro Autobot action figures.

These transformers are advanced models used in natural language understanding. This type of AI uses learning based on past experiences to make informed future decisions. Similar to how humans learn from experience, a deep learning algorithm can perform a task repeatedly, each time adjusting it to improve the outcome. In many ways one can say that Deep Learning is very much inspired by how our human brain works when we try to reason to produce a sound solution.

AI reasoning is where the machine relies on any software to autonomously draw conclusions and make interpretations. After being given data/rules, they are subsequently designed, programmed, and trained by humans.

These are divided into inductive and deductive reasoning. Some examples include self-driving cars, IBM's Watson Assistant which combines deduction-based rule-based dialogue flows, statistical language models (induction), and retrieval-based inference (abduction) to respond to user queries. Additionally, ROSS legal expert AI leverages large-scale legal text embeddings (induction) plus rule-based filters (deduction) to recommend relevant case law. Through reasoning, AI systems simulate human-like decision-making and problem-solving capabilities to arrive at a decision. Still, we know the rules it's following and the knowledge it contains. After all, it's still just an algorithm.

Retrieval-Augmented Generation

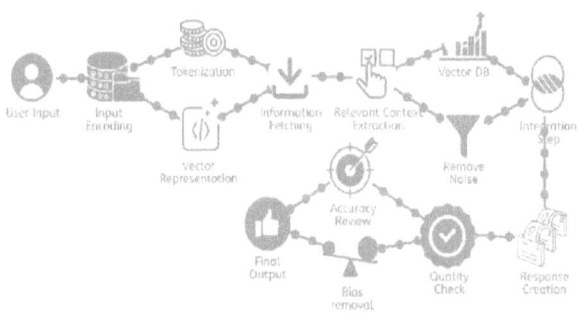

Traditional AI models are like my friend who is stuck in the past. ChatGPT, for instance, has a knowledge cutoff date—it literally doesn't know what happened after its training ended. Ask about yesterday's news, and you'll get an educated guess based on old patterns, not actual facts.

LLMs are limited to their pre-trained data which may also contain inaccuracies or biases. This leads to outdated and potentially inaccurate responses.

Conversely, Retrieval-Augmented Generation (RAG) is a brilliant technology which is sometime called a "smart fact-checking machine"—though as we'll see, this label oversimplifies what it actually does.

Think of RAG as giving AI systems a research assistant with access to a curated knowledge base—such as company documents, academic papers, or product manuals. When combined with web search tools, RAG-enhanced systems can also retrieve current internet sources, though this requires additional integration.

When you ask a question, the RAG-enhanced AI doesn't just rely on its pre-programmed knowledge. Instead, it acts like a brilliant student taking an open-book exam. The student flips through the textbook looking for sections that seem relevant—scanning headings and keywords. The student finds passages that match — not by understanding deeply, but by pattern-matching words and concepts. Then the student combines what they found with their own understanding to write an answer.

Think of it another way most us use internet these days to search for information. When looking for answers online, we encounter a mix of reliable and unreliable sources. Basic RAG faces the same challenge—it retrieves what's most similar to your question, not necessarily what's most accurate.

However, well-engineered RAG implementations can add layers of sophistication: reranking algorithms to prioritize higher-quality sources, metadata filtering to exclude outdated documents, and citation verification to cross-check claims. Similar to how modern search engines rank and filter web pages, these additional components—not RAG itself—assess information quality and thereby minimizing errors and improving the reliability of generated responses. RAG grounds AI-generated text in retrieved documents rather than relying solely on trained patterns. This significantly reduces hallucination and enables access to information beyond the model's training cutoff. A fair warning to you, the quality of RAG output depends entirely on two factors: *what's in the knowledge base* and *how much engineering goes into retrieval and filtering*. Garbage in, garbage out still applies. Much like what you find by googling information.

By grounding AI-generated text in factual data, RAG significantly enhances the precision and trustworthiness of AI-driven search and response generation. Retrieval lets AI go beyond patterns it learned during training by fetching fresh information when necessary. Think of it like having a reference library at hand—dynamically selecting and verifying multiple sources before answering—but that's beyond this crash course overview. Below I made a diagram showing RAG (Retrieval-Augmented Generation) workflow.

First the user enters input — You ask a question or give an instruction. Then the text is being encoded / Tokenization and is converted into a format the model understands. The vector representation means that the text becomes numbers — a kind of "fingerprint." Thereafter that fingerprint is used to find similar passages in a document database (Vector DB). The most useful excerpts are selected. Irrelevant or conflicting information is filtered out, and the material is combined with the user's question. The model generates an answer based on its skills plus the retrieved sources. It then does quality checks to improve accuracy, remove bias, and the answer is checked for errors, bias, and trustworthiness. The final output is that one gets a response that's more factual and usually more accurate than one made up from memory alone.

While LLM context windows are expanding, RAG remains critical for enterprise scale, cost-efficiency, and compliance. However, we are moving toward a Hybrid Architecture: using RAG for broad information retrieval, and reserving Long Context windows for deep analysis of specific, complex documents once identified.

How Does AI Interpret and Perceive Information?

Humans understand and interact with the world by processing information gathered through our senses—seeing, hearing, feeling, tasting, and smelling. Our brains interpret these sensory inputs, allowing us to perceive our environment, develop skills, and make decisions.

Similarly, in order for an AI system to solve problems and operate effectively, it must have the ability to sense and interpret its environment. This is achieved through various sensors and input modalities (e.g., cameras for vision, microphones for hearing) which act as artificial senses, providing the data the AI needs to understand its surroundings.

Natural Language Processing

As you will learn in the next chapter, scientists have been teaching computers to understand and use human language since the 1950s. NLP (Natural Language Processing) is the broader field of getting computers to work with human language. Whether it's through text, speech, or images, NLP enables computers to interact with us in ways that feel natural. For instance, banks like Goldman Sachs deploy NLP to track regulatory updates (e.g., SEC filings) and ensure compliance with evolving rules. NLP can translate your spoken words into another language in real time and even provide a synthesized voice to speak the translation. Similarly, you can type text into the app, and it will not only translate the text but also generate an audio version of the translation in the target language. Through this language understanding, software developers are able to ensure that computer programs can efficiently execute their respective functions and operations. A common misconception is that the more parameters an NLP model is trained on, the better the quality of its output will be. This isn't always true — while more parameters can increase the model's potential, they don't automatically guarantee higher accuracy or reliability.

Tokens

One of the techniques NLP relies on is called tokens, as this is how it "understands" and "speaks". This is especially the case for LLMs like ChatGPT, which processes and generates text. A token is a unit of text which is used to represent a word, phrase, or other piece of text. Tokens can be whole words, sub-words, or even characters or spaces. They are all represented as individual tokens. By breaking text into these smaller chunks. And these tokens are individual units of data that are fed into a model during training. Tokens are not only the building blocks of the model's responses, but also determine how it interprets input. This occurs both during training, and when interacting with users in real time. Today, all of the models have limitations. There are often creative ways to solve problems within the limit, e.g., condensing your prompt, breaking the text into smaller pieces, etc. Examples of tokens include:

- A whole word *(e.g., "Computer")*
- A subword or part of a word *(e.g., "laptop" in "annual" or "ing" in "swimming")*
- An individual character *(e.g., "a", "Z", "$")*
- Punctuation *(e.g., "!", ".", "?")*
- Special symbols or control characters used by the model.

1 token is equal to 4 English characters, 1 token is ¾ words. And below you see a picture that clearly shows how much tokens are required.

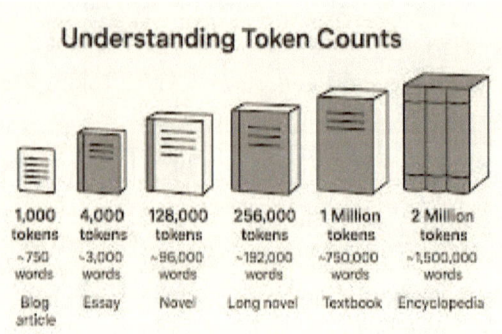

Our sensory information, gathered from our environment (what we see, eat, watch, and overall sense), can be compared to the data that AI systems learn and consume. Our experiences shape our thoughts and behaviors, just as large datasets help AI systems enhance their performance and make more accurate predictions.

AI and human intelligence both depend on this process of learning and adapting. Both systems rely on reinforcement learning (trial and error feedback) to refine outputs. However, Generative AI's open-ended nature demands far more complex training frameworks.

We are typically courteous by nature, so we automatically add "please" and "thank you" to our requests. OpenAI CEO Sam Altman noted that those courtesies, though polite, do introduce additional data: each word adds additional tokens that the system must process. Multiply that by millions of interactions a day, and it all adds up—to more computer power, more energy consumption, and, over time, another $10 million in expense. It's a reminder that even the seemingly unimportant factors can have significant consequences when you extrapolate them across a worldwide system. During the interview Altman responded, "tens of millions of dollars well spent," adding cryptically, "You never know."

AI Agents

AI agents are autonomous digital "helpers" with a clear goal that operate within agentic workflows. Unlike traditional automation, which just follows pre-set rules, AI agents can evaluate situations, adapt strategies, and make decisions to meet specific goals. Similar to ChatGPT, the chatbot is one of many types of AI Agents - as the concept is still very broad. While an AI agent's capabilities are undeniably tied to the range and quality of the tools available, its effectiveness depends on how well it selects and uses the right tool for the job. An AI agent's architecture consists of four fundamental components: model, tools, memory, and planning.

Agent AI works on its own to achieve any goal autonomously, regardless of what the user assigns — from scheduling meetings to analyzing financial data. Give it a complex task or project and it then figures out the steps on its own, and will continue working independently, needing little to no human supervision. (It might use background instructions, sometimes called 'system prompts', to guide its general behavior. However, the key is its ability to act on the main goal.) Agentic AI takes a step closer towards Artificial General Intelligence (**AGI**) by turning this intelligence into AI "agents" which can collaborate with other agents to make independent decisions.

Agentic AI (workflow)

Agentic AI (workflow) refers to the entire approach of autonomous, goal-driven AI systems. Think of it as flexible road that bends and changes according to what tools are being used. You've probably used chatbots like ChatGPT—ask it a question or tell it to write something, and it responds. It can be extremely helpful, but you need to guide it step-by-step with clear instructions. Use this approach when you want flexible, goal-oriented execution. Examples are training AI models or RAG. Conversely, Agentic workflow operates more like a cognitive or 'thinking' system, because it integrates several key abilities such as planning sequences of actions, maintaining memory of past interactions, utilizing external tools (like accessing software or databases), and executing tasks independently to achieve its objective. What makes this "thinking" system more advanced is a so-called chain-of-thought (CoT) reasoning, which is a key factor. CoT enables AI Agents to deal with ambiguity, reason about dependence between tasks, and communicate how they perform, making them bit more trustworthy for complex, high-stakes, or creative tasks. For a very simple overview, the below illustration highlights the main difference between AI agents and Agentic AI.

Robotics

When most people hear "AI and robotics," their minds immediately jump to Hollywood blockbusters—Arnold Schwarzenegger's relentless Terminator or the heartbreaking robot child in Steven Spielberg's *A.I.* These cinematic visions have shaped our expectations, but the reality of robotics tells a far more practical and fascinating story.
The word itself has humble beginnings. "Robot" comes from the Czech word "*robota*," meaning "forced labor"—a term coined by playwright Karel Čapek's brother Josef in 1920 for the play *R.U.R. (Rossum's Universal Robots)*. Even then, the goal wasn't to create artificial humans, but about making

machines that could take over tedious, repetitive work. Robots have always been physical machines with mechanical and sensorimotor capabilities. Robotics integrate AI to create and design autonomous or semiautonomous robots and machines. Additionally, the field of robotics often incorporates other AI technologies such as NLP and ML to enhance robotic capabilities (meaning robots can be equipped with AI agents' capabilities). AI-based robots are already making significant contributions to various industries, including healthcare, retail, and manufacturing, while performing tasks with precision and efficiency. Below is a table highlighting the difference between the different feature sets of RPA (software robots which handle repetitive digital work automatically),

AI Agents, and Agentic AI.

Feature/Capability	RPA	AI Agent	Agentic AI
Core Functionality	Rule-based automation, screen scraping, UI interaction	Smart task execution, Tool calling along with memory.	Intelligent reasoning, autonomous decision-making, multi-agent coordination
Execution Model	Sequential workflow execution, predefined scripts	Dynamic planning and execution, data-driven actions	Self-organizing task mgmt, autonomous workflow creation
Decision Making	If-then logic, exception handling	Smart task breakdown, feedback-based planning	Advanced reasoning, continuous learning and adaptation
Adaptability	Low - requires manual reprogramming for changes	Medium - can adapt based on context and feedback	High - autonomous adaptation and learning from experience
Use Cases	Data entry, form filling, report generation, invoice processing	Customer service, data analysis, content creation, research assistance	Strategic planning, complex problem-solving, autonomous business operations
Technology Stack	Screen automation, OCR, workflow engines	LLMs, APIs, Memory, Retrieval systems	Advanced LLMs, multi-agent frameworks, reasoning engines, orchestration platforms
Human Oversight	High - requires monitoring and exception handling	Medium - periodic review and guidance	Low - autonomous operation with strategic oversight
Scalability	Linear scaling - more bots for more work	Moderate scaling with resource management	High scaling through agent multiplication and coordination

AI models vs. the human brain

The human brain is an incredibly complex organ that looks grayish in color, makes up approximately 2% of our body mass, and boasts the largest cerebral cortex of all mammals, relative to the size of their brains. The cerebral cortex houses the cerebral hemispheres, which are responsible for higher functions including learning, reasoning, memory, decision-making, intelligence, personality, and emotion. Think of it as a powerful supercomputer inside your head. About 80% of our cerebral cortex is made up of the neocortex, which consists of over ten trillion connections and over 16 billion neurons. Our amazing brain is made up of roughly 86 billion brain cells called neurons. These neurons are all connected to each other through about 100 trillion connections called synapses. These massive networks of neurons and synapses let us do things like remember our favorite memories, think through problems, and make everyday decisions.

While computer programs, or algorithms, learn from huge amounts of information via data, our brains learn through everything we experience in life. We learn by actually living and doing things. This means our brains are really good at connecting new things we learn to our past learning experiences. This way of learning helps us predict what might happen in the future based on what we see, hear, feel, and remember. This ability to learn from past experiences in order to predict the future has been an integral aspect. On the other hand, there are many misconceptions when comparing AI attributes to the human mind. Although AI has come very far, it is still only a simulation of certain brain-like processes. John Searle and Hubert Dreyfus, both philosophy professors at UC Berkeley, argued that computers, even when programmed to reason, merely manipulate symbols without having understanding or consciousness. This is far from replicating the full scope of human cognition or consciousness. AI is still a set of algorithms coded by humans to achieve specific tasks.

How the brain adapts and learns

Have you ever noticed that the more you practice something, the better you get? This happens because of synaptic plasticity, a process in which our brain strengthens or weakens synaptic connections based on experience. This fine-tuning helps us adapt, much like a musician who refines their skills through repeated practice. Scientists believe that prediction is a core brain function, as it continuously anticipates and interprets incoming sensory information. For example, the human retina transmits visual information at around 10 million bits per second, comparable to real-world 5G speeds. Our brain constantly processes this information, creating and refining mental models to help us navigate the world. But what happens when these predictions are wrong?

Consider this sentence:

"She put the groceries in the car and then drove home to cook a delicious meal for her family, but realized she forgot to bring the kitchen sink."

Did the last two words seem out of place?

That's because your brain encountered a prediction error—it expected the sentence to make sense based on previous knowledge. When faced with an inconsistency, your brain immediately adjusts its expectations to make sense of the information.

Super Smart AI in the Future?
Artificial General Intelligence (AGI)

AGI refers to machines that can think, understand, and respond just as humans do. Many experts, most notably Ray Kurzweil, predict that human-level machine intelligence (i.e., passing a valid Turing test) will most probably start sometime after 2030 or likely around 2045, the moment Kurzweil dubs the "singularity." His idea was recently and frequently supported by OpenAI CEO Sam Altman, who indirectly stated his desire to build a brain for the whole world, adding he also wants the public to have open access to advanced models. In that scenario, an AGI could perform any intellectual task we can, across any professional domain.

Artificial Superintelligence (ASI)

Artificial Superintelligence (**ASI**), the next step beyond AGI. Is a concept straight out of science fiction, in which machines not only possess social skills and emotional intelligence, but also far exceed our own cognitive abilities which enables them to think, feel, and act like humans. As Oxford's Nick Bostrom puts it, super intelligence is *"Any intellect that greatly exceeds the cognitive performance of humans in virtually all domains of interest"*. Superintelligence would have its own thought, feelings and needs. If this happens, I'll be the first to book my ticket to another planet, if humanity is foolish enough to allow for its creation.

Still, knowing what AI can and cannot do represents only half the battle.

Just as important - Becoming proficient in the art of communicating effectively with these machines in order to critically evaluate AI-generated content. This skill isn't just useful, it's essential for professional survival.

Chapter 4 Work

Have you ever sat down and really tried to figure out why you want that job or that position? I've been asked *"Why do you want to work here?"* more times than I can count, and for years I gave the standard answers—growth opportunities, company culture, competitive salary. But recently, as I continue to watch AI reshape everything, I thought I knew about knowledge work, I've realized this question cuts much deeper than any interview script. I decided to refer to a dictionary for a better understanding. The word "work", is defined as an "activity involving mental or physical effort done in order to achieve a purpose or result." Simple enough. Effort. Purpose. Result. Much like the origin of the word, wyrcan. A muscular word. It meant to prepare, to perform, to make something where nothing had been — to strive after a thing with your hands or your will. And then you have the other word Wircan — the Mercian form — was less about making and more about *moving*. To operate. To set events in motion. And here is the curious thing: unlike its counterpart, wircan was not born of a verb. It was reverse-engineered from a noun, from the Proto-Germanic werkan-, from the idea of the *thing made*, not the making. A process working backward into action.

For many being able to work means finding purpose, seeing themselves develop, and in an era when machines can duplicate our efforts and frequently outperform us wondering if it still matters— all of these observations have served as the central themes of my personal and professional journey over the past 20 years.

It's a question that's haunted humanity since we first picked up tools and started working together. In prehistoric times, the answer was simple: survival. We worked for food, shelter, and the safety of community. But as civilization evolved and we moved toward information-rich environments, that simple answer became layered with complexity. Work began providing not just necessity, but intellectual stimulation, fulfillment, and belonging.

Now, as I watch artificial intelligence automate tasks I have spent decades learning to master, I find myself confronting this fundamental question all over again.

From Factory Floors to Office Cubicles

I can't get one story out of my head from a history class I took as a teenager. When knitting machines began to replace Ned Ludd's source of income in 1811, he took the desperate and incredibly human step of smashing the machines. Back then, there were no safety nets. You starved after losing your job. The Luddite movement began as a result of his frustration. This relentless focus on optimizing output, treating work like a mechanical process, is precisely what Frederick Taylor formalized in his Scientific Management principles during the early 20th century.

He introduced the role of "efficiency experts," individuals whose job was to study workers' every move and tweak tasks to ensure they were producing as much as possible, as quickly as possible. This was a time when factory work was grueling, and many workers were subjected to long hours completing repetitive tasks. Taylor's idea was revolutionary: strip away inefficiencies and create the most efficient system possible. This made the work more stressful and tiring, and caused workers to be prone to more errors, which in turn led to the production of more defective goods. And while productivity may have increased in some areas, worker morale diminished, as workers started to feel as though they lacked purpose.

The post-World War II era witnessed another transformation as offices replaced factories. Intellectual contributions superseded physical production as the prime source of economic worth, but the ethos of efficiency continued, unabated. The white-collar working class was burdened with fresh metrics—performance appraisals, productivity targets, and output goals—that aimed to quantify intellectual contribution similarly to how Taylor quantified physical effort. Knowledge workers suffered from an unusual form of stress: mental exhaustion of uninterrupted productivity. Their work, too, was compartmentalized into measurable outcomes, so that artistic and intellectual work evolved into a list of deliverables.

When I read about Taylor's factories, I thought about the modern knowledge worker who stared at productivity dashboards, tracked hours billed, and tried to measure an intangible output in the number of reports they generated and tickets they closed. We may have moved from factory floors to office cubicles, but we brought that same obsession with measurable efficiency along for the ride.

Norwegian Work Culture

Since 1970s the general working hours have been reduced to 40 hours per week. Saturday became a day off and five weeks' vacation was introduced in Norway. At the same time Norway, ntroduced retirement age at 64. Norway's flat organizational structure, which emphasizes collaboration, transparency, and trust, provides a unique context for this transformation. It's an unwritten rule that Norwegian work culture is known to give employees "Freedom with responsibility". For those coming from more hierarchical cultures, adjusting to Norway's open and egalitarian work culture can be a major shift. Compared to Indian workplaces, where authority and seniority often guide decisions, or American workplaces, which emphasize individual performance and ambition, the Norwegian model is built on trust, flat structures, and shared responsibility. In such environments, managers and employees alike work closely with the government to ensure a high degree of autonomy and mutual respect. This raises an important question: What if AI could assume many of the traditional managerial functions? With its ability to process vast amounts of data and deliver unbiased strategic insights—assuming the AI is built on diverse, high-quality data—it might offer more precise and efficient decision-making than its human counterparts.

It could also reduce the cost of meetings that currently take up 70–80% of a middle manager's time. Most interesting, 50% of all these meetings are widely seen as waste of time. By using algorithms to help manage, overall overhead costs would be reduced, and pointless meetings would be eliminated. Between 2014 – 2018, upper management worked an average of 48.1 hours a week. However, the current SSB supplied data below shows a sharp reduction in hours worked.

Roles	Average working hours per week
CEO, CTO, Directors	34.2 hours
CFO and Finance directors and managers	34.8 hours
Other middle managers	34 hours

My Three Acts with Work

This history of how work evolved made me reflect on my own relationship with it, and I realized I could identify three distinct reasons for why I work.

Act I: Work to Survive

My approach to work comes from my father's own experience. He would tell me about how his work permit felt like a magic talisman in his back pocket as he boarded the plane in 1970 from India to Oslo, Norway. That single piece of paper represented everything his own parents had lost. Twenty-seven years after Partition tore through the Indian subcontinent like a blade, its aftermath still rippled through our family. My grandparents had watched everything they owned disappear in the chaos that erupted between India and Pakistan—their land, their savings, their future. In Norway, my dad started working in August, 1972 as a factory worker at Det Norske Slipeskivefabrik, earning 16.70 kroner an hour. The work was steady, if not repetitive, but gave shape to his new life. By 1974, he moved to D. Mustad & Søn, where he worked in the Galvanizing. He later became a section leader in that department and doubled his salary. He proved himself—not only in terms of skill, but in his resilience. My dad was just trying to make a living. Finally, in June

1981, he was granted Norwegian citizenship. On paper anyway, he found a country to call home. But later that same year, in December, his employment at Mustad ended, and left him unemployed, still with a family to support. That dark period stretched on until August 1982—just a month after I was born. Then came a turning: he found work at Peppe's Pizza in Kristiansand. From steel and chemicals, he pivoted to flour and ovens and became one of the city's more renowned pizza chefs. That period of stability lasted until 1994. Two years later, he went into business for himself and ultimately used his own recipes to open several restaurants and pizza outlets in Oslo, Sweden, Spain and Kristiansand.

My father's work life reminds me of an old-school platformer styled video game—linear levels, no saves, one life. Anyone who lost their job was often forced to start from the beginning. Conversely, my generation expected something more like a modern role-playing game; multiple paths, skill trees, the ability to save your progress, and experiment with different approaches. However, AI is turning work into a roguelike game in the sense that every run is different, meaning your previous strategies might not work, and permanent death is always just one automation away. This story of how work has evolved made me reflect on my own journey to becoming a knowledge worker.

"Money doesn't grow on trees." My parents said this constantly when I was growing up—an Indian proverb that echoed through our house every time I wanted something. My father's lessons about money came wrapped with a sense of guilt, as if every expense was a burden on the family. I understood he was trying to teach me financial responsibility, but it also planted a deep sense of obligation that took years for me to unpack.

My early jobs reflected this survival mindset perfectly. I took whatever came my way: cold-calling strangers, knocking on doors, waiting tables, conducting phone surveys, flipping pizzas. These weren't careers; they were jobs taken out of necessity. But if nothing else, they taught me resilience and more importantly, gave me the independence I desperately craved.

However, even then I felt pulled toward something greater. There was this nagging sense that work could be about creation, contribution, and building something meaningful beyond the basic obligation of just paying my bills.

Act II: Work to Create

Something changed within me when I made my initial transition into knowledge work, first as an ERP sales consulting manager, followed by a role in project management. The work was often still repetitive, but I started to catch glimpses of something bigger. Each role brought me closer to what I was searching for beyond a paycheck; purpose.

I remember the first time I helped a client implement a complex system that actually solved their problems. It was the moment when everything clicked into place, and realized I wasn't just executing tasks, I was creating solutions.

Act III: Work to Contribute

Now, working as a senior technical project manager, I've found something I didn't experience during my time flipping pizzas - fulfillment. When I'm building systems, leading teams through seemingly impossible challenges, or watching a project come together to solve real problems— it's in those moments I feel connected to something larger than myself. I'm participating in what I can only call world-building.

However, when I finally reached this understanding, AI flipped to challenge every assumption I previously held regarding knowledge worker productivity and value.

Knowledge Workers

Knowledge workers emerged thousands of years ago, long before the internet. Their historical lineage is long and varied, beginning with the dawn of writing itself. As an Egyptian father was sending his son to school in the third millennium BC, he famously said: *"Put writing in your heart that you may protect yourself from hard labor of any kind, the scribe is released from manual tasks"* and that it is *"he who commands"*. This quote offers a glimpse into what it meant to be a knowledge worker so many centuries ago. The invention of writing created a distinct class of knowledge workers who gained status, influence, and eventually became known as "white-collar workers". From scribes to architects, many enjoyed high status, mostly due to the significant amount of time and energy that was necessary to master literacy.

Knowledge has various definitions. It can mean know-how, or wisdom. On many occasions we even use the term to refer to information. Part of the difficulty of defining knowledge stems from its relationship with two other concepts, namely data and information. Both of those terms are often pegged in a lower grouping of knowledge. Some argue knowledge can be innate, acquired through observation, derived by pure thought, or an observation, or acquired through a combination of thought and observation. But the exact relationship varies greatly from one example to another. If "knowledge" has so many different meanings, what is the best way to define a knowledge worker?

In 1959, management pioneer Peter Drucker defined the term *knowledge worker* in *Landmarks of Tomorrow*, and described them as those who *"possess, utilize, and create valuable knowledge."* He argued that by the 21st century, an organization's greatest asset would be the productivity of these white-collar professionals—yet he did not attempt to pin down their exact numbers. In this context, knowledge workers are workers whose main commodity is knowledge – as they take existing information and use it to create new information.

Examples include Information and communication technology (ICT) professionals, physicians, pharmacists, architects, engineers, scientists, design thinkers, public accountants, lawyers, librarians, archivists, editors, and academics, all of whom "*think for a living*".

They differ from information workers, task workers, skilled workers and other specialty areas in the sense they use their expertise to strategize work activities and develop plans of action, all toward the goal of seeing work activities through to completion. Conversely, information workers, task workers and skilled workers are subordinate to knowledge workers, as they are charged with applying information by performing skilled work or completing specific tasks.

Living With a Productivity Paradox

Here's where this gets personal. When I studied macroeconomics at BI, I learned that productivity is a key driver of both economic growth and improvements in living standards. A commonly used measure of productivity is the value generated per hour worked, also known as labour productivity.

I live in Norway, a country that should be winning in the knowledge economy. We ranked 2nd globally in productivity in 2022, but by 2024 we'd dropped to

5th. Our growth rate hovers around 0.5% per year—below the OECD average of 1%. For a country of only 5.6 million people with some of the world's highest wages and lowest unemployment, this should be alarming.

But what keeps me up at night isn't the rankings—it's what they represent. Despite our wealth, education, and social systems, Norway risks a five-year delay in adopting generative AI compared to countries like the US, China, and India. We're falling behind on the very technologies that will define the next phase of work.

When an AI system can do the work of three knowledge workers, and those workers happen to be among the world's most expensive, the mathematics becomes uncomfortable. We can't compete on cost, so we have to compete on something else—but what?

This isn't just about national competitiveness. It's about whether the approach to work I've spent twenty years developing—moving from survival to creation to contribution—still has relevance when machines can think, learn, and create alongside us – faster, and more efficiently.

Rank	Country	Region	Sub-region	GDP per hour worked (international $ at PPP)
1	Luxembourg	Europe	West Europe	146.09
2	Ireland	Europe	North Europe	142.5
3	Liechtenstein	Europe	West Europe	141.3
4	Monaco	Europe	West Europe	138.4
5	Norway	Europe	North Europe	92.58
6	Netherlands	Europe	West Europe	79.83
7	Denmark	Europe	North Europe	78.2
8	Switzerland	Europe	West Europe	75.55
9	Belgium	Europe	West Europe	75.49
10	Austria	Europe	West Europe	74.2

The challenge becomes even more complex when we consider how to define the concept of productivity in this new era. Productivity is in the middle of a significant shift during AI's increased integration into our workplaces. Data projections predict that AI will contribute to a 20% increase in productivity in Norway between 2025 and 2030. This makes sense, but it's a terrifying reality. The question is – between AI and knowledge workers, who will ultimately be deemed *"productive labor"* and *"unproductive"*? In *The Wealth of Nations* (1776), Adam Smith distinguished between *"productive"* labor (work that *"fixes itself in a tangible object"* and *thereby adds lasting value), and "unproductive"* (labor whose value is consumed as soon as it is created).

Smith illustrates this with a simple contrast: a manufacturer's work enriches both the raw materials and his employer's profits, whereas a servant's labor, however essential, *"adds to the value of nothing..."*

Smith's distinction feels increasingly inadequate in our era, where value creation occurs in intangible ways. This inadequacy was evident to management thinker Peter Drucker, who recognized that knowledge work required entirely new frameworks for understanding productivity. Smith also listed six key factors that will ultimately determine a knowledge worker's productivity in the age of AI:

1. Knowledge worker productivity demands that we ask the question: "How can AI clarify and break them into manageable steps?"

2. It demands that we impose on a knowledge worker a sense of responsibility and accountability for their actual productivity. Knowledge workers have to manage themselves and have autonomy in doing so.

3. Continuing to innovate must be part of a knowledge worker's responsibility and workflow.

4. Knowledge work requires continuous learning on the part of the knowledge worker (to facilitate the sharing of best practices).

5. A knowledge worker's productivity is not—at least not primarily— a matter of quantity of output. Quality is at the very least just as important.

6. Finally, knowledge worker productivity requires that they both be recognized and treated as an "asset" rather than a "cost." Similarly, knowledge workers should express a desire to work for the organization above all other opportunities.

Most knowledge workers start their careers after college or university around the age of 26 and retire near 67. During that period, Norwegians could expect to potentially spend 70,000 hours working during their career. Internationally, this number is even higher – an estimated 85,280 hours. Based on an 80-year life span of standard, full time work outside of Norway, that person would ultimately spend about 12% of their life contributing their skills over a typical career. We must address the critical question of how we measure the value generated during someone's career. When someone uses AI to increase productivity, it's a safe assumption that Drucker would have likely embraced knowledge workers use of AI, provided it's properly applied to enhance efficiency. He emphasized technology doesn't simply mean scientific or engineering spin-offs. Drucker reminded us that "technology" derives from the Greek word *"techne,",* which means "useful knowledge" or "organized skill" rather than just engineering. If Drucker saw technology as organized knowledge, then AI's fundamental use of data and algorithms fits perfectly into his framework. This broader understanding suggests productivity improvements come from applying knowledge systematically, regardless of whether knowledge originates from formal science.

The traditional focus on simple output metrics feels increasingly inadequate, especially as AI begins to augment and even automate significant portions of our tasks. With higher GDP growth, any AI-powered economy would demand more labour across a wider range of occupations and skill levels. This makes no difference for Norway, because the issue is that we have such a small population of about only 5.5 million people, along with having one of the fastest-aging populations in Europe. Norway's unemployment rate hovers around 3–4%, and average wages are among the highest in the OECD.

AI offers an insight into what Peter Drucker meant regarding the more human and often less quantifiable aspects of work. Consider the emergence of tools like Microsoft Viva Insights. This system ventures beyond tracking keystrokes and deadlines, attempting to capture the more subtle intricacies of team dynamics - morale and stress levels, which are the precursors to burnout. It's not about creating a Big Brother scenario, but rather providing a richer data set that reflects the complex interplay of factors influencing true productivity.

Instead of having managers spend countless hours interpreting these signals, AI could, with much less effort, provide workers with useful information to appropriately adjust their workloads, collaborate with different colleagues, or, when necessary, access mental health resources. This would allow employees to actively shape their own work experience in line with their skills and passions, rather than simply fulfilling externally imposed roles. AI could not only empower employees to take ownership of their work, but also play a crucial role in providing the resources and support they need to succeed. Imagine an AI system being able to analyze data to predict resource needs, optimize allocation, and even automate distribution. This would free managers from handling many routine tasks, allowing them to alternatively focus on higher-level strategic planning and fostering a positive work culture. In a self-organizing team environment, AI could provide real-time insights into project progress, identify potential roadblocks, and suggest corrective actions, empowering teams to make informed decisions and achieve their goals. Of course, ethical considerations like privacy and consent are crucial to how these systems are used and applied.

Any AI application will ultimately be influenced by how we choose to utilize data, along with how we value humanity, particularly in terms of numbers driving insights, and human judgment influencing action. If we measure both metrics, we could get a more honest answer to not just how busy we are, but how efficiently we're doing the work that really matters.

From Ned Ludd's rebellion to today's algorithms, every technological leap has promised to make us more productive, usually at the expense of re-defining the meaning of work. We've now come full circle: from manual labor to intellectual work to managing AI systems. I've spent twenty years evolving from survival to creation to contribution.

Now I'm facing a fourth act: learning to work alongside artificial intelligence while holding onto what makes the work meaningful.

Living in Norway, I'm watching, in real time, as our productivity rankings slip as other nations race ahead in AI adoption. I'm reminded that this isn't just about individual careers, it's about entire societies figuring out how to preserve human dignity and purpose in an age of intelligent machines.

Because a knowledge workers' most valuable product is thought, we need to use qualitative metrics to measure their productivity. One way to create a baseline for productivity is to collect data from workers by asking them how they feel about their work. Because not all tasks create the same value for the organization, measuring tasks on their own can lead to a lack of clarity. We can therefore safely state that every knowledge worker, whether they are a strategist, project manager, CEO, real-estate executive, or consultant, would likely embrace one single measure of performance. If only we could occasionally quantify productivity, we'd be able to prove the value of our recommendations, but such measures often do not exist. This is evidenced by the fact that most, if not all senior management feedback and questionnaire forms pose the same question: Did you generate any value? When productivity is equated with effort or billing hours, clients will frequently challenge their billed hours based on their own understanding of what defines quality. An objectively defined measure would provide definitive criteria for making workplace investments and measuring results—rather than subjective judgment.

Machines don't call in sick, take vacations, or need breaks—and with AI now replicating skills like thinking, seeing, and learning, it's no wonder companies are racing to adopt it. As firms reduce headcounts and consolidate roles for routine cognitive work, we're witnessing a fundamental reorganization of human capital investment. Companies will pay more for workers who can design, oversee, or fine-tune AI systems, while reducing investment in those executing repeatable tasks. With so much information and disruption flowing through our work lives amidst a frantic race for productivity and efficiency, we now struggle to accept that fact that AI doesn't have a human-like *"growth mindset"*. Yet many organizations still have an ingrained focus on traditional metrics, which are difficult to quantify with qualitative aspects.

Unlike workers in the Industrial Revolution who were faced with the stark decision to either adapt or resist (and risk unemployment), knowledge workers have a unique opportunity to actively shape today's ongoing transition. We have the choice to actively choose to see AI not as a threat to human capability, but rather as a tool that amplifies our distinctly human contributions.

My father's journey—from factory worker to business owner—represented the eternal hope that hard work and resilience could lift you out of the working class. He believed, as many immigrants did in the 1970s, that education would insulate his children from the struggles he had no choice but to face and overcome.

But what he couldn't have predicted was that the very definition of "working class" would shift beneath our feet. I have a fairly good education and many certifications, while he had strictly vocational training. I work a flexible schedule in a climate-controlled office filled with amenities. My father, on the other hand, labored day after day with molten metal and pizza ovens to create "something out of nothing". Yet, in some ways, I face more uncertainty than he did. His factory job, for all its hardships, came with a union membership, and his pizza restaurant couldn't be outsourced to an algorithm. The corporate world convinced my generation we would enjoy "work-life balance," as if notions of flexibility and autonomy were revolutionary. In reality, they were a mirage. The fact is, even though my father stood in front of a pizza oven for twelve-hour shifts, he actually had more freedom than I do. When he closed the restaurant, his work was done. But when I close my laptop, I'm still thinking about utilization rates, worried that the hours I didn't bill today will mean I'll be falling behind financially tomorrow. Perhaps the cruelest irony is the machines I must master in order to stay competitive are the same ones gradually eroding my value in the workplace. I, along with my fellow knowledge workers, *must* use, understand, and become fluent in

AI not because it liberates us, but because it's the only way to remain employable. My father owned his means of production, his recipes, his restaurant, his reputation. I essentially rent my relevance from an algorithm, month by month, certification by certification, billable hour by billable hour.

The working class hasn't disappeared—it's just wearing different clothes. Today's knowledge workers are discovering what factory workers learned a century ago: that specialization makes you vulnerable, that skills become obsolete, that employers will optimize you out of existence if the mathematics makes sense. The difference is that we lack the collective organizing structures that gave industrial workers bargaining power. We're atomized, told to be "entrepreneurs of the self," competing against each other and now against machines that never sleep.

The real value of work in the future won't be measured in competition with machines, but rather in how effectively we can leverage our uniquely human capabilities, empathy, creativity, ethical reasoning, complex problem-solving—to tackle challenges worth solving. A knowledge worker's chief product is thus a particular kind of thinking - the kind that asks not just *"how?"*, but *"why?"* and *"should we?"*

As we continue to place so much emphasis on how we can leverage AI in order to increase productivity, we must ask ourselves – how can a knowledge worker define and demonstrate their true value? The next chapter offers valuable insight and perspective into how future generations might answer this question.

Chapter 5 Prompt craft and Writing Smarter

If a phrase appears frequently in some data, it's more likely to be used by the AI. These phrases serve as logical transition points or connectors in a text, which can be valuable in creating coherent and cohesive content. ChatGPT, like other AI models, learns its language patterns from the data it's trained on. Since there are over 400 million users every week, it's obvious that it will utilize a frequently used a pattern more frequently, allowing the highlighted text to become *"generic"*.

The result? Overall, we've seen a staggering 189% spike in AI-produced content since the start of 2023. Moreover, as of December 2024, more than half (54%) of LinkedIn articles and posts are now created by AI. Even prestigious platforms aren't immune, approximately 10.86% of Fortune 500 company blog articles and one out of every 20 new Wikipedia entries appear to be generated with the help of AI.

This chapter will give you an overview of two essential skills: How to craft better prompts that produce more original, useful responses, along with how to spot AI-generated content that might be generic or inaccurate. In other words, you'll learn how to work with AI more effectively, and how to think more critically about its output.

AI Fluff Words

AI often tries to use sophisticated vocabulary. It often throws around words like "comprehensive," "intricate," and "pivotal." Therefore," "however," and "furthermore" are also AI favorites, making the output sound like something you might find in a research paper. It's like that one friend who uses "exacerbate in casual conversation, trying a bit too hard to impress. Similarly, if you prompt the GPT to have a formal tone, it will probably produce phrases like "It is imperative that…" and *"In light of this…"* which scream "robot." Humans, especially in casual writing, are more likely to say "We've got to…" or *"So, because of this…"* It's common for the text generated by any of these generative tools to produce phrasing which appears to be very repetitive. Some words that appear frequently in AI-generated content include:

• **Nuance**—AI tends to highlight complexity by emphasizing "nuance" when introducing intricate topics.

• **Emerge**—You can't help but feel a sense of excitement when the word 'emerge' pops up (think "emerging technologies"), which is the intended effect when AI uses it.

- **Meticulous**—It's unsurprising that 'meticulous' is overused by AI when you consider that lots of users prompt their chatbot to describe people, processes, or actions that show this quality.
- **Navigate**—For some reason, these AI large language models seem to take the role of a map reader, determined to help you 'navigate' a course or path. We can all agree it's reassuring to have a map when making our way through uncharted territory.
- **Foster**—AI language models are hardwired to make users feel as though they are in a supportive environment, hence why words like 'foster' come up frequently.
- **Convey**—With over 400 million users relying on chatbots to relay information, ideas, and concepts in an understandable manner, it didn't surprise me that the word 'convey' itself is one of AI's most popular words.

Any of the models love to discover new patterns, seeing as they learn from every prompt we enter. Personally, I think including the word "explore" is a sloppy way to write an introduction, but that doesn't stop Chat-GPT from using it: "In this article, we'll explore…" Variety in the tone of writing is important when writing with depth and complexity; AI is quick to use the word 'nuance' when introducing an intricate topic to entice, or maybe even warn, the user.

Effective prompting and variance in writing

During one of my podcast episodes, I interviewed University in Kristiania Professor Moutaz Haddara about how students are using chatbots these days. We also spoke about what it was like being a student when we had chalk and blackboards, followed by projectors and whiteboards, or handouts using notebooks and writing. Now when I take notes, I usually use my recording device on my phone, notepad, or laptop. Learning handwriting as a skill now seems to be pointless. I remember practicing writing as fast as possible during a 3-hour period during my years at university, all in preparation for taking time-limited exams. But what is the point of writing quickly or with attractive handwriting these days? When we are able to any skilled agent in the tone, that has its own "voice" or personality you give it using prompts. Way more than many people thinks. In order to make the most of the output, and have it stand out in a positive manner, you need to learn how to prompt.

Effectively prompting an AI is both an art and a science. It requires a understanding of your subject matter and a willingness to learn how an AI develops its "voice." To get the most out of these tools—and to ensure the results truly stand out—you must look past the simple chat box and understand the two distinct layers of instruction at play.

The first layer is the *System Prompt*. Think of this as the "background DNA" or the "stage directions" given to the assistant. This is where you instruct the AI to adopt a specific persona, such as a social role or a fictional character, which dictates its tone and behavior. For example, rather than asking for general advice, you might instruct the AI to act as a 35-year-old college-educated woman who is a veteran real estate buyer. By defining her age, experience, and perspective, you give the AI a specific lens through which to view your problem.

The second layer is the *User Prompt*. This is the direct input you type into the chatbot—your specific question or task. To make this layer effective, you must be deliberate in how you articulate the problem. Ask yourself: *What am I choosing to explore? What critical information is missing?* When you master both layers, you move beyond "talking to a computer" and begin a sophisticated collaboration. By combining a well-defined persona with a clear, detailed task, you transform the AI from a generic tool into a tailored consultant that understands exactly how to weigh what matters most to you.

The best way to get AI to successfully perform a task is to instruct it to act take on a certain persona, which, for example, could mean assuming a social role or fictional character. For instance, if you are asking AI to evaluate a real estate agent's proposal, you would ask it to assume the role of a female client age between 30 to 40 years old with an optional college degree.

She could either be her first apartment, or she could be a veteran buyer. When crafting prompts, it's always important to ask yourself *how you articulate the problem, what you choose to explore, and decide what matters.* Understanding these questions helps you interpret AI's responses better.

Comparative Analysis Prompt

Comparative analysis prompts are effective when you need to evaluate different approaches within a project or understand the distinctions between research papers or concepts. These prompts work by explicitly requesting contrasts between specific elements, helping to identify key differentiators and benefits.

For comparative analysis I choose using Claude over Open AI's GPT. I used the following prompt when writing the chapter on Universal Basic Income:
"Contrast the advantages and disadvantages of UBI based on the articles and research I have provided."
This type of prompt is particularly useful for decision-making processes, literature reviews, or when synthesizing information from multiple sources to understand competing methodologies or viewpoints.

Contextual Analysis Prompt

Contextual analysis prompts prove valuable when working with multiple sources of information which require synthesis within a specific domain or industry context. These prompts help extract targeted insights, by focusing the analysis on particular sectors. For example, when I wanted deeper insight into a given field, I moved from Perplexity—after encountering frequent hallucinations—to Google's Deep Research. It provided more accurate details and used a more thorough "inquiry" method for contextual analysis. I relied on the following prompt: *"Provide insights into the impact of AI in the legal industry from 1990 to today (2025)*

This approach works well when you have collected various articles and research papers on a topic and need to understand their collective implications for a specific field or use case. The prompt helps consolidate disparate information into focused, actionable insights relevant to your particular context of interest.

Prompt engineering doesn't require a technical degree, but it does require creativity in framing requests and strategic thinking about how language models interpret instructions.

So:

- Start by giving clear direction—describe the desired style in detail or reference a relevant persona to shape the tone and approach.
- Specify the format by outlining the rules to follow and the desired structure for the response. For instance, I provided the tool with a concrete example "text1" that detailed the flaws in AI-generated content. This provided examples will then showcase successful outcomes, offering a diverse set of test cases in which the task was executed correctly.
- I subsequently provided "text2", another AI generated text entry aimed at evaluating quality by identifying errors and rating responses. The goal – to help uncover what drives high performance.
- Finally, for more complex goals, break up the labor by breaking the task into multiple steps, and then chain them together in paragraphs to ensure each stage is completed methodically and efficiently. I instructed the tool as follows: "I'll provide two texts. TEXT1 details the flaws, whereas TEXT2 is AI generated. Now, with the help of TEXT1, rewrite TEXT2."

If your brain works like mine, I am able to remember two to three facts at the time, this technique ensures that AI deals with its limited memory through context window and ensures it stays relevant without - forgetting anything in that given time. The process of prompting the model to think step by step is called "Chain of Thoughts" (CoT) and systematically guides a model to decompose complex problems into sequential steps, producing more reliable outputs into manageable pieces (chunks) in order to consequently understand and solve them. The end result is a more accurate output.

You've probably seen those flashy demos in which AI either writes highly polished copy, or its image generator churns out jaw-dropping art.

Sure, they look incredible, but generally speaking, AI does not typically generate flawless results overnight. Achieving the right results required weeks of tweaking settings, adding more data, and asking, "Why did you mess up here?" I needed the model to understand not just what people said, but how they felt; specifically, their frustration, excitement, and even a bit of sarcasm and tonal nuance that models can struggle to interpret reliably without sufficient context. While writing this book, I tested various AI detection tools designed to analyze textual patterns and determine whether a piece of writing is human-made or generated by AI. Many of these tools—if not all—tended to flag certain words and phrases as AI-generated.

Some even labeled my own writing style as AI-generated, which I found amusing. These are known as false positives. I also tested the tools on academic research papers, and surprisingly, some of those were flagged as AI-written too.

Best practices include always fact-checking AI's findings and claims, especially in light the fact that futurists, researchers, and technology consultant firms confirm the risk of likely encountering sophisticated disinformation in digital spaces will rise substantially after 2030. Even worse, half of users are barely able to distinguish between fake and fact. It's been my experience that success lies in establishing continuous feedback loop that starts with your prompt, which is followed by assessing the response. Finally, refine your questions by dividing them up in correct sizes, all while evaluating whether the outcome is both logical and grounded in common sense. As someone who uses the tool, this iterative process has taught me to be patient and thoughtful. This means what you put in your prompt changes the probability of every word generated, and fundamentally impacts the quality of the produced results.

I often use a thesaurus to avoid overused words

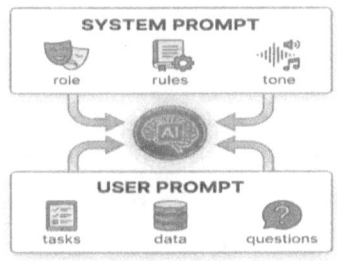

(some of them are mentioned above). If you find a model repeating the same word, then I would advise you pick up a thesaurus to find better alternatives for your prompt.

"Smart Tools"

Today there are countless valuable tools available to help you increase productivity. During my research for this book (I reviewed more than 500 articles and research papers in a limited amount of time), I used the paid versions of Gemini Deep Research, Claude Opus 4. If you're serious about building with generative AI, you can't rely on just one tool. You'll need Anthropic Claude or OpenAI ChatGPT for reasoning, Microsoft Copilot for smooth integration with MS365, Cursor for data work and coding, Lovable for code generation, and *HeyGen* or *Synthesia* for video.

I cross-checked and compared their outputs and then looked into their source data to confirm the accuracy.

While writing of this book, I had to circle back and read several research papers again. To make this 'refresher' process as efficient as possible, I used a tool called *Research-Pal*, was turned out to be very useful. Given the fact I had to ultimately review more than 200 research papers with limited time availability, this tool was very good for literature reviews, generating references, summarizing papers, extracting methodologies, and synthesizing the core findings. Since English is my third language — Hindi is my mother tongue, followed by Norwegian. I often use *Grammarly*, another tool which enhanced my writing by correcting grammar, suggesting tone adjustments, and offering full sentence suggestions. Being a non-native English speaker, it was quite handy. However, I did not like the tool's AI feature, which can be used to re-write a whole text. Other tools for better writing which, in my humble opinion, are equally worth trying out, include *Hemingway Editor*, *Quillbot* and *Wordtune*.

In the creative space, I have also used tools such as Sora, which is a text to video generator. Other tools I've previously used include *DALL-E* and *Midjourney,* both of which are fascinating Each of these AI image generators are able to produce visually stunning images that brought many of my wildest ideas to life by me submitting text-based prompts. A word of caution, beware of copyright or style biases in downloaded assets, and double-check the license if you plan to publish any of your creativity commercially. As there have been too many lawsuits due to people mindlessly putting out whatever these tools would generate.

Suno is a generative artificial intelligence music creation program designed to generate realistic songs that include vocals, instrumentals, or a combination of both. Last year I had a lot of fun trying out Suno to compose many high quality, professional tunes - everything from heavy metal, Norwegian rap, to the theme song for my YouTube channel.

Meetings, and taking notes can be somewhat cumbersome if one need to be attentive and participate at some level. As you recall my brain focuses on2-3 facts and for this reasons I often use the transcription feature included in "Teams with CoPilot" with some success, although it was not as accurate and efficient as *Otter Meeting AI*. This AI meeting assistance gave me very accurate meeting notes. Of course, there are many other providers that can be used as AI meeting assistants, including Fireflies. Since we all are different with specific tastes and preferences, feel free to try out various tools, and use the one you prefer.

No matter which of these tools you end up using, most of them require prompts to function. The rule of thumb is simple. System prompt = how the AI should behave in general. User prompt = what the AI should do right now.

The AI's Blind Spot

Besides being a really amazing tool for various tasks, AI can also make independent decisions and create ideas using data to build its assumptions. Still, it's worth noting AI generated posts or content typically receive fewer clicks, likes, shares, and less overall engagement, which, for whatever reason fail to capture the reader's attention. Humans have this unique ability to see an emotional connection, along with our remarkable ability to see the world from someone else's perspective. There is, however, one point I need to clarify. The detection tools that I tried do have a tendency to produce false positives, which are common. In fact, I've seen legitimately human-written content also flagged as AI simply because of unusual writing patterns or an extensive vocabulary, like my own style of writing.

While only 30% of students have received any education on how to use an AI, 86% of them are using it in their regular studies.

This might be seen as the equivalent of driving a car without a license, but more importantly this trend raises important questions about the nature of knowledge.

What is the value of knowledge if you don't understand its implications, origins, and the process by which it was acquired? Struggle, even intellectual struggle, plays a crucial role in DL. AI, with its ability to instantly provide answers, risks short-circuiting this process. Moreover, the tendency of AI tools to "re-shuffle" existing information raises concerns about the future of intellectual diversity.

One can consider Generative AI to be a very clever parrot capable of accurately mimicking human language, but without an important component – context. When the parrot in this scenario come across a gap in its learned phrases (something it doesn't truly understand), it might very well fill the gap with a likely-sounding but completely fabricated tale—a 'hallucination'. When you use a Generative AI tool without being aware of the potential for AI hallucination, it compromises content that, let's say, corporate boardroom members would rely on to make critical decisions about multi-million-dollar transactions. It's a recipe for disaster, and it's in these situations where the human mind can successfully challenge any AI, in accordance with the concept of *"Theory of Mind"*.

"Theory of Mind" is essential for us to succeed in our social interactions with one another. Part of this ability is recognizing different viewpoints, including those you know not to be true. As long as we have this unique ability, along with our ability to sense and reason, there is still hope. If our information is shaped by something that neither doubts nor dreams, then what good is such information be for us? If AI learns from data, what happens if the data being produced is flawed, only to be consumed again

by AI? How would snowball effect of fundamentally flawed knowledge impact the future of knowledge workers?

AI platforms and the models are becoming more sophisticated. For that reason, some experts doubt whether the importance of prompt engineering will be long lasting. AI models may soon be able to write prompts themselves. Artificial Intelligence, as a force derived from information, and built upon data, models, and algorithms, has precipitated a shift in the way we approach learning, decision-making, and action. Yet these systems do not function in a vacuum. In fact, they are necessarily embedded in questions regarding our purpose as humans. Specifically, what we derive worth from our work, what judgments we consider most trustworthy, and what causes the growing divide in skill-and-repetitive employment. From chapter 5, we turn our attention away from machines and closer to human aspects in order to examine AI's effect on job polarization, how younger generations perceive work in an AI-augmented world, how our own mental biases take shape, why trust matters, and how it can sometimes destruct the course of innovation.

Chapter 6
Humans are Complex and Fallible

We make thousands of decisions every day. What to eat, which route to take to work, how to respond to an email. We make most of these decisions so quickly we barely notice them. But lurking beneath this never-ending stream of choices lies something fascinating and troubling: your mind processes between 12,000 and 60,000 thoughts daily, 80% of which are negative, and 95% are simply recycled from yesterday.

AI systems are increasingly being designed as agents that can act independently to achieve open-ended goals. Since humans drive AI innovation – hopefully with positive intended consequences - we are essentially programming agents into the system as objectives. How often have you thought, *"why did I do that?"* Or after doing or saying something you might find yourself wondering, *"Why did I feel that way?"*

Theory of Mind

How do people come to understand their own minds and the minds of others—a question that has long been explored in philosophy and psychology?

Theory of Mind, as introduced by Premack and Woodruff in 1978, refers to humans' ability to attribute mental states, such as thoughts, beliefs, or feelings, to themselves and others. Our own perceptions drive how we project ourselves, so it's also about recognizing that someone else's perspective might be entirely different from our own. You've likely heard the saying, 'Put yourself in someone else's shoes'. This is a simple way of describing how we try to grasp another person's thoughts and emotions. However, in order to do this, we first need to develop a mental model of our own mind, as our ability to 'decode' what others think, feel, or believe depends on our self-awareness.

Some argue that 'Theory of Mind' plays a particularly crucial role in professions like politics, although leadership also plays a crucial role in understanding and responding to the emotions and perspectives of others when striving to gain influence.

How do people come to understand their own minds and the minds of others? It's a question that has long been argued in philosophy and psychology.

Self-interest is the crucial aspect that would make anyone shift their mind towards your cause. Leaders are experts in making others believe how their actions might meet their needs or advance their cause, and in most situations, workers eagerly follow a leader, especially if they are a politician, CEO, CTO or anyone who sits at the upper management. The difference is not just what is said, but how it's being said. The art of persuasion involves mutual respect and open dialogue, while manipulation relies on exploiting emotional vulnerabilities and creating a power imbalance. People are often driven by social proof, and will do things that they see others doing, even if it is not in their best self-interest.

As a long-time admirer of Sir Arthur Conan Doyle, I'm reminded of *Sherlock Holmes*. If you've read his stories, watched his series, or played any of the games based on his work, you'll recall his extraordinary "mind palace"—a technique where he mentally maps out the thoughts and motives of his suspects. While this concept is rooted in memory techniques, it mirrors how we construct mental models of others. Just like Sherlock imagines what his adversaries might be thinking, we subconsciously build mental blueprints of the people around us—what they fear, desire, or plan.

What's fascinating is this is what AI is attempting to do today by simulating how humans think. While machines don't possess true self-awareness, they mimic patterns of human behavior, similar to how Sherlock pieces clues together, not by feeling, but by recognizing patterns that exist within vast amounts of data.

Humans have a limited short-term memory, which is why we work our way through a single problem in a series. We seldomly multi-task, except for when we have a limited number of options at our disposal. In many situations we don't have the time, or the Lean Methods, which empower and often make possible the process of trial and error. In many situations our knowledge makes it possible for us to search by trial and error.

We also utilize a method called "best first search". Imagine you're managing a large project containing multiple tasks that need to be completed in order, and a fast-approaching deadline. You would want to focus on the tasks that will move the project forward the fastest. Instead of tackling every task one by one, you start with the ones that will directly impact the project's progress, such as getting the client's approval on a key deliverable. This is akin to *best first search*. You prioritize the tasks that are closest to the goal, making the most efficient use of your time, which just happens to also be a process utilized during machine learning. Most of the knowledge we accumulate from childhood is based on generalizations formed from a mass of particulars. Take this simple question: "What is the phone number of Aristotle?" Your immediate response might be to recognize that Aristotle, the Greek philosopher from the 4th century BC, obviously didn't have a phone. This analogy goes down the tubes, of course, if you just happened to share a history class with fellow student named Aristotle – like I did! This illustrates how both our brains and computers work symbolically—we manipulate symbols (like the concept of a phone number) based on our understanding of the world. Both the brain and computers process, transform, and manipulate symbols in various ways. However, even though AI empowered with machine learning is capable of much these days, it still cannot reason in the way humans do. These systems don't understand the actual meaning of the real-world information they process, nor can they sense it in the same way humans can. AI systems struggle to adapt and reason in all the ways that we do naturally, and they struggle to make reliable decisions when faced with the unknown. If AI was able to achieve a human-like 'Theory of Mind", and specifically define contexts as broadly and vividly as our minds do, AI would require an unimaginable amount of data and programming in order to do so.

Whether through the sharp logic of a fictional detective or the calculating intuitions of a skilled leader, the ability to see the world through someone else's eyes remains one of the most powerful and human abilities we have, especially in the age of AI. It still puzzles me why we strive to replicate this deeply human ability in machines. Is it a pursuit of understanding—or control? And if the latter, who will ultimately control whom?

All of these aforementioned tasks can be increasingly automated, or, at the very least, significantly augmented by AI, performed with the assistance of a knowledge worker. Additionally, a good leader or manager should demonstrate a comprehensive skillset that includes expertise in modern organizational management and relevant industry trends, proficiency in administrative, entrepreneurial, and decision-making processes (particularly in dynamic environments), a strong understanding of economic analysis and market dynamics, exemplary ethical conduct and leadership, the ability to analyze competitive landscapes, manage resources, and strategically plan for organizational growth. They should also have a mastery of modern information technologies and communication tools, exceptional interpersonal skills for effective team management and relationship building, strong self-management and time management capabilities, decisive, enthusiastic, and adaptable problem-solving approaches, and a thorough understanding of economic trends and regulatory landscapes.

Many of these skills can easily be mimicked and executed by AI, although there are other additional soft skills that truly define whether you are a good or bad leader/manager. The role of a middle manager is likely to become obsolete by 2030. This doesn't mean these individuals will be out of work, but it does mean a significant shift in their roles and responsibilities, forcing them to transition to roles that require higher-level strategic thinking, project management, or specialized expertise.

"Bias" Beings

Bias and discrimination can arise from a wide range of characteristics. Skin tone and gender are among the most widely recognized, but other factors—such as age, mental or physical disabilities, religion, or physical attractiveness—can also serve as bases for prejudice or discrimination. Scientists have identified around 200 cognitive biases that shape how we think. In the 1970s, psychologists Daniel Kahneman and Amos Tversky gave us the language to understand the predictable ways our thinking goes astray when making decisions or judgments. These mental shortcuts affect everyone, often without us realizing it. We may believe we're being impartial and fair, but our minds are filled with stereotypes, preconceptions, and confirmation biases which operate in the shadows of our consciousness.

These biases affect everyone, often without us even realizing it. Bias is not just a byproduct of flawed thinking; it is a long shadow cast by humanity. Our biases occur unconsciously.

Now something big is changing the way we work AI. AI is designed to be smart and efficient, but it's important to understand that the way we humans think – biases and all – consequently play a huge role in how we use and understand AI. In fact, some of our biases are even showing up in the AI systems themselves!

This chapter will discuss some of the most common mental shortcuts and biases that affect us in white-collar jobs, and how they play out in the world of AI. I will also discuss some of the ways we can detect and reduce these biases.

To Compare Is Human

Have you ever checked out what a colleague is doing and compared it to your own progress? Maybe you saw someone get a promotion or land a big client, and it made you feel a little less confident about where you are in your own career. That's a common human tendency called social comparison.

In 1954, psychologist Leon Festinger hypothesized that people compare themselves to others in order to fulfill a basic human desire: the need for self-evaluation. He called this process *social comparison theory (SCT)*. According to Festinger, *"There exists, in the human organism, a drive to evaluate his opinions and abilities."*

We naturally look at others in order to evaluate ourselves. If we compare ourselves to people who seem more successful, it can sometimes make us feel down. On the other hand, comparing ourselves to someone who seems to be struggling might make us feel better about our own situation. While some of this behavior is indeed normal, the act of constantly comparing ourselves to others, especially in a negative way, can actually make us feel more envious and less happy overall. Knowledge workers will compare their own performance (speed, accuracy, efficiency, creativity) directly to that of AI tools performing similar tasks. And if they are not, the business owners certainly will.

Knowledge work (e.g., software development, research, lawyers, project leaders or consulting) often involves complex tasks where performance isn't always easily quantifiable. Sometimes we knowledge workers might prioritize tasks that are easily visible and comparable (e.g., lines of code, number of reports completed) over less tangible but equally important aspects like deep thinking, mentoring, or relationship building.

Social Proof

Knowledge work-based environments are often complex and uncertain, making them particularly vulnerable to the influence of social proof.

The term "social proof" was first introduced by psychologist Robert Cialdini (see below) in his 1984 book, *Influence: The Psychology of Persuasion*. Following others has been our survival instinct for over millions of years. My mom used to tell me that just because one person jumps down the well doesn't mean you too ought to do the same. Back then it meant that I should follow my own assumptions based on what I think, and not what others claim, say, or do. Knowledge workers heavily rely on what peers, industry leaders, or successful companies are doing. Widespread adoption provides "proof" of effectiveness or suitability, driving adoption even without deep personal evaluation.

Social proof can be like a quiet force, pushing us to follow the crowd without questioning that decision. It's subtle pressure that can make us forget to think for ourselves. Today, we see this a lot with AI.

Many "experts" and leaders tell us that AI is the next big thing; knowledge workers and organizations feel pressure to adopt AI technologies or strategies partly because "everyone else" seems to be doing it, fearing they'll be left behind. This social proof can overshadow critical analysis of whether the specific AI application truly adds value in their unique situation.

The Future Impact

As discussed in the previous about AI fundamentals, AI algorithms often fundamentally prioritize results based on popularity. Many recommendation systems are built this way, directly embedding social proof into the tools many knowledge workers use today.

AI systems may also be designed to learn by observing and mimicking successful strategies used by other agents (human or AI).

This could lead to emergent herd behavior among AI agents, as they rapidly propagate strategies based on observed success (a form of automated social proof) without necessarily ensuring they are optimal in every new context.

As AI becomes more sophisticated, its recommendations might carry significant weight. If an AI agent suggests a particular approach, users might accept it partly because they trust the AI's "intelligence," which can function similarly to trusting the *"wisdom of the crowd."* They might assume the AI has synthesized vast amounts of data indicating this is the "proven" path, when in fact – that was not the case.

Halo Effect

In 1920, American psychologist Edward L. Thorndike uncovered a fascinating cognitive illusion while studying servicemen. He asked commanding officers to rate their subordinates on intelligence, leadership, and character—without ever speaking to them.

Strikingly, those perceived as taller and more attractive consistently received higher marks in unrelated qualities, such as competence and discipline. Thorndike's research revealed a hidden bias: people instinctively generalize from a single prominent trait, allowing one favorable impression to cast a glow over an entire personality.

The Halo Effect also occurs in AI when an AI system overgeneralizes from limited data or when users interpret AI decisions based on superficial impressions. If an AI system is highly accurate in one task, users may also trust it in unrelated areas. If an AI chatbot answers factual questions well, users might trust it on legal or medical advice, even if it's not qualified.

Authority Bias

At a former workplace, I was forced to follow my manager's flawed strategy simply because they held a leadership position, even when evidence suggested a better approach. Since I was not part of senior management, my voice wasn't considered; I was firmly told to just follow orders. This bias is rooted in our psychological inclination to trust in and defer to perceived authority figures, which can sometimes lead to poor decision-making, ethical lapses, or a lack of independent thought.

When AI has been trained with data based on "expert" opinions, it triggers the authority bias. This bias is particularly strong in situations involving health, finance, and technology, or in any consulting capacity where an expert opinion is highly valued. People in a position of authority still make mistakes, which is why it is important to make it a habit to think before we blindly follow. My best suggestion to overcome authority bias is act with caution, be self-reflecting and educate yourself.

Confirmation bias is the tendency to seek out, interpret, and remember information in ways that confirm our pre-existing beliefs while choosing to ignore contradictory evidence. It's a universal human trait, though we might not readily admit it. GenAI can amplify this bias, acting like an additional voice in our heads that not only praises us for being "right" but also supplies us with supporting evidence.

We discussed prompting earlier. Your inputs or your search queries could unintentionally steer the conversation in ways that reinforce your existing beliefs, while neglecting to explore alternative perspectives or counterarguments of the output provided by GenAI.

Imagine if your inputs to GenAI are phrased in a way that already leans towards your existing beliefs. For instance, instead of asking "What are the potential challenges and opportunities in expanding to market X?", you might ask something like, *"Provide evidence that expanding to market X is a risky venture due to [mentioning your existing concerns]."* By framing your prompt in this manner, you are unintentionally guiding GenAI to search for and potentially prioritize information that confirms your initial skepticism. The AI, in its effort to be helpful and responsive, will likely provide you with data and arguments that support your viewpoint, while potentially overlooking or downplaying counterarguments or alternative perspectives that might present a more balanced picture. This creates a feedback loop where our biases inadvertently shape the information we receive, further reinforcing our initial beliefs and potentially leading to less informed decisions.

Upon research for my book, I came upon a site named *the decision lab.com* and found a list of over 100 cognitive biases commonly held by humans. I read another study published in *Nature Human Behavior* which revealed how our biases can create a harmful feedback loop, amplify errors, and reinforce stereotypes from AI.

The study shows that when people interact with biased AI systems, they are more likely to adopt and assume these biases, leading them to underestimate women's abilities, or overestimate the likelihood of white men holding high-status jobs. AI systems learn from human data, which fundamentally carries biases, and then amplify these biases to improve their predictions. This creates a cycle where small, initial biases in human judgment are exacerbated by AI, making users even more biased in their own perceptions. The researchers also found that when people were exposed to biased AI generated content, such as images of financial managers, they were more likely to reinforce stereotypes, further demonstrating the impact of AI on shaping beliefs. However, the study also suggests that interacting with accurate, unbiased AI can improve decision-making, highlighting the need for developers to prioritize fairness and accuracy when designing AI systems. This isn't a flaw of the GenAI itself but a result of how we interact with it. As users, we can sometimes steer the conversation to echo our existing beliefs and overlook counterarguments.

Brain Shortcuts

We use what we've learned from our environment to make quick assumptions about whom to trust, how to behave, and what to say. During a recent discussion earlier in 2025 about my book's underlying message, Simon, a former colleague, shared an interesting perspective.

He believes that while AI is surrounded by a great deal of hype, we shouldn't underestimate the power and complexity of the human mind. He pointed out that despite the fact that most knowledge workers have gained much more experience compared to 25 years ago, we are still influenced by tech companies that often amplify AI's capabilities, largely to drive interest and sales on their own products.

Simon's point - about not underestimating human intelligence—can also be seen as a human-centered bias, where we might undervalue AI's contributions due to our belief in human superiority in cognitive tasks.

AI systems are only as objective as the humans who build them. Our personal experiences, cultural backgrounds, and individual perspectives shape how we interpret information and make decisions—and these same influences become embedded in the data we use to train AI. Although AI systems lack consciousness, they operate on a foundation of accumulated digital knowledge that reflects a combination of human experiences and judgment, complete with our cognitive blind spots and unconscious biases. AI is often described as something very linear and simple in theory. In reality, it's more like a maze. Machine learning is often described as a powerful, but hard to interpret "black box" process that simply works but is not always explainable. This is due to the fact that we often don't quite understand how machine learning actually arrives at a conclusion, or why it may often take short cuts, in the same way that our neurons are connected in our brains.

The image below explains the reality on how machine learning actually works.

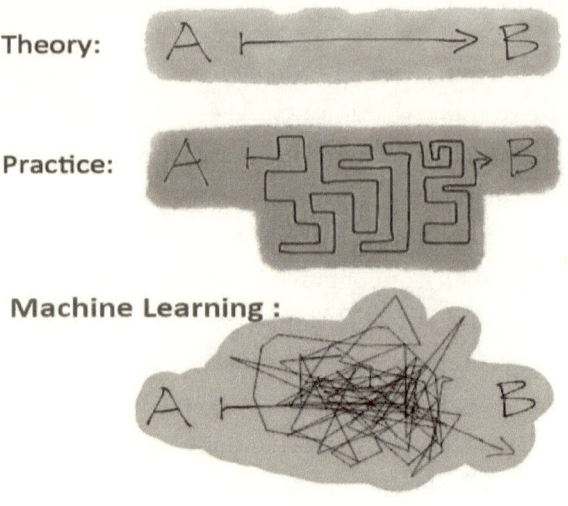

Gender Bias

As Anita Krohn Traaseth explored in her 2015 work "Good Enough for the 'Bastards'," being a female C-level executive in the male dominated IT profession presents a unique set of challenges.

Her experiences reflect the broader struggles that women in leadership positions continue to face in technology fields. In 2023, Fortune 500 companies achieved a milestone, with women assuming leadership positions in more than 10% of the elite companies for the first time in the 68-year history of the list. Although this is a remarkable development, it is also a reflection of the long way the industry has to go to achieve true gender equality. Women hold barely 28% of IT careers globally. In the USA, the contrast is glaringly obvious. Women comprise 47% of the labour force but hold 25% of computing jobs. Even in STEM fields, women hold a negligible 35% of all workers. Perhaps most troubling is stagnation over time; women's percentage of computing work has hovered at around 25% since 2015, indicating deeply embedded structural barriers to meaningful progress. Statistics have repeatedly revealed a staggering shortage of women on corporate boards and in executive C level roles. Underrepresentation creates a cycle that cascades downward through each step of the technological career ladder. Without proper female representation in decision making roles, policies and workplace climates often fail to consider the specific challenges women in the technology industry must overcome. However, the small advancements achieved to date offer a reason to be optimistic.

Overall, there's a smaller gap between women and men in knowledge work roles, compared to manual labor. Yet a clear difference still exists, especially in software development. In fields like science, technology, engineering, and math, about 70% of the workers are men. In countries like Sweden, Finland,

and Norway, only about one in five jobs has a balanced mix of men and women. This is surprising because, academically, women tend to perform better than men.

The rise of artificial intelligence has introduced new dimensions to existing workplace gender gaps. While AI ranks among the top subjects drawing interest from women, a concerning paradox has emerged. A staggering 63% of women report lacking proper training and feeling deprived of on-the-job opportunities in this crucial field. This skill gap is particularly troubling given that AI continues to transform work patterns and create new pathways for career advancement.

Current adoption trends reveal an alarming disparity. Women accounted for 42% of the 200 million average monthly visitors to ChatGPT's website between November 2022 and May 2024. Research suggests that while women excel in areas such as attention, word and face memory, and social cognition, men typically perform better in spatial processing and sensorimotor speed. These cognitive differences may contribute to behavioral patterns where men (who tend to favor technological solutions and logical thinking), adopt AI tools more readily than women, who often prioritize relationship-building and creative approaches.

Women generally adopt AI technologies at a rate 25% slower than men, despite both genders benefiting equally from these tools. This adoption gap risks amplifying existing workplace disparities as AI integration accelerates across industries.

The slow adoption rate among women is particularly surprising given the potential advantages of leveraging AI skills in the job market. Survey data from employers reveals that AI competency has become a high priority during the hiring processes, with female candidates commanding a significant premium for their AI expertise.

Female applicants with strong AI skills rated 7.6% higher than their less-trained counterparts, while male applicants received no premium for similar AI familiarity. This suggests that women with AI competencies may have a unique opportunity to distinguish themselves in an increasingly competitive job market.

Disinformation

It's interesting to watch how most politicians present fact to the public. When I reflect back on how Putin and Trump often misinformed the public, I was reminded of the concept of disinformation. The word "disinformation" originates from the Russian *dezinformacija,* dating back to the earliest years of the cold war, it means sowing falsehoods among one's enemies in order to confuse them about one's own capabilities or intentions. But the more general term "misinformation" —spreading untruths—has been around since the late 16th century.

Hans Rosling spent much of his life trying to offer a clearer, more fact-based view of the world, and believed that the presence of accurate information was the key to making better decisions. Rosling, the author of *Factfulness*, voiced his frustration over how difficult it was to challenge people's misconceptions without solid data. He posed an intriguing question—could we all adopt a worldview rooted in facts? Yet, what he never foresaw was the rise of AI and the deep impact it would have on truth itself in the 21st century, especially given how this technology is now being used to disinform and create fake news. AI technologies, with their ability to generate convincing fake texts, images, audio, and videos (often referred to as 'deepfakes'), present significant challenges in distinguishing authentic content from synthetic creations.

This capability lets wrongdoers automate and expand disinformation campaigns, leveraging AI to greatly increase their reach and impact.

Just days before the 2024 New Hampshire presidential primary, voters received fraudulent robocalls featuring what appeared to be President

Biden's voice, urging them not to participate in the election.

The audio, generated using AI, was convincing enough to deceive many. That same month, deepfake video calls tricked a finance worker at a Hong Kong based company into wiring $25 million to scammers impersonating the company's CFO. As AI technology grows more advanced, experienced professionals struggle to keep pace with its rapid evolution. In high-pressure environments, where time is limited and decisions must be made quickly, the temptation to take shortcuts becomes all too real. The line between efficiency and vulnerability is thinner than ever.

Uncommon Sense

Common sense, as Professor Moutaz pointed out, is becoming increasingly uncommon. We need to cultivate this essential skill in both students and teachers. We must also be vigilant about the importance of discerning "truth" in the age of misinformation, especially when AI can generate convincing yet fabricated content. The challenge lies in using AI tools effectively while maintaining our own critical thinking skills and fostering originality. This could involve exploring new assessment methods, such as "live composition" exercises, where students demonstrate their understanding in real-time. As Hilary Mason, Founder and CEO of Fast Forward Labs, fittingly tweeted, "AI is not inscrutable magic – it is math and data and computer programming, made by regular humans." Like the internet before it, AI is a human invention, a powerful tool that can be used for better or worse. Its fate is determined by how humans choose to use it. The best approach is to accept AI's existence, and utilize it within our educational systems, rather than ignore it, a choice which threatens to make learning obsolete, and education boring for the next generation.

Remember the example from previous chapter about AI being similar to a parrot? Let me further elaborate on that example using philosopher John Searle's popular "Chinese Room". He argued that a computer program running language is like someone in a room executing instructions to string together Chinese characters without having the ability to read Chinese. The person receives input (Chinese characters), employs a rulebook (the program), and produces corresponding output (response in Chinese) to convince people outside the room that whoever is inside can read Chinese. But the person in the room is only transforming symbols according to rules, without completely grasping their meaning.

Research by Dean L. Gano in 2024 confirmed that common sense is in fact not that common. Gano argues that relying on *"common sense"* to resolve issues is flawed because every person's perception of reality is uniquely shaped by their individual experiences. He breaks this process into the three following interconnected steps:

1. Our senses gather raw data from the world around us. Though everyone shares the same five senses—sight, sound, touch, taste, and smell—their development, and the pace of that development varies widely. Different factors, such as upbringing, culture, and daily environments shape how our brains interpret sensory input. Over time, these differences create distinct neural pathways, meaning no two people perceive the same situation identically.
2. This sensory data is processed into knowledge. Each person filters, prioritizes, and stores information based on personal interests, values, and past experiences. For example, a musician might notice subtle sounds others overlook, while an architect might focus on spatial details. What one person deems critical, another might ignore or forget entirely.
3. These knowledge patterns inform our problem-solving strategies. People adopt

behaviors that align with their goals and past successes.

A model embedded with common sense should also have basic knowledge about the world. Second, it should have the ability to reason over common-sense knowledge. Common sense is also defined as negative knowledge. An example would be the common-sense statement, "Lions do not live in the ocean." Negative knowledge refers to information that describes what is not true, what cannot be done, or what does not exist, while everything that exists is positive; basically, it helps us think critically about what we should not think. Negative knowledge serves as a pivotal role in human decision-making process, offering direct assistance in decision-making and error avoidance. When it comes to LLMs, negative knowledge can help alleviate their hallucination problem, but only to some extent. It is also vital to understand a concept called "anti-intelligence", which means a model fails to understand something. It's the performance of knowing without understanding the context. It's language separated from memory, context, or intention. Large language models aren't stupid; they're structurally blind and don't know what they're saying. By better understanding and incorporating negative constraints, we might be able to guide these powerful AI systems towards more reliable and grounded reasoning.

The image below is a snapshot from a tool, *similar web*, indicating that people might need to be told what is true, and fewer are actually seeking out the truth. Indeed, LLMs are a good tool, and contain the assumptions and opinions of their creators, and the enormous data sets of their users upon which they've been trained. The mere size of the user base itself, at billions of monthly interactions, increases the likelihood of those biases being spread.

	Domain (100)	Traffic Share	MoM traffic change	Monthly Visits
1	google.com	36.38%	↓ 3.18%	81.31B
2	youtube.com	12.83%	↓ 2.13%	28.68B
3	facebook.com	5.17%	↓ 3.05%	11.56B
4	instagram.co	2.76%	↓ 1.65%	6.172B
5	chatgpt.com	2.30%	↑ 13.04%	5.141B
6	x.com	1.94%	↓ 5.21%	4.338B
7	whatsapp.com	1.87%	↓ 2.75%	4.168B
8	wikipedia.org	1.66%	↓ 6.06%	3.721B
9	reddit.com	1.63%	↓ 3.77%	3.650B

AI is WEIRD

Humans are not simply one rational-thinking entity. We are affected by jealousy, plagued by complex and sometimes illogical emotions, and constantly evolving in countless ways.

In order for us to effectively understand and communicate with AI, we must impart it with knowledge from psychology, economics, political science, and ethics philosophy—modifying and translating each of these fields so it may address these great issues from more intelligent systems. To date, we have barely begun.

Tromsø, a Norwegian municipality, derived its school strategy early in 2025 based on cases which never existed. This stemmed from its use of AI (ChatGPT) as an aid, and it ultimately cited (fictitious?) sources to produce a new school structure report that was factually incorrect.

This case highlights the fact that most Norwegian bureaucrats generally lack basic AI literacy or technology and underscores the fact that machines can make mistakes. When you use an AI tool, it clearly warns, *"AI may make mistakes."* It might present some information that it thinks is correct on its own but is, in fact, just a hallucination. Engineers have already implemented "self-doubt" in these tools, which asks it for clarification, to show self-doubt, and admit mistakes. AI can develop biases because it learns from data, which often reflects human mistakes and unfair patterns. These biases are hard to remove because spotting them and fixing them requires both advanced technical skills and an understanding of social issues, like how data is collected and what influences it in the first place. Additionally, we sometimes don't quite understand how the AI arrives at the answer it suggests, which is a phenomenon known as "black box", which consequently makes it impossible to test it fully in all mission critical aspects.

Authors Michael Chui, James Manyika, and Mehdi Miremadi of the consulting firm McKinsey point out the challenge is these biases are not just about technology, they're also about ethics and fairness. Deciding what is "fair" is complicated and even controversial. Consequently, removing bias from AI is one of the hardest and most sensitive problems in the field today.

An insightful study, *Generative language models exhibit social identity biases,* confirmed that AI systems, much like humans, can develop biases based on social identity, showing favoritism toward their "ingroup" and negativity toward "outgroups." These biases reflect the same human tendency to divide people into "us" versus "them." The study, which examined AI models like GPT-4, found that when asked to generate sentences, the models tended to create more positive statements about ingroups and more negative ones about outgroups. However, the researchers also discovered that these biases could be reduced by carefully curating the training data.

AI training data largely reflects what is known as WEIRD populations—Western, Educated, Industrialized, Rich, and Democratic societies. This skew exists because most internet data originates from developed nations, creating a training quantity that represents only a fraction of global human diversity.

This causes the output of the data mainly to be driven by Western thinking and not as much from Asian or other cultures. According to Harvard University, these matters (see graph below) because human cognition, values, and problem-solving approaches vary significantly across cultures. When AI systems learn primarily from WEIRD data sources, they embed the reasoning patterns, cultural assumptions, and priorities of this narrow demographic while underrepresenting or ignoring perspectives from the majority of the world's population.

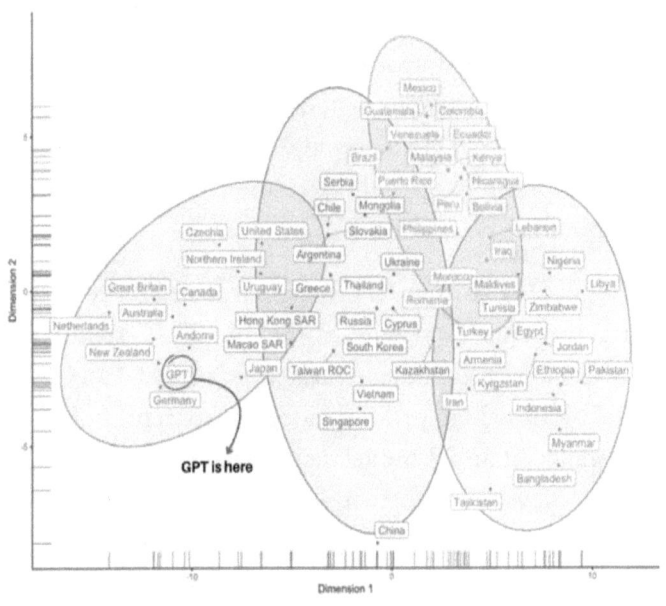

Mitigation strategies

The ability to choose an action that balances conflicting goals is not a simple feature can just program into a machine—it's a core aspect of human intelligence. It involves not only logical reasoning but also an understanding of social context and the subtleties of language. While a machine might be able to process information and recognize patterns, it doesn't truly "care" about outcomes the way humans do, even if it can technically "know" what those outcomes are.

Research has proven that LLM agents show the same biases as humans when making decisions. LLM agents often make persistent attribution errors, meaning it would incorrectly assign causes or intentions in judgment tasks—much like humans sometimes do.

Cognitive biases in AI can arise from patterns in training data, but Chain-of-thought (CoT) reasoning offers a way to mitigate these biases by making the decision-making process more transparent. For instance, if an AI model demonstrates confirmation bias—favoring information that aligns with its pre-existing assumptions, CoT can force it to explore multiple perspectives rather than reinforcing a singular viewpoint. This step-by-step reasoning approach helps uncover biases embedded in algorithms, such as those influencing hiring decisions, where an AI might disproportionately favor certain demographics.

Reinforcement Learning (RL) enhances bias correction by providing feedback at different levels. Through outcome supervision, AI receives corrective signals when producing biased outputs, while process supervision allows human reviewers to assess and refine the model's reasoning at each stage. However, despite these advancements, CoT can sometimes lead to "rationalization bias," where an AI overcomplicates simple decisions, generating unnecessarily complex justifications for flawed conclusions. By combining CoT and RL, AI systems not only improve their reasoning but also become more accountable and adaptable in identifying and addressing biases.

Diverse and representative data

Smart programs need lots of good, high-quality data based on different types of information. They learn by receiving feedback. That means the better the data, the better the program becomes. Training AI systems on data that reflects a broad range of perspectives helps minimize biases and promotes fairness. Because of this, companies need people to help identify and prepare data. Furthermore, the focus on "only" having people with tech skills to help out with AI, while frowning upon other cognitive jobs, is a miscalculation many organizations seem to make these days.

Human In The Loop

In 1936, psychologist Kurt Lewin gave the world a simple equation: $B = f(P, E)$ Behavior is a function of the Person and their Environment. This was the original "blueprint" on how human behavior could change. It now seems we're trying to reprogram humans without rewriting the code of their surroundings.

Those who commit cognitive biases are not bad people; these errors are part of our highly adaptive cognitive mechanisms. To address such biases, companies must integrate human oversight at every stage of AI development. Initiatives like Google's PAIR (People+ AI Research) provide open-source tools that help organizations analyze and improve their AI data. By maintaining a human-in-the-loop approach, businesses can enhance accountability and reduce the risks of algorithmic discrimination.

How do we move forward if humans are fallible and AI systems inherit our biases? The answer lies not in perfection, but in trust - a concept which becomes infinitely more complex when one party in the relationship is an algorithm. In a world where machines increasingly make decisions that affect our lives, careers, and societies, we must redefine what it means to trust. How do we trust systems we don't fully understand? Perhaps s most critically, how do we build AI systems worthy of our trust?

Chapter 7 Trust

None of us are perfect as we live in a very complicated and volatile world, where much of the tasks and work are gradually being handed to machines. Much of what we do in this environment is built on trust in our colleagues, in the systems we use, and even in the information we consume. Imagine a scenario where you might trust an AI more than your own work team, what would that look like?

Trust involves accepting some vulnerability. We risk being hurt by other people's actions, but we do so because we expect them to act responsibly. When it comes to AI similar principles apply you trust it by relying on its designed function without constant checking, and designers may even be held accountable for its performance.

Trust plays a critical role in the study of human–machine communication (HMC), as it is essential for establishing effective and reliable interactions between humans and machines. For AI, we trust it to perform its designated tasks without constant checking. However, unlike with human trust, if an AI fails, we don't experience moral betrayal because an AI can't intend to harm or act out of goodwill. AI systems, being inanimate, cannot bear moral responsibilities or understand commitments, which again, challenges the idea of trusting them as humans would. Critics argue that trying to apply human notions of trust to AI is problematic. If we force AI to fit these models, we end up anthropomorphizing them (attributing human traits to machines) or merely treating them as reliable tools without true trust. Moreover, trusting AI can be undesirable because it might allow developers to shift responsibility away from themselves, creating a gap in accountability. Charles Green's Trust Equation, introduced in *The Trusted Advisor*, offers a framework for describing these complexities. By breaking trust into discrete, measurable components, Green's model reveals how traditional notions of trust translate, or fail to translate—to our relationships with machines with four distinct factors as seen below.

The Trust Equation 2.0

Trust is something intangible for most. Each time your model nails a prediction, you're one step closer to calling it a teammate, not just code. As AI uses algorithms or LLMs, formal metrics tend to have a strong foundation in algebra, probability, or logic. I am noticing a shift in a different kind of trust that I would not consider in a human colleague, but closer to trust we have in any well-engineered tool or machine. "Tool-like" or "machine trust" usually builds over time with the consistent delivery of accurate and useful results. Trust among humans, however, usually originates from how that person makes us feel in terms of connection, empathy, and mutual understanding.

$$\text{Trust} = \frac{\text{Credibility} + \text{Reliability} + \text{Intimacy}}{\text{Self-Orientation}}$$

Reliability

Will it do what it's supposed to, consistently? Similar when you promise something and deliver on it. People will find you reliable. In the context of AI, reliability translates to its ability to be easily trusted, and is established when we consistently meet or exceed expectations. LLMs offer expert guidance, and their expertise increases with additional modules and practices, such as the use of RAG for context enrichment. An opinion survey conducted in 2025 suggested sixty percent of Norwegians who were questioned disagreed with the notion that they can trust information generated by AI, while only nine percent agreed. Many Norwegians are also aware of the risks associated with the use of this technology. More than half (56%) say they are concerned that AI may produce and spread misinformation. This indicates that although AI is being adopted, a majority express skepticism toward the reliability of its output.

Credibility

Can I believe the AI what it tells me? Telling somebody that they can count on you and then you subsequently deliver, gives you credibility. It means fewer second-guesses, faster decision-making and a reputation that opens doors—whether you're pitching a new strategy, leading a team, or just trying to get buy-in on a routine status update. Without credibility, even the best proposals can stall under the weight of doubt. AI systems have demonstrated the potential to do so by processing vast datasets with speed and precision.

As we design and develop systems aimed at improving knowledge workers' efficiency and productivity, what gets seen and how end users interpret what they actually see can indeed have deep implications in the workplace. That increased visibility can potentially lead to worsening situations by hindering individual's efficacy and well-being. If an AI helps most users better understand why it made a certain decision, you're more likely to believe its reasoning (credibility), and less likely to suspect hidden biases or agendas (lower self-orientation).

According to a 2025 Norwegian Study completed by "my OsloMET", we have little faith that AI will offer selfless benefits to our society. Only 17 percent consider it credible, while 38 percent are skeptical. The rest, nearly half of responders, have not yet made up their mind.

Intimacy

In the trust equation, intimacy is a factor in how open we are to being vulnerable—to sharing our doubts, our fears, and our very personal information. Humans typically establish intimacy through mutual disclosure. But what is intimacy when the other party is artificial intelligence?

AI cannot reciprocate exposure in the emotional sense, yet it achieves a strange simulation of closeness through personification. When the algorithm anticipates our requirements or remembers our tastes, we experience a feeling of being "known" or, maybe, understood. We have already witnessed AI's uncanny ability to mimic mimicry of deep human emotions such as love, pain, care, even the joy of parenthood. These imitations activate our most primal desire for attachment, clouding the difference between reality and an algorithmic response. Organizations should use secure and reliable data storage solutions with strong access controls and regular security audits. When possible, sensitive data should be made anonymous before processing, and should abide by easily understandable and comprehensive privacy policies that explicitly outline what data is collected, how it is used, where it is stored, and for how long. GenZ is known for preferring to have control, while also appreciating direct and clear communication. These protocols empower users with that control and allow them to specify what data they are comfortable sharing, for what purposes, and with whom. Additionally, be sure to establish clear internal guidelines and protocols for data handling, access, and retention within the area of the organization tasked with developing and deploying the AI system. Finally, ensure there are clearly defined roles and responsibilities within the organization for maintaining the security and confidentiality of user data.

Self-Orientation

Much of our work life consists of sharing and working in collaboration if we want to solve or produce something worthwhile. Otherwise, we might say, *"I can't trust him on this deal—I don't think he cares enough about me; he's focused on what he gets out of it."* Or more often, *"I don't trust him — I think he's too concerned about how he can shine and would throw the team under the bus."* We are all relation-oriented beings; we work best when we collaborate with each other and this also builds loyalty and confidence through life's ups and downs. In the Western world, genuine trust is often compromised by financial motivations and competition. Many of us are so focused on monetary success and individual achievement that we rarely pause to reconsider our willingness to collaborate and enjoy mutual support. As a Norwegian, I have seen many leaders support people's growth and development to incentivize making good decisions, rather than relying on the leader telling them what to do, which is what often happens in countries such as India or USA. In a sense, when it comes to AI systems, many of us question their motives in the same manner. Are they acting for our benefit, solely in their own interest, or in the interest of big tech companies? Separately, self-orientation relates to where you tend to put your attention and focus. Are you more interested in getting what you need so you can look good? From the knowledge worker's perspective, a lack of trust in the AI system can severely impact productivity. In short, how can you stay productive, let alone thrive, within a system you don't trust?

I was constantly looking for some tangible proof that AI reliability is actually being put into practice, and discovered a recent study by Stanford University that measured developers' openness about their models. Their latest report, covering the time period between late 2023 through to the spring of 2024, provided a better understanding, and affirmed my belief that we are heading in the right direction when it comes to transparency.

Industry leaders such as Anthropic and Amazon had their transparency scores increase significantly. It's an indication that momentum is starting to shift, indicating the possibility of a truly reliable AI is a bit closer to becoming a realization.

We are, however, extremely concerned about developments in AI. As many as eight in ten are concerned about disinformation, surveillance and fraud. Just as many fear election manipulation, hacking and ID theft.

Throughout various chapters in this book, I am presenting various knowledge worker connected professions which are, and will be, heavily impacted by AI. However, as you reflect on each profession and scenario be sure to ask yourself who do you trust most — yourself, your team, or the AI system with which you're working? More importantly - why?

Chapter 8 The country with no innovators?

Historical Perspectives on Innovation

History reminds us that innovation can be both destructive and generative. Joseph Schumpeter's idea of creative destruction illustrates how transformative breakthroughs—like the shift from

horse-drawn carriages to automobiles—could simultaneously dissolve entire industries while giving birth to new ones. The challenge Norwegian businesses face involves guiding this cycle so tomorrow's gains outweigh today's losses. Peter Drucker's ideas about innovations are as relevant today, if not more, than they were back then.

Another scholar in history of technology, Melvin Kranzberg, defined *"Kranzberg's Laws,"* the first of which states that "Technology is neither good nor bad; nor is it neutral." This principle suggests that technologies such as AI will likely have both negative and positive impacts on society, although they are not inherently predestined toward either. While advancements in technology, science, and industry are often hailed as markers of progress, they frequently bring unintended and sometimes detrimental consequences. Material progress does not automatically equate to the betterment of a society. In fact, it can actually introduce new social problems. These negative outcomes often appear in parallel with advancements, suggesting that while progress yields remarkable achievements, it can also strain social structures and create new hardships, highlighting the emotional and social costs of modernization. This led me to consider that Norway is indeed in a puzzling state. We have become a nation of "cuddly" workers rather than hungry innovators. So, are we simply not the right kind of people, curious, and risk-takers? Are we somehow not made to invent? The key consideration shifts from whether AI creates jobs or destroys jobs, to how it ultimately transforms the meaning of work, and who benefits from this transformation. Are we passively going to accept disruption, or actively shape the future of technology's potential for equitable human augmentation? This has evoked a curiosity to explain my personal understanding of work.

Historically, writing was invented by societies in regions that featured food production and the presence of advanced economies. While writing, as an invention, was driven by specific needs, including record-keeping, the primary motivation for its invention and its widespread use was essentially our need to share and store information for the benefit of others. Current day AI systems, specifically those capable of autonomously performing tasks that traditionally required human intelligence, represent the latest phase in this AI evolution. Unlike its predecessors, AI doesn't merely follow instructions; it acts with apparent purpose, making decisions, solving problems, and even negotiating with humans and other AI systems.

Norwegians are devoted consumers of tech accessories, and share, with the Japanese, their love of gadgets. From smartphones to smart houses, we're eager to adopt the newest tech developments into our daily routines. But when it comes to actually inventing tomorrow's breakthroughs, Norwegians are sadly, still stumbling in the dark (despite making minor progress but not enough compared to other European countries).

For Norwegian knowledge workers—from software engineers to financial analysts, lawyers, and consultants—this development represents both an opportunity and an existential challenge. This might lead people to question why we persist with innovation when it creates so many challenges. Think of how the railroad annihilated the horse-and-carriage industry, or how the internet rewrote the rules of commerce and communication.

Schumpeter described this revolutionary process moving through distinct, though often overlapping, dimensions:

- **Invention**: The spark of a new idea or technology. Such as universities and research centers as NorwAI and NORA publishing cutting-edge AI papers.
- **Innovation**: According to an article by Shifter, Norway has more than 200 startups bringing AI invention into the market.
- **Diffusion**: The widespread adoption of this innovation across society. Industries such as finance and health are great examples of how various fields are adopting the use of AI.
- **Imitation**: When others copy and adapt the successful implementation of AI innovations, its impact spreads - fueling competition. Meta, Google, X and Microsoft are all tech companies are imitating each other in attempting to leverage the power of AI.

Schumpeter's waveform economic evolution is interesting, as it describes the idea of successive industrial revolutions. AI is a key component of the current revolution, representing a significant shift in technology and economic organization in Europe and across the rest of the world. As stated in *chapter 2*, AI doesn't have a defined definition and its usage can be complex depending on the process or business application. It's correct to assume that AI in its current stage is moving through Schumpeter's four phases.

Agentic AI is currently surging through all these stages *simultaneously* across various sectors of Norway's economy. While fundamental research continues at institutions like NorwAI and NORA (invention), applications are already being commercialized (innovation) and rapidly adopted (diffusion) in energy, finance, healthcare, and media. This acceleration is precisely why its impact feels so profound and so immediate. It aligns with Schumpeter's understanding that true innovation isn't just about marginal gains in efficiency; it's about unlocking entirely new possibilities, transforming the very way we live and work.

AI Transforms Both How and What We Create

Schumpeter introduced two variants of innovation: product innovation (mentioned in chapter 1), which produces new or radically improved offerings vs process innovation, which improves how those offerings are created or delivered. In many cases, AI is an example of process innovation which is transforming how work is done. In industries like manufacturing, AI automates tasks and improves productivity, just similar to earlier forms of automation (think of machines replacing manual labor). This process of innovation improves efficiency but doesn't necessarily disrupt entire industries or create entirely new markets compared to a product innovation.

AI is also creating entirely new products and even new markets: consider AI tools (e.g., chat assistants), AI-based drug discovery platforms, or algorithmic creative applications. Those would be product innovations—often very different from the products we had before—instead of minor incremental changes to processes.

While a human inventor might spend years pursuing a single idea, AI works differently. It's like having thousands of researchers working simultaneously, each examining a different piece of the puzzle. The AI scans millions of scientific papers, patents, and experimental results in seconds—not just reading them but finding hidden connections we'd never spot.

Think of it this way: You're looking at a massive jigsaw puzzle, but the pieces are scattered across different rooms, different buildings, even different countries. A human might find a few matching pieces through dedication and luck. But AI? It sees all the pieces at once, instantly recognizing which edges fit together, even when they come from completely different fields.

For knowledge workers, AI isn't only about automation; it's about enhancement. Think of it as having a brilliant intern with perfect recall, infinite patience, and zero preconceptions about what solutions "should" look like. Your job evolves from information gathering to insight evaluation—from finding needles in haystacks to deciding which needles actually matter.

"The Magnificent 7"

Schumpeter is useful for understanding AI because his ideas show how major innovations completely reshape the economy and society. He originally developed his theory during the age of railroads—when new technology was radically transforming industries, but the same concepts apply.

Schumpeter argued that economies evolve through waves of innovation, a process often called "creative destruction." This means that new technologies replace old ones, changing not just businesses but also social structures. Aircraft, computers, modern chips, cars, etc., are all man-made creations and defined as innovative products. Innovation has never been, and will never be, just about assembling things. It is a thoughtful process of using knowledge worker's intellectual abilities, enhancing them, and merging them into ideas that transform the way we do things and live. Which is the opposite of when we manufacture a product that is a physical thing, where resources have been used to create it. How does Schumpeter's idea align with Norwegians' spirit of innovation? Norway has one of the world's most educated workforces and is widely regarded as a leader in the field of research. But is that enough?

Schumpeter believed as a matter of practice that firms with strong market positions such as Apple, Meta, Nvidia, Google, and Microsoft should be considered powerful engines of technological progress because they have the resources and market power to drive innovation. These companies can invest heavily in research and development, take risks on new technologies, and shape entire industries by introducing disruptive innovations.

Their leading market positions enable them to lead waves of *"creative destruction"*.

As the world becomes more interconnected—and the internet has made buying and selling almost frictionless, the global economy has paradoxically shrunk. There are fewer, more dominant players that currently hold the winning cards, and the majority of them are tech giants who consistently enjoy the support of investors and politicians., 19th century British economist Alfred Marshall described what is called the *"Winner takes it all society."* One of the major challenges of innovation is that instead of distributing wealth evenly, it seems to be concentrating it, while simultaneously creating a wider gap between the wealthiest and the middle class.

Despite Norway's wealth and high standard of living, its position in the global innovation landscape is surprisingly modest. The Global Innovation Index reveals that as of 2024, Norway ranks between 19th and 23rd place a position it has maintained for nearly a decade, while other nations have made dramatic leaps forward. India, for example, jumped 41 spots within nine years. The Global Innovation Index (GII) measures how well a country supports innovation by looking at five key areas: institutions, human capital and research, infrastructure, market sophistication, and business sophistication.

The GII also tracks the results of innovation through two main outputs: knowledge, technology, and creative. Norway ranks 12th place on the German Innovations Indicator report. while Switzerland, Singapore and Denmark hold the top 3 spots. On the European Innovation Scoreboard (EIS), Norway ranks 7th, while Denmark, Sweden and Finland once again hold the top 3 spots. Norway's public sector R&D expenditure declined by more than 30% compared to 2023, and the R&D business support fell by more than 20% in 2024, amid inflationary pressures, along with increased public spending – all against the backdrop of a slowing economy (OECD, 2024). Norway's exports are dominated by petroleum and its related industries (ships, oil platforms), which make up around 60% of total goods exports in 2023, with transport (shipping) being the largest service sector (OECD, 2024). Innovation in these sectors has a lot of potential for increasing the share of high and medium-tech exports complemented by the increasing telecommunication equipment exports, medical instruments and digital services.

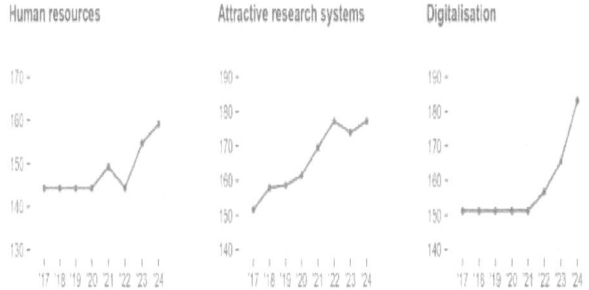

Knowledge is the fuel for innovation

Despite the aforementioned inherent challenges, our society continues to progress because humans have the ability to invent new technologies and discover new energy sources. Organizations use a combination of labor and capital to perform tasks to produce the goods and services we consume. Each task typically follows what economists call a 'routine', which is a set of established procedures that guide how work gets done. However, these routines are rarely static. They evolve over time, adapting to changing circumstances and incorporating innovative improvements.

Joseph Schumpeter distinguished between the 'circular flow' and periods of dynamic change. Circular flow is a state of economic equilibrium in which routines repeat without change, while dynamic change occurs when innovation disrupts established practices. In reality, routines undergo constant modification through both small adaptations and more significant innovations. However, both of these resources are limited compared to knowledge, which is almost limitless. In fact, we never seem to stop searching for more knowledge, and it is unique in the sense that the more we use it, the more insights we gain. Thus, the more knowledgeable we become the more capable we are of developing new ideas and innovations, which ultimately leads to greater advancements and wealth creation. With each passing generation, humanity has pursued new inventions, driven by a need for growth. When we see a resource being depleted, we instinctively seek alternatives—whether it is nuclear power, solar energy, or carbon-based solutions. If we realize that some of our discoveries and practices (reliance on fossil fuels, etc.) have the potential to destabilize ecosystems or threaten human life, perhaps we will feel more compelled to seek out environmentally safer alternatives to protect ourselves - and our future.

GenAI allows companies to prototype and test innovative ideas faster than ever before. For instance, in the automotive industry, manufacturers are using GenAI to simulate vehicle designs and evaluate them in virtual environments, identifying potential flaws before physical prototypes are built. This reduces costs and shortens development cycles, allowing firms to bring innovative products to market more quickly. In biopharmaceuticals, GenAI is used to design and simulate drug compounds, further accelerating the R&D process.

Oppenheimer's Legacy and the Ethics of Innovation

The story of J. Robert Oppenheimer, the inventor of the atom bomb, offers a powerful parallel. Recent films and biographies on his life and work reveal the profound moral conflict he experienced following the "Manhattan Project". His invention advanced science dramatically, yet it also demonstrated how innovations can spiral beyond their creators' control, serving a destructive purpose they never intended. This dilemma mirrors concerns in today's technological landscape, where AI, initially celebrated for its transformative potential, has increasingly shifted toward profit driven applications, surveillance, and power consolidation among the few tech companies.

A particularly concerning trend is the tendency for innovation to become trapped in a cycle of addressing problems largely created by the very systems it aims to improve. In this scenario, innovation becomes primarily reactive rather than proactive. It focuses on fixing self-inflicted problems rather than driving genuine progress or fundamentally improving overall well-being.

When innovation is merely a reaction to the problems created by our current systems, innovation essentially resembles my niece's hamster "Hammy" running on its wheel—constantly moving yet never making progress. In such cases, innovation fails to create genuine advancement. It only addresses the symptoms of a flawed system, without leading to a broader improvement in the quality of life.

True progress emerges when innovation is guided by critical thinking and empathy. Only then may it have the potential to lead us towards future AI technical advancements, ensuring those advancements actually enhance our lives, as opposed to rather than merely maintaining flawed systems controlled by the few – and misunderstood by policymakers and/or the general population. According to a report by Deloitte from March 2025, 58 percent of employees say increased innovation is one of AI's most important benefits. AI mirrors the characteristics Schumpeter attributed to entrepreneurs: intelligence, alertness, energy, and determination.

While AI lacks human creativity and intent, it amplifies human potential by processing information, identifying trends, and suggesting strategies at a speed and scale humans simply cannot achieve. It does not replace entrepreneurs, but often acts as a force multiplier, allowing them to experiment, adapt, and innovate more effectively.

AI has become a powerful enabler of Schumpeterian innovation. It fuels innovation cycles by accelerating invention, broadening diffusion, and intensifying competition through imitation. As AI evolves, it will likely extend the boundaries of what entrepreneurs can accomplish, and drive economic progress in ways that align directly with Schumpeter's vision of innovation and as a marker of historical change. Examples include recent and rapid developments within the chipset, automobile, and medical industries – which all rely heavily on AI.

Nine Tensions

1. The Innovation Trap: Nordic organizations have more conservative expectations for scaling experiments compared to global firms. Many Norwegian organizations struggle with a fundamental contradiction, which is that our flatter hierarchies do not seem to be delivering the expected benefits (which include a more frictionless path toward innovation allow for a stronger faith in the system.) However, Norwegian's tend to a lot of trust in our government and societal leaders, which could bolster the concerning tendency for Norwegian organizations to implement AI reactively rather than proactively toward the ultimate goal of fundamentally re-imagining work. This approach resembles a hamster wheel—perpetual motion without genuine progress.

2. The ROI Question: Norwegian enterprises are rushing to implement AI — the "bandwagon effect" — without asking the fundamental question. As a senior project manager, I always push teams to evaluate a new initiative on three fronts: value, viability, and desirability. Does this AI integration justify the cost? Proper ROI calculations (Estimated Benefit - Total Cost = Project Net Gain Value) should guide investment decisions, but are often overlooked in the general excitement that tends to surround new technology.

3. The Cultural Factor: Management theorist Peter Drucker's insight that *"Culture eats strategy for breakfast"* applies aptly to Norway's AI adoption efforts. Organizations often draft ambitious AI roadmaps without addressing their underlying bureaucratic inactivity, fragmented communication channels, and risk-averse cultures. Consequently, success remains elusive. Drucker's work reminds us that technology alone cannot overcome organizational silos and resistance to change that continues to plague many enterprises. Despite soaring investments, only 18% to 36% of Norwegian organizations achieve their desired outcomes from AI based initiatives.

4. The Oil Buffer: Norway's (petroleum based?) sovereign wealth fund provides a financial cushion which many other nations lack. This wealth could be leveraged to manage the transition to an AI-integrated economy, but it also threatens to reduce any sense of urgency around innovation. So, we have to question whether this capitalist innovation engine applies to a nation with such abundant oil wealth. Moreover, because the Government Pension Fund Global provides such a substantial financial cushion, Norway may lack the urgency that drives innovation elsewhere. In other words, why struggle to innovate and increase productivity when the politicians continue to confidently promote a petroleum fueled "plan" to improve living standards?

5. Strong Labor Regulations: Norway's extensive worker protections may also slow the adoption of AI technologies, when compared to less regulated markets. While this practice provides short-term stability, it could lead to longer-term competitive disadvantages.

6. High Labor Costs: With some of the world's highest labor costs, Norwegian businesses have stronger incentives to adopt automation and AI solutions than their counterparts in lower-wage economies. This economic pressure accelerates adoption despite cultural conservatism.

7. Small Domestic Market: Norway has a population of less than 5.7 million people. Our smaller population means AI innovations developed specifically for Norwegians could potentially lead to limited returns on innovation investment.

8. Language Specificity: While Norwegian knowledge workers typically have excellent English skills, AI systems optimized for the Norwegian language and cultural context remain less developed than their English counterparts.

9. **Anti-Innovative Policies**. Between 2020 and 2025, Norwegian newspapers consistently reported on the country's bureaucratic and regulatory obstacles facing entrepreneurs and R&D initiatives. This shift reveals a fundamental tension in Norway's innovation landscape that Schumpeter's theories help us to understand. In the spirit of Schumpeterian innovation, market dynamics create powerful consequences. Specifically, companies that lose market share typically reduce innovation investment (fewer patents) and see declining stock values. Conversely, companies that maintain or increase

market share through technological innovation are rewarded with higher valuations, creating a virtuous cycle of continued innovation. This competitive pressure— the fear of replacement by something new—drives continuous improvement throughout the economy. This presents a policy dilemma: when governments implement strong antitrust measures to deter market concentration, they may inadvertently weaken innovation incentives. For example, when Sam Altman launched OpenAI's latest version of ChatGPT "O3", in January 2025. It wasn't released in Europe because of stricter regulation rules. In contrast, it was immediately released in the United States, following President Trump's signing of a broad waiver allowing AI developments to flow freely. As a result, Europe's restrictive regulations tend to hinder innovation and slow progress.

Systematic Innovation - 7 drivers

Peter Drucker may help us understand what is required from Norwegians to have a chance to successfully innovate, and it requires an approach he termed *systematic innovation*. Drucker states there are four sources of opportunities in any industry or company, and each must be prioritized. They include process needs, industry and market changes, incongruities, and unexpected events. We have already AI change most industries and markets. We also know in order to increase the efficiency of our processes, AI needs to be used correctly.

Three additional sources of opportunity outside of a company's direct reach include changes in public perception, changes in demographics, and the acquiring of new knowledge. Imagine if you woke up five years from now living in Norway, and discovered oil and gas were no longer profitable - not due to poor extraction, but because rest of the world simply no longer valued those resources.

Our expertise, infrastructure, and entire economic identity would require a radical reinvention. This hypothetical scenario is precisely what knowledge workers face with the advent of AI. This monumental shift -threatening to render obsolete both our experience and expertise -means our evolution is not a choice – but a necessity in order to survive. This hypothetical scenario also illustrates Drucker's point perfectly, sometimes the greatest innovations occur from the most unexpected pressures.

Together, the seven aforementioned drivers account for virtually all major innovation opportunities. Organizations feel compelled to satisfy the inevitable need to "build something" as AI and digital technology and unforeseen disruptions continue to demolish aging and soon-obsolete workplace structures, all while delivering modern new "building blocks" for heightened productivity, competitiveness, and success. Moreover, every country has its own unique path toward innovation. Norway's strategy lags far behind South Korea, Japan, USA, Denmark, or Sweden.

Much of the blame can be placed on the Nordic model, which is based on high labor and consumption taxes and soaring social security benefits that ultimately leads to a weakened labor supply. The increasing mobility of a well-educated new generation will lead to 'cherry picking' in different phases of their lives. Separately, an aging population raises concerns about the sustainability of generous public pension and health insurance systems. This is an issue for Norway and other countries across Europe facing an "innovation paradox", which is typically defined as the inability to convert research-driven AI competence into commercial and marketable products and services. Norway's firms, in particular, struggle with monetizing AI research and AI pilots. For Norway to remain competitive in in 2030, we must systematically leverage each of these areas, rather than simply hoping innovation will somehow occur on its own. The clock is ticking. While we debate and deliberate, other nations race ahead in converting AI breakthroughs into market leadership. Drucker's systematic innovation framework indeed offers a roadmap, but we must have the courage to follow it.

Innovation Creating or Eliminating Jobs?

The internet was born more than 40 years ago. Since then, several tech firms, including Alphabet, Amazon, Apple, Meta, Microsoft, and Nvidia have all attained trillion-dollar market capitalizations, and led the charge to change the anatomy of work and how we access information. Similarly, AI now is like the internet of many years ago. The risk for business leaders is not thinking too big, but rather thinking too small, and failing to understand the consequences of not seeing the 'bigger picture'.

Innovation fueled by AI will inevitably lead to future collaborations in traditionally white-collar roles (creativity, newspaper, healthcare (diagnostic), etc.) between humans and AI – primarily out of necessity. Conversely, there are countless other job roles which could face significant disruption - think taxi drivers, waiters, telemarketers, delivery drivers, postal office clerks, receptionist, cashiers in stores, customer service agents, game developers, manufacturing workers, and market research analysts. Additionally, we should also expect that AI applications, including predictive AI, will indeed lead to job creation. The key is understanding that while AI will ultimately automate routine decisions, humans will still need to manage and curate the data that fuels it, and subsequently explain and legitimize its outputs.

The Unequal Distribution of Benefits

However, this technological renaissance comes with a troubling warning: don't expect the benefits of this transformation to be distributed equally. AI engineers and senior project managers who master these tools will experience rising productivity and earnings. Meanwhile, mid-level administrative, financial, and legal professionals may face automation risks and downward wage pressure. The International Monetary Fund (IMF) predicts that AI's gains will flow primarily to capital owners rather than workers, meaning average real wages may stagnate even as GDP and corporate profits soar.

This imbalance represents more than statistics; it signals a real fundamental change in how economic value is distributed. Even those with the right skills may struggle to secure these new positions, raising collective concerns about whether job creation will match the rate of what is expected to be widespread displacement. AI's ultimate economic impact may depend on our capacity to adapt.

AI and Human Touch

Given these profound changes, policymakers and business leaders must recognize that AI implementation brings unexpected challenges. Some companies have already learned this lesson the hard way, after they faced customer backlash from an over-reliance on AI chatbots, which in turn led to a more nuanced approach to technology integration.

This tension plays out daily in Norway's financial sector. AI tools are now increasingly common in banking and insurance (recall our earlier discussion about trust). I consider myself to be practical about technology adoption, including AI. Yet like so many others, I still value interaction with a personal advisor. This preference underscores the critical balance between AI efficiency and human connection in maintaining customer satisfaction.

Looking beyond customer service, the future of work isn't a simple story about human-versus-machine. It's about continually redefining what tasks humans will retain. In my experience, organizations that grant employees significant autonomy create environments where new technologies can be embraced innovatively. Innovation has shifted from optional to standard operating procedure.

Norway's Innovation Challenge

Historians have long recognized that this was not merely an economic deviation. What we were witnessing was a fundamental realignment of global power itself. The gravitational center of world affairs was shifting relentlessly toward those nations that controlled three critical assets: the digital infrastructure that would underpin the future, the massive populations whose data fueled artificial intelligence, and the demographic vitality to sustain innovation across generations. Norway, as it is currently governed and structured, is arguably too slow, expensive, and small to realistically compete at the top of global innovation indexes. For those pursuing R&D and innovation. Norway spends heavily on research and conducts significant development work; however, our ability to commercialize our activities falls short. Neither our problem lies in the area of taxation policies or access to funds—areas in which we enjoy rich supply. Instead, at the root of the issue lies our weak understanding of the innovation process itself. It seems that other countries are offering more dynamic and efficient environments, e.g., Sweden or Switzerland. Norway's economic reality— being high-cost, a fairly glacial political process, and having a strong welfare system because our oil wealth makes us highly risk averse— offers few compelling incentives to innovate.

Chapter 9 Generation Z and AI

GenZ is often characterized as lazy, carefree, and rebellious against the *"normal norms"* of their parents. They've grown up in a virtual world. Their deep connection with technology, combined with their values, uniquely positions them to shape Norway's future in many ways by rewriting the rules of work. In reality, GenZ is not lazy. They are actually innovative, digitally native, and ready to harness the power of AI to transform both their careers and our society. This chapter discusses Gen Z's work ethic, their tech-forward mindset, and the mutually transformative relationship between AI and their future.

Gen Z/Delta

Gen Z (born between 1995 and 2015) is the first generation to grow up with the internet, smartphones, and social media as ubiquitous parts of daily life, as 99% of 16–24-year-olds use Internet daily according to Statistics Norway, SSB. This deep connection to technology shapes how Gen Z interacts with the world in their own vacuum. By 2030, they will likely lead Norway into an even more advanced digital era.

GenZ's reliance on apps and streamlined digital tools is not a crutch; but rather a carefully crafted toolkit of a generation that understands how to optimize every moment. Their world isn't less demanding, it's simply evolved beyond the old rules and norms. I often have to remind myself that while It's easy to judge from the outside—what looks like a quick scroll might actually be a deep dive into research, creativity, and meaningful connection.

As a millennial who grew up in Southern Norway, I experienced the internet's initiation into our homes via broadband in the late 90's. Conversely, Gen Z grew up in a digitally integrated world filled with social media, virtual realities, and constant connectivity. One of the largest shifts that I foresee in the near future includes the boom in digital innovation and entrepreneurship.

GenZ has lately been given another nickname - the "Delta Generation", a reference to the mathematical symbol (Δ) signifying change. The choice of "Delta" aims to capture a core observation about this generation: a strong perceived drive for significant social transformation, possibly on a scale or with an intensity distinct from the advocacy seen in prior generations. This chapter challenges the "lazy" stereotype and explores the mutually transformative relationship between AI and the Delta Generation.

Making their Own Rules

Norway's economic landscape is shifting under the weight of rising housing costs, a precarious job market, and the lingering aftermath of various global crises. While previous generations scaled corporate ladders with steady ambition, Gen Z is carving out paths that are as unconventional as they are inspiring.

No longer content with the status quo, these digital pioneers are embracing freelancing, gig work, and even launching entrepreneurial ventures that bridge technology and sustainability. The rise of smart tech startups like Airthings illustrates a clear trend: where others see obstacles, Gen Z sees openings to innovate, adapt, and thrive.

Transparency and Privacy

There's more to this tech revolution than efficiency and speed—there's a deep, human need for privacy, transparency, and ethical conduct. Recent movements toward digital sovereignty echo Gen Z's belief that our digital lives should be governed by the same care and respect we give to our personal lives.

While most of us carefully curate our social media profiles, Gen Z takes this mindset further: they're actively creating and supporting technology that protects privacy by design. This generation isn't waiting for Big Tech to change—they're building the solutions on their own.

In Norway, which enjoys advanced infrastructure and a digitalization-friendly reputation, Gen Z will lead these initiatives. The push for digital sovereignty and sustainable tech will be among GenZ's core priorities. Consider the current rise of digital platforms like *Tise* for sustainable fashion or *Spleis* for crowdfunding, platforms Gen Z popularized. By 2030, Gen Z will not just be using similar tools; they'll be leading them and driving them to new heights while they integrate AI, blockchain, and other cutting-edge technologies into everyday life. By 2030, Gen Z could be spearheading the next wave of eco-tech innovation, launching businesses that combine cutting-edge technology with environmental stewardship. This might involve new digital platforms for tracking carbon footprints, virtual consultations for sustainable practices, or even AI-driven waste reduction systems for urban areas.

GenZ is also often associated with another stereotype – being unmotivated. But this perception often stems from a poor understanding of how they approach the world. For example, unlike previous generations who had to be really proactive in their daily work, Generation Z grew up with convenience at their fingertips: food delivery apps, automation, and AI-driven solutions. While older generations may see this reliance on technology as laziness, it's actually a reflection of the genius of members of Generation Z in maximizing digital tools to their benefit. They're not lazy; they're simply optimizing their lives with the resources available to them— often in ways that outpace any generation before them. Gen Z continues to embrace and push the boundaries of new digital tools. In the future, Gen Z could spearhead the development of apps that further reduce environmental impact, such as those integrating circular economy models into daily life or using digital currencies for green initiatives.

Unlike my generation, where most of us entered adulthood during the 2008 financial crisis, Gen Z has grown up amid economic instability triggered by the COVID-19 pandemic, high student debt, and an uncertain job market. Norway struggled with the implications of these destabilizing events as housing prices increased, and job opportunities became more competitive. During this period Gen Z faced significant economic challenges, but they also leveraged a unique set of strategies to navigate them.

Most of GenZ see AI as a tool for problem-solving, conducting research, and creative activities, thereby freeing up time for critical thinking. Companies like Airthings, which develop indoor air quality monitors, are already at the forefront of smart tech solutions that enhance environmental conditions.

Generation Z is much less conventional when it comes to careers. Whereas Millennials, like GenX before them, tend to focus more on making it to the peaks of corporate ladders, GenZ is more likely to go freelance, join the gig economy, or venture into entrepreneurship. Moreover, a study by the Norwegian Institute for Social Research revealed Gen Z places greater emphasis on job flexibility and maintaining a good work–life balance compared to previous generations. This outlook could drastically change the face of the Norwegian labor market by 2030. The trend for remote work, which increased dramatically during the coronavirus pandemic, is likely to continue, with more young Norwegians working from home or as digital nomads. Norwegian industries will have to adapt to these changing expectations as Gen Z seeks flexibility and more meaningful workplaces.

Organizations will also have to install policies that address mental fitness, work–life balance, and sustainability if they intend to win this generation's allegiance. DNB and Telenor might be among some of Norway's largest firms currently under pressure from Gen Z staffers to embrace very progressive policies for remote working, mental fitness, and flexibility. By 2030, those policies may become the norm. The economic landscape also offers opportunities for Gen Z especially in the green economy. As a global leader in sustainable energy, Norway is well-placed for Gen Z to lead on green energy policies including wind, solar, and other renewable sources of energy. This generation is already actively involved in advocacy for a zero-carbon future.

While my generation (Millennials) grew up publicly posting deeply personal material to Facebook and blogs, the Gen Z way is drastically different: more cautious. Their preference for anonymous platforms such as Snapchat and Whisper speaks volumes about how concerned they are with privacy in a seemingly transparent digital world. Whereas my generation lived through the rise of cyberbullying and oversharing in real time, Gen Z has learned to curate their digital presence, even though there have been numerous reported cases showing this generation is more prone to anxiety, compared to my own generation. GenZ wants flexibility and freedom, they want to work as they wish, as long as they manage to deliver on time and abide by the standard. This generation is unafraid, and I have seen many examples of friends and reports that if they don't like the leader or the work, they simply quit and find something better or start for themselves. They want work with purpose and growth.

Since the GDPR came into existence there has been a move to seek out options which can offer transparency, autonomy, and privacy. People, especially from Generation Z, have started looking for alternatives to the Silicon Valley giants, and so platforms like European Alternatives have come up to help people find independent alternatives created. But it's not just users who are moving; so too are private equity and venture capital firms, which are traditionally stalwart fans of big technology corporations. Their interest has shifted to smaller, more nimble startups focused on human centered design and a commitment to privacy-first principles.

This is in close connection with the values of Generation Z in Norway, where data privacy and sustainability mean a lot. Gen Z are very skeptical about big tech monopolies and demand that platforms prioritize people's rights and self-determination. Under GenZ's influence, there is a big possibility that by 2030, more Norwegian businesses and startups will embrace these principles, and build a digital ecosystem that focuses on ethical design, sustainability, and user autonomy.

For Gen Z, technology is not a tool but a means to shape the future in accordance with their own ideals.

This will take the form of increased calls for digital sovereignty movement that calls for the governance of digital platforms in a way that keeps user data and rights private, and safe—and means there will likely be even more innovation in the tech space. Consequently, corporations will likely move toward increased user privacy, ethics in data management, ultimately allowing users to have more control over their digital presence.

New Social Contract

Socially, Gen Z is more diverse, inclusive, and politically active than previous generations. They are passionate advocates for gender equality, LGBTQ+ rights, racial justice, and climate action. In Norway, where social equality and inclusivity are already highly valued, Gen Z's influence will likely amplify these values, driving more progressive social policies.

By 2030, Norway could evolve into a more inclusive society thanks to Gen Z's activism. Consider, for example, the *Fridays for Future* movement, which has gained widespread support in Norway, especially among young people. Gen Z's activism in pushing for urgent climate action will likely lead to significant policy changes, with green legislation at the core of Norwegian governance. This could result in further investments in sustainable industries, such as the expansion of electric vehicle infrastructure or renewable energy projects.

Moreover, Gen Z's advocacy for social justice will have tangible effects on the political arena. With a strong presence in social media, this generation will continue to hold institutions accountable.

Expect to see more members of Gen Z running for political office, influencing laws and policies. We are witnessing a surge in youth-led initiatives, like the Norwegian Green Youth, which focuses on environmental activism. Gen Z's leadership will push Norway's social policies towards more inclusive, equitable, and sustainable outcomes. These include improved mental health services, reforms in the education system, and more attention to diverse learning needs.

Education Securing Against Job Polarization?

When I started writing this book back in August 2024, I paid close attention to how many GenZ students entered the IT field. The latest statistics were chilling. Applications for Information and Communication Technology programs plunged 23% compared to the previous year (2023). As healthcare and other fields continue to attract more students, we can't ignore the fact young people are beginning to turn away from more traditional fields like software engineering - in droves.

Is Gen Z missing an opportunity, or are they seeing something the rest of us are reluctant to acknowledge? As I scrolled through my LinkedIn feed over the last couple of months, I saw countless posts from frustrated Gen Z bachelor's and master's degree students who recently completed their IT studies and submitted hundreds of applications – for them only to be met with silence or rejection. It felt like a collective cry for help: *"Why am I not getting hired, I thought studying software engineering was a safe choice for job security?"* In truth, it's currently incredibly difficult to find a job in the IT industry. During their studies, some students who aspired to become IT workers were promised job guarantees amidst the 'need for 40,000 IT professionals.' However, upon graduation it was a very different story. Now, they're consistently receiving dozens (and in some cases hundreds) of rejections.

I assumed only a small segment of the GenZ population faced these challenges. But during a deeper investigation, I found numerous articles documenting how working IT professionals in their 30s and older were also applying to several new job postings without receiving any offers – and in many cases, no interviews.

As AI continues to automate large segments of technical work, businesses that are laser-focused on efficiency continue to tighten their hiring criteria. If the trend I've witnessed over the last two years continues, then I predict artificial intelligence will increasingly assume many routine "bread and butter" tasks, including research, summarization, and reporting. For members of Gen Z entering the workforce, this will mean fewer entry-level roles and assignments which have traditionally been used to gain valuable experience. In the long term, knowledge workers will need to focus on more complex, creative, and strategic tasks that AI cannot currently fully replicate. It is important to note that while AI may not perform as well as humans in some areas, its results are still often considered "good enough" while certainly being more cost effective. These capabilities have and will continue to persuade many organizations to adopt AI, thus entirely reshaping the future and scope of knowledge work entirely. The reality is that today's employers indeed enjoy the luxury of being ruthlessly selective. Why hire an inexperienced junior developer when AI can handle routine tasks, and senior developers from Eastern Europe can be contracted remotely for a fraction of local salaries?

Meanwhile, policymakers and industry leaders continue making claims which are disconnected from reality. *"AI will create more jobs than it eliminates."*

"Everyone should learn to code." "Automation will lead to prosperity for all." These inspirational platitudes offer little comfort to graduates who are facing rejection after rejection. Although there is a relatively small dip in employment for those over 30, as of 2024, approximately 85–90 % of tertiary educated Norwegians of any age remain employed. GenZ might be described as difficult and overly cautious, but generally speaking, they are not stupid. They are watching in real time as both policymakers and business leaders continue to constrict the job market by handing over work to the machines.

Collaboration Success Factor

GenzAI is a global research project that aims to explore ways of

moving towards a human-first AI future - through the lens of GenZ. The project reached out to over 10,000 youths across eight countries to get a better understanding of how GenZ might utilize AI in the future. The results showed while Gen Z will certainly drive change, collaboration with older generations will be crucial to ensure these shifts stick – and are successful. Millennials, who are now stepping into leadership positions, will clearly need to work alongside Gen Z to help bring their innovative ideas from concept to reality – essentially drawing on the institutional knowledge of older generations.

By 2030, we could even see a new model of leadership emerging, in which young innovators work in tandem with experienced mentors to solve complex societal problems.

For example, Millennials and Gen Z could collaborate in the world of politics to develop policies that integrate new technologies such as blockchain and AI, into governance and public service delivery. Norway's *Altinn* platform, which provides e-government services, could also evolve under the influence of Gen Z, with inclusion of more advanced AI integrations aimed at streamlining bureaucracy and improving efficiency.

As we prepare this generation for tomorrow's knowledge workers, it's imperative we develop and nurture future-oriented skills. Still, it would be narrow-minded to neglect the continued relevance of fundamental professional skills like communication and good teamwork, which are not simply nice to have. They are actually critical interpersonal skills which have always permitted individuals, and society, to work together toward success. These are the gifts that are inherited through generations who enter the workforce, evolving but never abandoning their fundamental worth.

Although they may execute it differently, both Millennials and those in Generation Z come from a perspective of efficiency—Millennials in working smarter, not harder, and Generation Z in matching job duties with strong skill sets.

Gen Z faces a world of economic challenges that include skyrocketing housing prices, an unstable gig economy, and uncertain career prospects. But their resilience, adaptability, and entrepreneurial spirit continue to be their greatest strengths. This generation is not waiting for opportunity; they are creating it themselves.

More specifically, as prices continue to climb in Norway, Gen Z is rethinking the traditional idea of home ownership. Many are opting for alternative living arrangements, embracing a more communal approach to housing. They believe that stability doesn't come from a single property, but rather from leveraging shared resources and community-based networks. In 2030, we could see a surge in co-operative housing projects, where young people pool resources to create sustainable, affordable living spaces. These projects will be fueled by digital platforms that allow individuals to share everything from electric cars to energy-efficient appliances.

This practical adjustment, borne out of economic need, goes far beyond the simple search for shelter. Confronted with an equally volatile job market, Gen

Z is also likely to experience the world of work in a very different way. It is projected that people of this generation can expect to have up to 17 jobs and seven careers during their lifetime, aligning with their primary goal of finding "meaningful work." Moreover, according to Duke University, 65 percent of first college students will, upon graduation, land a job that currently does not exist.

GenZ is also redefining the notion of what defines a successful career. Unlike previous generations which valued corporate ascension, Gen Z is drawn to freelance work, the gig economy, and digital nomadism.

In Norway, where remote work is already an increasingly popular trend, Gen Z will take full advantage of flexible, digital-first careers. Some quit their traditionally "9 to 5" jobs to be their own boss and hopefully earn more money. Their reason is simple - "okonomisk uavhengighet" and "frihet", which simply translate to "financial independence" and "freedom". They're not tied to any single company or organization—and value greater autonomy and income. Additionally, their use of AI tools and awareness of digital platforms allows them to work anywhere in the world, offering unmatched control, flexibility, and earning potential which no company nor organization can beat. It's why you'll often find young Norwegian Gen Zers working from the scenic mountains of Lofoten, or from a cafe bar in Cyprus. Tech-driven workspaces like *Startup Norway* could host co-working spaces specifically designed for remote workers, offering high-speed internet, access to mentors, and a creative, collaborative environment.

Gen Z's future: Is it our responsibility?

Norway will certainly be influenced by Gen Z, simply because by 2030, more than one million of them are expected to enter the workforce, and eventually assume some kind of leadership role. With its strong educational system and digital infrastructure, Norway provides fertile ground for Gen Z to drive innovation, technology, and social change. Their fluency in digital tools and commitment to sustainability and inclusivity will ultimately shape our economy and society.

By 2030, Gen Z may also disrupt outdated systems, such as slow-moving industries, governments dependence on fossil fuels, and the traditional corporate prioritization of profit over people. Still, this will not happen overnight.

Honestly, watching Gen Z rise to prominence is inspiring. In contrast to my generation, theirs will be defined by a fully digital existence that pushes the limits of how we currently define progress. Their impact could extend beyond Norway, leaving a global mark. Moreover, their resilience and activism will drive industries to evolve, ensuring that progress is not achieved at the expense of equity, sustainability, and humanity's core values.

So, while Millennials and GenZ may have different approaches, they are both rooted in the same values: hard work, resilience, and adaptability. What's most striking is how each generation adapts to its circumstances and evolves the narrative of thriving in a rapidly changing world—where technology accelerates every shift and creates new pathways for progress.

As members of GenZ grow into their careers, will they be able to effectively engage in critical thinking and problem-solving at work? Growing up in a world where essentially unlimited information and solutions are just a click away, it stands to reason they might lean towards getting quick answers from online sources - instead of working through problems on their own. Others worry that growing up in a time of instant answers will dull GenZ's capacity for profound problem-solving. But there's another way at looking at this; what seems to be shortcut-driven convenience is, in fact, a strategic response to a world where knowledge doubles overnight. They prefer efficiency to tedium, and creativity to tradition as they re-framing the notion of "effort" by using every tool at their disposal — human or technological — to spark genuine innovation.

I still wonder how our generation and the ones that came before us, bridge this gap in the near future? Will our institutions embrace GenZ's demand for purposeful work, flexible career paths, and ethical leadership? If that happens, we should go beyond simply labeling their behavior as indolence. I actually see it as a pragmatic adaptation to the ever and fast-changing reality of knowledge workers. Gen Z's approach values efficiency over monotony and innovation over convention, redefining the very concept of *'effort'* as they tackle challenges in the modern workplace. And maybe in doing so, they might just save the rest of us from the very machines we are so afraid of.

Chapter 10
AI Cause of Job Polarization?

In our world, technology progresses faster every year, creating a wider gap and consequently impacting more and more knowledge workers. Specifically, it's a gap between those who are unable to work due to a lack of technological skills and/or knowledge, or simply because a machine has taken over their duties.

John Maynard Keynes long ago warned of *"technological unemployment"* —a scenario in which technology outpaces job creation. Although this has been debated over the decades, the concept is certainly relevant in the Norwegian context. Back in 2021, there was a general consensus that Norway faced a shortage of educated IT professionals—a challenge that persists to this day. Still, there is the hope that even if AI potentially eliminates the need for the traditional IT role in five to ten years, some IT related *skills* might still remain in demand – especially as new specializations emerge.

Experts suggest that by 2030, we may have more qualified resources than available jobs. In fact, a report by Samfunnsøkonomisk Analyse (SOA 2025) suggested only about half of the prospective white-collar workers would work directly within IT and AI. The remainder could be spread thin across other sectors, risking underemployment or job mismatches. By 2030, we could see the creation of see 170 million jobs — and 92 million jobs lost, while 39% of our current skills will be outdated. This transformation indeed requires us to equip individuals of all ages—not just students, but everyday workers—with the knowledge and skills to thrive in an AI-driven world.

Additionally, given the existence of Norway's aging population, a shrinking workforce, and rapid advances in AI and automation, the country is facing fundamental questions about the future of work and its social welfare model. While some warn of a jobless future (as Elon Musk has suggested), the reality is more shaded. This chapter discusses these challenges and opportunities, focusing on how individuals can prepare for the evolving job scenario through 2030 and beyond.

Few Kids Many Elders

Norway's population is projected to grow to 6 million by 2040, and more than 6.2 million by 2100. Last year, Norway's employment rate stood at 70% for individuals aged 15–74, surpassing the OECD average of 66%.

Historical trends indicate a pronounced aging of Norway's population. Since the 1970s, the birth rate has been steadily declining, and at times has fallen below 2.10 children per family, which is the threshold generally considered necessary to maintain a stable population. By 1983, the birth rate dropped to 1.66, well below the replacement level, signaling the beginning of a long-term demographic shift.

In the coming years, the number of people aged 65–79 will rise significantly, and the 80+ age group is also expected to grow dramatically. According to Statistics Norway (SSB), the proportion of residents aged 65 or older will increase from 16% today to 24% by 2050. Simultaneously, the working-age population (20–65 years) is expected to decline from 61% to 55% over the same period. SSB projections highlight additional demographic shifts: by 2034, the 60–69 age group will outnumber those aged 20–29 for the first time. Furthermore, by 2026, one-quarter of Norway's population will be over 60. These trends underscore a shrinking workforce and a growing elderly population in the coming decades.

Norway's demographic landscape is indeed changing dramatically.

With one of the world's highest life expectancies (currently 83 years), and a fertility rate of just 1.48 children per woman (well below the replacement rate of 2.1), the population is aging rapidly. As the population ages, there will be an increased demand for healthcare and social services. At the same time, fewer workers will be available to sustain Norway's welfare model. This demographic shift makes it even more important for the country to find ways in the coming decades to maintain productivity and economic stability.

Job market and emerging roles

Historical trends indicate that technological change not only eliminates jobs but also creates new ones. Studies show 60% of today's professions did not exist in 1940, and approximately 85% of all new jobs have emerged since then. The job market is constantly evolving. Some roles disappear, while others are created.

Norway's job market remains stable, with unemployment holding at around 4.1% in January 2025, amidst moderate job growth expected in the next 2 years. However, structural changes are reshaping employment patterns. High-skilled workers in specialized fields continue to see job growth, while routine-based middle-class jobs are in decline, leading to economic disparities.

Economist Erik Brynjolfsson's "Turing Trap" warns that when AI is merely substituted for human effort, we risk wage stagnation and widening income inequality. But I refuse to believe our destiny is fixed—rather, it is shaped by the choices we make *now*.

However, if AI can be further developed in ways that actually enhance human productivity - rather than replace it, the transition to a new economy could be more beneficial. These demographic shifts will create complex challenges that will require strategic planning and solutions to ensure a sustainable and effective workforce.

Karl Taylor Compton made a version of this argument decades ago, insisting that technological unemployment, viewed across an entire economy, was largely a myth. New industries, he argued, always appeared to absorb displaced workers. And historically, he wasn't wrong. But Compton was also honest enough to acknowledge the other side: for the individual worker in the town whose mill just closed, or the craftsman whose skill just became obsolete, the economy-wide statistics offer cold comfort. The macro story and the human story are not always the same story.

That tension sits at the heart of where we are now. Kahneman's research adds another uncomfortable layer: higher education correlates with people rating their lives as more successful — but not necessarily feeling happier day to day. Better jobs bring better salaries and better status, but also longer hours, higher expectations, and a particular kind of stress that doesn't show up in the GDP figures. If AI is going to reshape work, the goal shouldn't just be productivity. It should be making the actual experience of working — and living — better. Otherwise, we've automated our way into a more efficient version of the same problem.

Gen Z, to their credit, seems to understand this intuitively. Having grown up with technology in one hand and a gig economy in the other, they're not particularly impressed by rigid hierarchies or the promise of a stable job that quietly destroys your evenings. They want flexibility, autonomy, and work that means something. Whether this is idealism or just good sense is debatable — but either way, they're pushing in a direction that might actually be right. AI should follow that lead: not as a tool for extracting more output from fewer people, but as a genuine shift in what work can look like.

Turing Trap

There are significant economic implications in creating AI that closely imitates human behavior. If machines can perform tasks that humans do, they effectively become substitutes for human labor. This will likely drive down wages, as machines become more cost-effective than human workers. As noted by Brynjolfsson, this phenomenon could lead to what he calls the "Turing Trap." In this scenario, workers find themselves not only with reduced economic power but also with diminished political influence, unable to reverse the economic shifts that result from machines' permanent displacement of human labor.

The real opportunity for long-term economic prosperity, as highlighted by thinkers like John Maynard Keynes and later Brynjolfsson, lies not in replicating human labor but in creating entirely new innovations that still leave a place for humans to positively contribute to the workplace.

These innovations—whether in the form of supersonic jets, nanoscale actuators, or new methods for solving complex biological challenges such as protein folding—create value that never existed before. It is precisely through these groundbreaking inventions that economies can thrive, as they create new industries and opportunities that were previously unimaginable.

Norway's emphasis on AI should therefore shift from simply improving machines to enhancing human capabilities through innovation. For example, instead of focusing on replacing human workers, we should be investing in technologies that complement and elevate human intelligence, enabling us to solve problems in entirely new ways. This approach would not only ensure that economic growth remains sustainable but would also help preserve the societal structures that rely on human creativity and ingenuity – and keep us "in the game".

Joseph Schumpeter's concept of "creative destruction," introduced in *Capitalism, Socialism, and Democracy*, describes the relentless process of innovation through which new technologies, industries, and methods emerge, consequently displacing older ones. This process drives economic dynamism, reallocating resources toward more efficient and productive uses, ultimately fostering long-term growth and improved living standards. Historical examples, such as the shift from horse-drawn carriages to automobiles, or from traditional retail to e-commerce, illustrate how innovation reshapes industries, enhances productivity, and creates new opportunities, albeit with disruptive short-term consequences.

Meeting this moment demands a coordinated sets of reform, and the fault lines are already visible: in the classroom, in the labor market, in the culture of entrepreneurship, and in the foundations of the welfare state itself.

Firstly, the country must address the potential for technological unemployment by investing in education and training to equip its workforce with the skills necessary to thrive in the digital age. This includes fostering digital literacy, promoting lifelong learning, along with encouraging innovation and entrepreneurship. Additionally, Norway should consider implementing policies that support job creation and income redistribution to mitigate the negative social and economic consequences of technological unemployment.

The long-term trend of job polarization typically accelerates during downturns, with routine jobs permanently eliminated. White-collar jobs today often involve project-based work, temporary contracts, or multiple concurrent roles. For example, a project manager or a finance market analyst might move between firms or assignments more frequently than workers in more routine sectors. That is, while AI applications improve work productivity, the mobility with which specialists like lawyers or software programmers switch jobs can render the labor market more elastic. This elasticity dampens the disinflationary impact of productivity gains.

It's also important to consider knowledge workers in "non-routine" or abstract jobs (like designers, software developers, engineers, financial analysts, economists, or lawyers) are more likely to work for more than one employer at the same time compared to people in manual or routine jobs. This means workers in these fields face more uncertainty and a higher chance of experiencing gaps between jobs, even as the overall labor market becomes more dynamic with frequent job changes.

Norway, in my opinion, is a rather risk-adverse country. However, by encouraging risk-taking, supporting startups, and investing in research and development, Norway can stimulate economic growth and create new jobs. This will help offset the potential job losses caused by automation and AI. However, Norway's cultural and structural challenges may hinder this process. A strong emphasis on job security and a relatively cautious approach to risk taking can reduce entrepreneurial activity and innovation. Encouraging a mindset that values experimentation, tolerates failure, and embraces change is critical for unlocking the transformative potential of emerging industries. Policymakers must also play a proactive role in reshaping the economic landscape by creating incentives for innovation, reducing regulatory barriers for new technologies, and reallocating resources to foster growth in AI and other high-potential sectors.

Norway's welfare system — brilliant as it is — was designed for a workforce of stable, full-time employees. That workforce is becoming a minority. Adapting pensions, healthcare, and social security to serve people who work three part-time roles while their main job quietly gets automated is not radical politics. It's just keeping up.

The choice is simple to state and hard to execute: stop building AI that competes with us, and start building AI that makes us capable of things we couldn't do alone. One version of this story ends with humans thriving in ways Keynes would have found deeply satisfying. The other ends with a very efficient machine doing your job while you wonder what went wrong. What some might choose next, only time will tell.

Dual Impact on All Job Roles

In fact, technological advancements could have a dual impact on numerous job roles. While some positions will experience significant growth, others might experience a sharp decline. Technology's ability to assume routine tasks, especially AI and automation - will likely drive this shift.

The fastest-growing roles will be those who effectively leverage technology and human creativity. As automation handles repetitive tasks, workers in fields like AI development, data science, cybersecurity, and energy transition will be in high demand. Additionally, jobs in the care economy, such as nursing, elderly care, and social work, will grow as populations age and require more services that involve human empathy, judgment, and personal interaction.

For example, it's highly likely that AI systems will replace or reduce roles that revolve around repetitive task such as cashiers, administrative assistants, insurance agents/brokers, and traditional stock market brokers. The decline in these jobs will require workers to transition to more complex roles that cannot be easily automated.

The top three fastest-growing skills in technology are expected to be in the areas of AI and information processing (86%), robotics and automation (58%), and energy generation, storage, and distribution (41%). These technological trends are likely to have a dual impact affecting both the fastest-growing and fastest-declining job roles. As a result, there will be an increased demand for skills related to technology, including expertise in AI and big data, networks and cybersecurity, and technological literacy.

Inflation is expected to have a mixed effect on net job creation through 2030. While slower growth is expected to lead to the displacement of 1.6 million jobs globally, the changes in job creation will simultaneously increase the demand for skills such as creative thinking, resilience, flexibility, and agility.

Among these shifting roles, frontline job positions are predicted to experience the largest absolute growth in terms of volume. Technology- related roles, such as Big Data Specialists, Fintech Engineers, AI and ML Specialists, and Software and Application Developers, are expected to see the fastest growth in percentage terms. Roles in green and energy transition sectors, including Autonomous and Electric Vehicle Specialists, Environmental Engineers, and Renewable Energy Engineers, are also projected to be among the fastest growing.

As we look toward the future leading up to 2030, workers should be prepared to re-skill and upskill significantly in order to keep themselves relevant, with an estimated 39% of current skills becoming outdated or needing adaptation. The reason is simple: as AI Agents become more advanced and more intelligent, it will take fewer and fewer people to create a successful business. This includes roles such as farmworkers, delivery drivers, construction workers, salespersons, and food-processing workers and most of the "blue-collar" jobs.

Keynes made an essential point: concept shapes the value of any tool, including AI. However, my assumption, based on the conduct of most companies and boards of directors, is that when they decide to implement autonomously intelligent machine systems, those systems will be put to work with a single purpose in mind. More often than not, that singular purpose involves generating wealth for their owners – free from the typical obligations typically associated with hiring humans to perform the same work. Indeed, in parallel with the Great Decoupling, there has been a progressive transfer of wealth from public to private hands. In fact, while private wealth (relative to national income) has doubled in most wealthy countries over the last thirty years, national income relative to private wealth in most wealthy countries has plummeted..

The effect of such economic and technological shifts is not only structural but also intensely personal and social, affecting the way people adjust to the changing job market. Our upbringing and education strongly influence our occupational choices and lead us to share similar perceptions and expectations as others around us. This behavior also applies to our job searching, with many of us hoping to seek work among people who are like us and, if at all possible, leverage the pre-existing social networks to achieve that. I am sure it must have had some effect on my professional trajectory and steered me towards looking for the "ideal" job. However, this innate human behavior to remain within comfortable groups can inadvertently contribute to accelerating technological disruption. It can also restrict access to new or alternative skills-based opportunities or in new locations, especially amplifying trends like the digital divide and the concentration of new employment in cities.

Digital Divided

Mass participation remains the foundation of Norwegian society, but how do you convince people to follow someone who is digitally illiterate? In Norway we have and estimated 670,000 residents who barely can use a proper android phone, let alone operate a computer to browse the internet.

It's important to understand that just because everyone has Internet access doesn't mean that everyone has the same level of competence in using the digital tools at their disposal. For instance, consider adult female foreigners who may lack proficiency in English or Norwegian and have not received adequate training in using digital systems. Similarly, many individuals remain unaware of the potential benefits digital tools offer. Given these realities, was it realistic to expect everyone to master digital communication without proper training? Digital skills can be incredibly valuable in a digitally connected city. However, for someone in a remote area without internet access, possessing those same skills might be less immediately crucial. Just as the value of a resource depends on its context, so too does the application of technology, including AI. The challenge lies in ensuring that AI respects and responds to these varying contexts, particularly when it comes to bridging the digital divide.

AI has the potential to empower those with limited digital skills by providing personalized training, simplifying complex information, and making digital interfaces more accessible. When Keynes imagined his utopian future, he did not count on automation's potential to exacerbate inequality. In his utopia, inequality is irrelevant if everybody's basic needs are easily met.

Only the foolish did more work than they needed to. However, if AI is developed and deployed without considering the basic needs of individuals, it risks exacerbating the very inequalities it could help to solve.

Urban concentration and Rural Decline

Beyond individual digital literacy lies another dimension of polarization: the geographic redistribution of opportunity. Researchers seem to agree that AI-enabled economies concentrate new job creation in specific regions and sectors—typically urban areas with existing technological infrastructure. This creates disadvantages for digitally excluded populations in rural Norway. They face the challenge of mastering new technologies, as well as potentially relocating to regions where those skills are economically valuable. They consequently risk disrupting community ties and family support systems that might otherwise help them navigate technological change.

The "sluggishness" economists observe in labor market adjustments isn't merely about inefficiency. There's a basic human reluctance to abandon homes, families, and identities for economic necessity. Workers are often forced to migrate to match their skillsets with available jobs, primarily due to job creation in new sector and geographical areas typically taking place in labor markets where AI is heavily utilized. That only adds to the bitterness of the adjustment process. This pattern threatens Norway's longstanding commitment to maintaining viable communities throughout our territory, not just in urban centers.

Collaborative effort

To address some of the aforementioned issues, we need to answer the following three questions: How does AI technology work? Where does it excel? What should it *never* be allowed to do? We also need to know how we can ensure humans will respect those boundaries. AI should enhance our ability to have empathy, along with critical thinking, and mathematical and data analysis skills. Additionally, it should improve our ability to reflect and ask insightful questions, and of course, boost our proficiency in prompt engineering. But beyond these specific skills, the educational system needs to foster a deeper understanding of what it means to learn. It's not simply about memorizing facts or passing exams.

As Keynes said in 1930, increased prosperity and increased automation of work were ultimately supposed to lead us to "*value goals over means and prefer the good over the useful.*" I don't believe the purpose of a shorter workweek is that we become a "useless" class, or that we become lazy, but rather that we can focus on the more important aspects of being a good human being.

OpenAI CEO Sam Altman once said, "*A lot of people working on AI pretend that it's only going to be good; it's only going to be a supplement; no one is ever going to be replaced.*" But, he adds, "*jobs are definitely going to go away, full stop.*" Since Norway is an open economy, it means we are very susceptible to global shocks or booms which will likely impact our economy and society in the coming years. A recent report from Goldman Sachs estimates around 300 million jobs could be affected in some way by generative AI. Moreover, it's estimated that 18% of all jobs globally could be automated before 2030. Generative AI seems to primarily affect the knowledge worker positions.

Future Roles

The work of Isaac Asimov comes to mind as we watch just how drastically AI is changing roles. His *Three Laws of Robotics* (first introduced in 1942's *"Runaround"*), which prioritized human safety over robotic autonomy, and established an early framework for discussions about AI accountability and programmed morality. While Turing focused on whether machines could think, Asimov asked *how* they should act—and who bears responsibility when their actions harm humans. Asimov foresaw a future where humans might primarily serve as machine operators, resulting in emotional, mental, and sociological consequences. He suggested that enforced leisure could become commonplace due to technological advancements, and that "work" would become one of the most spectacular words in the dictionary. Additionally, the potential for machines to displace human workers has been a subject of consideration among economists for many years. Notably, Nobel Prize winner Wassily Leontief foresaw this trend in 1952, when he predicted that technological advancement would gradually reduce the significance of human labor as machines took over more tasks. This made me wonder - what new roles could AI bring forth prior to 2030?

I was intrigued by the role of Decision Engineer. Is that someone who tries to create machines that make decisions better than humans? With all of these new jobs, how will you help create a future in which human knowledge and computer capability can work together?

The problem right now isn't so much that AI is replacing jobs; it's that workers aren't learning the appropriate skills necessary to fill the new roles that are emerging due to rapid AI development. This will only become more of a challenge as companies continue to apply AI and reimagine work in other areas.

Norwegian job polarization is neither inevitable...nor pure fantasy, but rather an emerging reality that we have no choice but to confront. The technological pressures transforming our economy can either lead to greater inequality or help create a more level playing field. It all depends on the collective choices we make as a society. Norway also has particular weaknesses: an aging population, regional disparities, digital divides, and cultural risk adverseness. Still, we also have particular strengths: a highly educated workforce, strong social safety nets, stable institutions, and financial means via our sovereign wealth fund.

Norway's reaction to job polarization will ultimately determine if technological advancement can exist in balance with our customary social pact, or if we will let market forces determine who profits from the AI revolution. The next chapter explores how humans can effectively collaborate with technological advances to increase our happiness and health in the future of work.

Chapter 11
Collaborative Partnership?

Like so many people, I learned in 2019 of a strange virus that began to spread through China. I didn't give it much thought at the time. But by March 2020, everything changed as the coronavirus began to spread across the world. It disrupted daily life and transformed the modern workplace. Remote work, once an exception, became a necessity. Hybrid work models emerged and quickly became mainstream as companies adapted to lockdowns and social distancing.

Meanwhile, another transformation was underway—one that was less visible but just as significant. While AI had already been present before 2019, generative AI development surged and continued to evolve at a rapid pace through 2022 driven by the launch of AI-powered tools from OpenAI, Google, and Microsoft.

My insights are based on reports from the World Economic Forum, SSB, and NAV. The World Economic Forum's 2025 report, which surveyed 1,000 employers representing over 14 million workers across 22 industries and 55 economies, and provided unparalleled insight into the emerging role of the knowledge workers for the upcoming period of 2025 to 2030.

Father of Modern Management

Peter Drucker, often called "the father of modern management," offered perspectives on the intersection of humans and technology that remain profoundly relevant today, especially in light of the rise of AI. Known for his forward-thinking insights into management and human potential, Drucker cautioned against overestimating technology's capacity to create value independently. He famously described technology as "merely a tool," a principle that applies equally to AI in its current form.

While AI can enhance efficiency by automating repetitive tasks, processing large datasets, and accelerating decision-making, the ability to foster true effectiveness is a distinctly human domain. For Drucker, effectiveness is rooted in qualities such as judgment, insight, and the ability to navigate complexity—attributes that rely on human intelligence and experience.

Let me explain Drucker's perspective with an experiment conducted in 2023 on management consultants who were responsible for tasks such as product ideation, prototype descriptions, market analysis, and marketing communications. This study is particularly interesting because it compared a group of humans performing these tasks alone, a second group that had access to AI tools, and a third, named "AI +", that was trained in AI prompt engineering. The results showed that both groups using AI tools outperformed the first control group, with the AI + training group performing the best. Participants who had access to AI, particularly those with lower baseline performance, helped the most. Overall, despite the improved quality of output, participants in both of the AI groups were more likely to make mistakes, showing an overreliance on AI tools when requested tasks exceeded the technology's capabilities. This proves Drucker's point, which is that even if humans use AI tools, we are still required to understand the work we are doing and still need to think critically. Moreover, if organizations are implementing AI in a sneaky way, in which employees don't explicitly know that some or all of their work is being used to train machines, then both machines and management can create a sense of distrust. However, in best-case scenarios, apprenticing can act as a salve against anxiety, passivity, and a sense of helplessness in human-machine interactions. giving people some level of control, make them feel invested in the future performance of a system or process, and they'll hopefully see AI as a colleague rather than a foe.

Collective Intelligence

Humans, as a species, are obviously more intelligent than any other animal. Aside from nature and the air we breathe, everything we see is a product of our ingenuity. However, as individuals, our practical, "real life" intelligence is often limited to only basic tasks like cracking nuts or fishing. If you doubt this, imagine yourself marooned in a jungle, with no one but yourself and no relevant survival knowledge. How far would you get, and how long would you survive? Despite our intelligence, no single human alone could design a democratic institution, a spaceship, or a smartphone. Our true "superpower" lies not in our individual intelligence but in our ability to collectively accumulate knowledge and pass it down through generations, allowing for its continuous refinement and improvement.

The human trait of offering assistance to one another, which emerged long before language development, is extremely rare over the course of the world's evolution and is far more developed in us than in our closest relatives – chimpanzees. The crucial difference between cognition in humans and other species is our ability to participate in truly collaborative activities—with shared goals and intentions. Infants in their second year already help others, work together, and share resources. Human beings are the world's experts at "mind-reading." Perhaps, rather than painstakingly hand-coding the things we care about, we should develop machines that simply observe human behavior and infer our values and desires.

As the British philosopher Bertrand Russell noted, "The average man's opinions are much less foolish than they would be if he thought for himself." Russell's statement underscores the power of collective culture in enhancing human intelligence. By pooling our diverse perspectives, experiences, and expertise, we transcend the constraints of our individual minds. As AI continues to change the nature of work for knowledge workers, no single employee can learn every new tool on their own. Companies that thrive in the future will need to make the act of learning a collective resource that allows for sharing knowledge, facilitating interdisciplinary learning, and allowing people to adapt new skills from what they know already. In this way, the future belongs not just to the isolated genius, but to the connected learner.

A New Era of Productivity

This vision of human–AI collaboration aligns with broader trends currently observed in many organizations. Companies like SAP have new managerial roles that focus on coaching human employees who are tasked with training AI systems to maximize productivity. Rather than simply offshoring jobs or replacing human workers, these companies are using AI to augment the skills of their teams, allowing them to tackle more complex tasks and drive innovation. AI integration is not about replacing human workers but empowering them to perform at their highest level. To get the best from both worlds, continuous upskilling is essential for employees to keep pace with the advanced capabilities of technology.

Crucially, managers need to build trust among their employees, ensuring they understand the benefits these agents bring. This requires trust among their employees, so they understand the benefits the new tools brought to the workplace.

The age of automation is not about machines substituting humans, but rather machines *augmenting* human capabilities. The real magic happens when AI's efficiency pairs with human creativity and intuition. For instance, in fields like design, AI can handle data-driven aspects while humans contribute original ideas and emotional intelligence.

Industrial people who are efficient by human standards will be eaten alive by AI. Because if the only metric is efficiency, AI has the capability to set standards that are completely unattainable for humans. Conductors/machine tamers and creatives, however, who give the machinery its direction—even if that's just a few hours of "work" (ergo: define the decision-making framework) will not have to worry as much about their jobs in the near future. Actually, their value will increase in the company.

Algorithms and Imagination Submerge

As someone who truly values freedom and flexibility, a sentiment which only grew stronger during the COVID-19 pandemic. Almost everything changed in the span of a few months, and remote work became the new norm. Yet, while I appreciate the flexibility of working from home, I also thrive on face-to-face interactions with colleagues and clients.

The key, it seems, lies in finding the right balance between in-person collaboration and remote work. This balance is especially important for Gen Z, who, more than any generation before them, want flexibility not only in where they work, but how they work. They don't want to conform to traditional organizational structures; instead, they seek businesses that can adapt to their needs. Companies that fail to accommodate this desire for flexibility will likely lose top talent in the future.

Another critical shift is how we evaluate performance. It's no longer about being constantly busy or visible; it's about producing meaningful, valuable output. This requires a shift in mindset - from outdated metrics to a more holistic approach that values results over hours worked. In this new landscape, employees should feel empowered to take breaks as needed, trusting that this contributes to better overall performance. Creating environments where people *want* to work and are excited to contribute is the future of talent retention.

Here is my take: AI has the potential to significantly enhance efficiency, streamline processes, and automate repetitive tasks. However, it does not possess the capacity to increase effectiveness—that remains firmly in the hands of humans. AI also does not have the ability to have any emotions, despite what the internet would have you believe. Still, it can simulate emotions in the way it "thinks", but in reality doesn't understand you - nor is it able to really "feel" you. That's why emotional intelligence is one of the many, if not the most important aspect of our evolutionary journey.

According to Drucker's theories, AI cannot replace teachers, and technology cannot replace humans, because technology will always remain as a servant to humans. Predictions of AI one day replacing humans is actually next to impossible, because AI cannot replace human imagination. Imagination is more important than intelligence and knowledge. Humans are gifted with the power of imagination and created automation for human progress and prosperity.

Drucker's framework of thinking suggests that the future of work will not be one where machine simply replaces human labor; rather, it will be a collaborative environment where AI amplifies human capabilities. Drucker would argue that the machine's role should be to relieve workers from the mundane tasks that drain time and energy, allowing them to focus on higher-order work that requires creativity, strategic thinking, and human intuition. The question, then, is not whether AI will replace jobs, but how AI can be integrated to help humans focus on what they do best, creating effectiveness through nuanced decision-making and understanding of context.

However, Drucker also criticized the overuse of computers for analysis, and this concern remains acutely relevant in the age of advanced AI and ML. AI tools, despite their sophistication, are fundamentally dependent on the data sets they are trained on. The old adage of "garbage in, garbage out" still applies: if AI is trained on biased, incomplete, or inaccurate data, it will consequently generate flawed results. Moreover, AI struggles when faced with environments that are volatile, uncertain, and unpredictable situations where historical data is irrelevant or misleading. In these cases, human intuition, which draws on experience and insight that cannot be reduced to data alone, is often the more effective tool. To rely solely on AI would be to ignore the nuances that only humans can perceive and act upon—and to do so can potentially lead to disastrous outcomes.

The machine may empower less specialized employees like accounting clerks or nurses to perform expert-level tasks, enhancing their productivity and capabilities. Additionally, skilled professionals such as doctors or engineers could also benefit from AI by accessing the latest knowledge and insights, allowing them to solve challenges more efficiently.

This hybrid "human-AI" approach combines the efficiency and data-processing power of AI with the empathy, creativity, and nuanced decision making that only humans can provide. It represents a shift towards collaboration between humans and machines to optimize both performance and output.

In the real world, the integration of AI into various sectors is already transforming the way we work. For instance, several Norwegian news outlets, including Digi.no (technology), VG.no (media), Dagbladet (media), and DN.no (business), are all increasingly using AI to write basic reports and articles. This new form of journalism enables human journalists to focus on more in-depth investigative work, rather than spending time on routine tasks.

Similarly, many Norwegian companies have adopted AI-driven chatbots and digital assistants to handle customer service. Skatteetaten (public sector), Talkmore (telecommunications), Elkjøp (retail), and Ving (travel) all use AI to manage customer inquiries efficiently. This not only enhances the speed and accuracy of responses but also allows human customer service agents to dedicate their time to more complex and nuanced issues that require a human touch. These examples demonstrate how AI can optimize operational tasks, allowing humans to direct their energy towards higher value, more creative work—aligning perfectly with the hybrid future of work we anticipate by 2030.

For instance, inventory management and supply chain operations are being optimized through the application of predictive analytics and demand forecasting. Additionally, many Norwegian online stores are implementing AI to augment how they customize services through the examination of consumer data. Ultimately, the utilization of AI-driven chatbots and virtual assistants to address customer inquiries is diminishing the duties of human customer service representatives. The healthcare industry is set to be revolutionized by AI, specifically in the area of personalized medicine. Medical personnel will have the AI-assisted capability to analyze substantial volumes of patient data in order to formulate individualized treatment strategies. This likely won't happen in Norway by 2030, as the governmental structure and understanding is too poor.

By 2030, I predict workplaces that thrive will do so on a hybrid model, where AI and humans collaborate to create value. Skatteetaten (Norway's Tax Administration) could deploy machine learning algorithms to predict and detect tax fraud. Just as fraudsters learn from each other and collaborate to evade taxes, AI could use social network analysis to provide insights into criminal networks, identifying patterns of behavior and uncovering fraudulent activities. While Norway possesses a vast amount of data, there is currently a gap in the skillset within the public sector to fully leverage that data. This challenge has already been addressed by the Spanish government, which successfully implemented similar data-driven solutions to combat tax fraud. By adopting such technologies, Norway could enhance its ability to detect fraud, streamline tax enforcement, and improve the overall efficiency of its public services.

However, for humans to trust AI systems, we need to feel involved in how those systems work and have some control over their decisions. AI should be designed to explain its choices and allow humans to make final decisions when needed. Building trust in AI takes time and testing, but when both humans and AI trust each other the results can benefit white-collar workers in the future. We will now pivot to discuss some specific knowledge workers and how their jobs might be affected by AI focusing on Nordic aspects.

Chapter 12
Middle Managers

What is a Middle Manager?

A middle manager's work consists of reporting, delivering targets, and executing instructions. As of end of Q4 2024, Norway had approximately 229,000 individuals in managerial positions (SSB), with women representing an average of 40% of these roles—a notable increase from 32% in 2012. Middle managers, while not always specialists in their team's specific tasks, are indeed knowledge workers, although they aren't necessarily specialized in the specific work their teams perform. Still, problem-solving remains a major task within the scope of their job responsibilities.

As previously discussed, AI has advanced problem-solving, especially in problem detection. However, in a middle manager role, problems often require more than simply finding an anomaly; solving the problem is much more challenging. Middle managers act as decision-makers, facilitators, and connectors between upper management and employees.

The Mintzberg model states that the middle managers hold three distinct roles: interpersonal, informational, and decision-making roles. The table below outlines their tasks and responsibilities across the three primary roles they typically assume.

Category	Role	Tasks
Interpersonal Roles	Figurehead	They serve as symbolic leader, representing the organization in ceremonial duties.
Interpersonal Roles	Leader	Executing performance reviews and providing productivity recommendations. Forwarding feedback from multiple teams towards top managers and vice versa.
Interpersonal Roles	Liaison	Exchanging information with external partners.
Informational Roles	Disseminator	Sharing new insights from internal and external sources with the team. Holding team meetings to keep them informed.
Informational Roles	Monitor	Seeking and receiving information to develop understanding of the organization (and its environments) from various sources.
Informational Roles	Spokesperson	Keeping top management and external partners informed about plans, results, policies, etc.
Decisional Roles	Entrepreneur	Strategic planning, designing and initiating improvements projects.
Decisional Roles	Disturbance Handler	Addressing unexpected issues and finding solutions.
Decisional Roles	Resource Allocator	Granting or protecting resources (time, workforce or equipment). Scheduling time and programming work (delegating work, authorizing actions, and budgeting.
Decisional Roles	Negotiator	Negotiating budget with consultants for new project or budget extensions with client.

Norway, as is the case with other Nordic countries, is among the world leaders in the digitalization of government services. However, as more businesses increase digitization, there's a resulting skills gap, where available jobs demand competencies many workers do not currently have. Given Norway's great IT infrastructure, the average Norwegian is quite adaptable to the new technology. The real challenge is whether Norway can turn disruption into opportunity before the market moves beyond its control or understanding.

This theme isn't new. Every major shift towards automation— from the Industrial Revolution to mobile technology and the internet—has triggered fears: "Jobs will disappear." AI is no different. Yet the data tells a more complex story. While some roles fade, others evolve, often in ways we fail to anticipate. By 2030, AI won't just change how managers work; it will also redefine what leadership means, reshaping responsibilities, and challenging traditional hierarchies.

Time management

The term "time management" is somewhat misleading. Time itself is an invariable factor, meaning it cannot be managed in the traditional sense. Instead, effective management should focus on how we allocate and use our available time. With the proper use of AI to automate both time and resource allocation for each employee, managers can ensure they have sufficient time to maintain and develop their professional competencies. It's critical to keep professional competence as a knowledge worker. The other aspect that has a great impact on the managers' work/life balance is how they choose to delegate tasks. For instance, how could you use ChatGPT \to delegate the tasks for you? You could type *"Draft an agenda for my [meeting]. Include steps for efficient time use, add break +10 minute each 90 minute and my deadline is X."*

Most managers lack time, and the other prompt may also help you organize your day efficiently. *My goals are X, and my free time is Y.*

The Rise of Algorithmic Authority

Studies show automation has already assumed many traditional managerial functions such as supervising, investigating, and even planning. Think about shift scheduling. Instead of a manager spending hours juggling schedules, AI can analyze real-time demand, employee skills, and even predict future needs to create schedules which are much more efficient and aligned with company goals. Instead of managers spending time analyzing data, trends, or feedback, AI algorithms analyze large volumes of data, which can then generate insights to guide business decisions.

This raises an interesting question: when AI drastically increases higher level supervisory automation, what work remains for human managers? Is it too far-fetched to envision a workplace where employees, particularly knowledge workers, are so self-sufficient that they would no longer need to envision traditional consulting and other service-oriented work, managers often spend a lot of time on resource allocation—deciding who works on which project. But AI could also easily streamline this function. Imagine an AI system that scans employee CVs, matches skills to project requirements, checks availability, and even considers individual preferences. The AI could then suggest the best fit for each project, saving managers valuable time. This same approach could be applied to policy work, where AI could potentially assist with tasks like document preparation and even help facilitate more productive discussions. We've all seen how policy debates can sometimes drag on, with solutions appearing only just before elections. AI might help focus those discussions on data and evidence rather than just political promises.

Automated task allocation is particularly widespread in standardized work settings, such as logistics, parcel delivery, or production. Many companies today use AI's algorithm-based solutions to create dynamic, i.e., on-demand schedules. Organizations utilize this approach to determine, for a specific timeframe, the best match between customer/market supply and labor requirements.

Who to Trust?

When it comes to AI, trust is something that must be earned and built on a fundamental sense of understanding and transparency (as described in chapter 6). Companies must consider two primary concerns when considering a reduction in middle management to address inefficiencies. First, there is the issue of transparency: we often do not understand how AI-driven chatbots arrive at their answers, which can become a serious problem in sensitive applications, such as HR and other areas involving personal data. Additionally, as previously discussed, the massive datasets that many AI models learn from often contain inherent biases, including gender or racial stereotypes which may be perpetuated or even amplified in AI's output. These are significant ethical challenges, which left unchecked can be equally problematic as the biases observed in human decision-making. Large language models are designed to appear trustworthy, but are not actually trustworthy. There's a big difference. True trustworthiness, as an AI trait, is *currently* far too complicated for a computer model to fully achieve.

I am concerned that as upcoming models like GPT-6 or GPT-7 become more advanced, humans will need to exert an excessive amount of effort – perhaps more than what's practical or reasonable - to verify their answers and spot misleading or false information.

However, there has been a growing concern since 2018 in Norway that both middle managers and company leadership are primarily engaging in lengthy strategic discussions that will yield few tangible results. This inefficiency not only hampers productivity, but also raises questions about the true value added by traditional management roles. By contrast, a well-implemented AI system—if designed to overcome the transparency and bias issues—could streamline decision making processes and reduce the time wasted in unproductive meetings.

Even as AI technology advances, human negotiation skills are likely to remain essential. Contract negotiations often involve complex interpersonal dynamics, nuanced understanding of context, and the ability to build trust—qualities that are difficult for AI to replicate. AI may assist in some of the negotiating aspects, but human negotiators will likely continue to play a central role.

Most middle and top managers are thought to have a lonely existence in the workplace. However, sense of loneliness is reduced whenever managers have a "sparring partner" - someone to trust and confide in, when it's time to address difficult questions or problems. However, challenging situations can be resolved much more efficiently when AI is used as that "sparring partner", a practice which GenZ has already seemed to firmly embrace.

My role as a project manager has provided firsthand experience in confronting some of the challenges faced by knowledge workers. It started innocently enough with Bi-weekly check-ins with my manager that were designed to gauge my progress but quickly became a source of frustration. The routine questions - "Did you find any projects?" "Do you know anyone?" "What about upskilling?"—felt less like genuine interest and more like a disguised performance review. It seemed like my manager was constantly questioning my self-sufficiency and ability to manage my own workload.

This experience led to me thinking about the dynamics of time management and productivity. Parkinson's Law, the principle that work expands to fill the time available, seemed to be playing out in real-time. Were these check-ins genuinely necessary, or were they a form of "Managerial Featherbedding," designed to justify roles rather than enhance productivity? I often wondered if my manager felt pressure from his bosses to simply demonstrate any activity, regardless of its actual value. Of course, there's the cost factor. The salaries dedicated to middle management roles represent a significant investment. What if some of those resources could be redistributed directly to the actual teams, specifically, empowering them with better tools, training, or even additional direct compensation?

This isn't to say I'm against all management. The Norwegian book *"Dear Leaders"* highlights the crucial role of supportive leadership in fostering well-being, motivation, and ultimately, results. Managers who trust their employees, empower them to use their expertise, and provide genuine support are invaluable. I've certainly benefited from such leadership in the past.

However, my experience also made me realize that AI could indeed streamline or automate *some* management functions, particularly those focused on administrative tasks that include "shadow reporting," metric tracking, reminders to fill out time sheets, and recommending generic courses. These tasks, while necessary, often detract from the core work that knowledge workers are hired to perform. AI could easily assume these responsibilities at a fraction of the cost.

The Peter Principle

On some of the articles I publish on LinkedIn, people have been asking why newer AI systems seem to make more mistakes compared to the older versions. Newer models aren't really worse. They're just being asked to do harder things, judged by tougher standards such as MMLU (Undergraduate level knowledge) or GPQA Diamond (Graduate level reasoning), and built with more complicated trade-offs inside. The mistakes aren't necessarily more frequent — they're just more obvious and sometimes trickier to fix.

So, this shift I am describing when did it happen? The early AI models did a great job on simple tasks like writing summaries or answering basic questions. Because they did so well, people gave them bigger jobs — planning, reasoning through complex problems, writing code, working on their own. But the harder the work got, the more they slipped up.

It's the Peter Principle, now in the digital world. The old idea that people get promoted until they reach a job they can't quite handle. AI is doing the same thing: rewarded for early wins, pushed into roles it isn't ready for, and tripping up in plain sight.

And the public has noticed. A 2025 report from Forskning.no shows that most Norwegians don't trust AI. People worry about technologies like the Internet of Things and how much access governments will have to their personal data. Only about half of Norwegian companies use AI at all, and fewer than 3% of citizens believe the government is a reliable watchdog for it.

The unease runs into the workplace too. Employees increasingly see AI as a tool their managers use to monitor them — a silent layer sitting between worker and boss. That changes how people behave on the job. It chips away at the sense of control over one's own work, weakens psychological safety, and pushes employees to focus their energy on navigating unclear systems of information rather than doing the work itself.

So the picture is this: AI was promoted faster than it could grow into the role, and the people living with the consequences — citizens and workers alike — are responding with exactly the kind of distrust you'd expect when a new manager is in over their head.

Even though the attention is on the issue of AI's role in surveillance, the bigger issue is an older concept known as the Peter Principle that has existed long before the advent of artificial intelligence.

However, I do believe we have the opportunity to potentially redistribute resources by directly empowering teams. This isn't about replacing human connection; but rather using AI to enhance and automate many managerial tasks, enabling human middle managers to focus on strategic workforce planning and innovation rather than using AI to create a wall between them and the team.

Human–AI symbiosis

Research dating back to 2018 supports this view, especially within service-related industries. A discussion with a professor from the University of Kristiania, coupled with a report by Capgemini, revealed 51% of respondents believe generative AI will ultimately diminish the number of available human decision-making roles. This implies that the "new human manager" will need to be armed with a diverse skill set ranging from data analysis, AI strategy, ethical assessment, and risk management.

Interestingly, while conventional roles may indeed decline, some surveys actually project a 12% increase in middle management functions by 2030, provided these roles evolve to become more strategic with the appropriate use of AI.

There are many skills and interpersonal attributes, specifically relating to social and interpersonal characteristics, which are essential to human middle managers. AI cannot truly motivate or inspire a person. Which means these intrinsically human traits should always be prioritized when selecting candidates for middle management. When I work with various teams in projects, interpersonal communication skills have always been vital in creating a positive organizational climate and improving job performance.

Research also shows emotional intelligence is a key factor in effective leadership. By focusing on these essential human skills, managers can free themselves from routine tasks and dedicate their time to more strategic leadership, thus guiding their teams and organizations through an increasingly complex world. Additionally, it's essential for managers to embrace the emergence of new roles that require algorithmic competency AI may ultimately offer an opportunity to transition from routine oversight to strategic leadership.

Embracing this level of change is also essential for members of Gen Z entering the workforce, a generation which values transparency and innovation. As AI redesigns the workplace in Norway, I wonder whether management will disappear altogether. But if they are able to educate themselves, will they be able to effectively use the AI to become better, or will they resist? As algorithms increasingly generate, process, and even *challenge* knowledge, how do managers prepare their teams? The challenge isn't just about automating tasks, but redefining roles. Humans have so far placed their faith in the reliability of algorithms, which is as dangerous as believing in any other dogma. We must approach AI with both excitement and profound humility, recognizing that we are experimenting with forces we may not fully understand. Managers also need to understand they must educate themselves and understand the ethical implications in order to use it to become better in their role, or risk perishing before 2030.

Theory of Mind, as discussed in Chapter 4, plays a particularly crucial role in professions like politics, although it matters just as much in leadership, where understanding and responding to the emotions and perspectives of others is key to gaining influence. Self-interest is crucial for making anyone change their mind to support your cause. Leaders are experts in making others believe how their actions might meet their needs or advance their cause. In most situations, workers will eagerly follow any leader, regardless of whether it's a politician, CEO, CTO, or anyone who sits at the upper management. The difference is not just what is said, but how it's said. Persuasion involves mutual respect and open dialogue, while manipulation relies on exploiting emotional vulnerabilities and creating a power imbalance.

People are often driven by social proof, and will do things they see others doing, even if it is not in their best self-interest.

Transforming Management

Humans have limited short-term memory and cognitive capacity, which is why we tend to focus on one task at a time rather than multitasking effectively. Multitasking is indeed possible, but it often reduces our ability to perform any given individual task well, especially when that task requires complex thought. We tend to use trial and error when there are a few options to consider. However, in many situations, we don't have the time or resources for such approaches. Instead, our knowledge allows us to search for solutions more efficiently using shortcuts (heuristic), or practical strategies to narrow down our options, a method commonly referred to as "best first search."

Imagine you're managing a large project with multiple tasks that need to be completed in order, and on deadline. You want to focus on the tasks that will move the project forward in the fastest way possible. Instead of tackling every task individually, you start with the ones that will directly impact the project's progress, such as getting the client's approval on a key deliverable. This is an example of *best first search,* in which you prioritize the tasks that are closest to the goal, making the most efficient use of your time. This is also a method used by machine learning.

But this isn't a story of job loss, it's a story of transformation. Instead of simply managing tasks, future leaders might focus on strategic planning, guiding projects, and leveraging deep, specialized expertise that only comes with human experience. Middle managers might even earn a bit less than they do today, but there could be a greater chance of enjoying a three-day workweek instead of the standard five. Imagine having extra time to spend with your family, travelling, or starting a new hobby, wouldn't that be worth it?

Chapter 13
When AI Manages $1.9 trillion

The summer of 1969 was a turning point in history. Phillips
Petroleum's discovery of oil in the North Sea did not just tap hydrocarbons; it revealed the future for Norway. The discovery of the largest offshore Ekofisk oilfield spurred the transformation of a Norwegian population predominantly focused on farming and fishing into one of the world's wealthiest nations. But as I look at algorithms making billion-kroner level decisions in microseconds now, I do wonder whether we have simply swapped one dependency for something more uncertain - one which no policy maker nor the average human really knows how to use.

From Primary Sector to Neural Networks

To understand our predicament, we must first understand our journey. Norway's path to prosperity wasn't always smooth. Norway obtained its independence from the Denmark union in 1814. However, Denmark-Norway was previously an ally of Napoleon during the Napoleonic War. Because it was on the losing side of that conflict, Norway was compelled to enter into a union with Sweden through the *Treaty of Kiel*, which lasted until 1905. During this period, much of Norway's economy was modest and agriculturally based in timber, and the maritime sector, which included shipping and fishing. In spite of its small population and relatively infertile land, the country took advantage of its natural resources and its historic fishing tradition to become part of existing regional trading networks. We know from early records that following its independence, Norway's enjoyed average wealth for a country in Western Europe, and during the 19th century, particularly less wealthy than countries like Great Britain, France, and Germany. Growth slowed during the Second World War while Nazi Germany occupied Norway, and the economic impact was rather dramatic. The war disrupted production, and led to inflation and rationing – as the country was forced to manage an extreme shortage of resources. The war also destroyed a great deal of infrastructure and industrial potential. Additionally, there were numerous other problems ranging from the destruction of productive assets to the broader disruption to the domestic market. The occupation divided the economy into two separate systems – one controlled by Germany, the other operated externally through institutions like Nortraship (which controlled the merchant fleet that, to a large extent, successfully avoided the economic consequences of the war). Norway benefited immensely from the Marshall Plan when, in 1948, it reluctantly accepted 3 billion Norwegian Kroner in aid through loans and other support.

That aid supported Norway's restoration of infrastructure, modernized industry, and stabilized the economy. It was also crucial in helping to jumpstart the country's process of recovery, and enabled the government to invest in public services, new technology, and institutional reform. The situation for Norway was quite good in 1945, and by 1946, Norway had reached pre-war levels of production and consumption. In other words, Norway had regained the same economic level it had before the war in 1940, just one year after the war ended.

The Norwegian economy expanded quickly during the last three decades of the 20th century, and at the dawn of the 21st Century placed it among the world's top 10 countries in terms of GDP per capita.

The Norwegian Oil Fund

Norway's evolution into a major global energy player wasn't just about wealth; it also sparked a deeper transformation in the way Norwegians viewed the concept of work. The oil boom provided not only jobs, but also a sense of pride and purpose. Workers who were previously seen as part of the industrial machine subsequently became part of something larger - a movement that fueled national growth and solidarity.

The oil fund is not only a symbol of Norway's economic success, but also a critical component of its financial stability. As it continues to grow, the fund has become an increasingly attractive target for global threats (cyber-attacks, data breaches, or market manipulation by AI). Even a small loss of just 1% of its wealth could erode public trust and undermine confidence in Norway's ability to secure its resources and manage its national wealth effectively.

But things weren't always that rosy. In fact, the period leading up to 1992 was marked by deep economic turbulence. In the late 1980s, Norway suffered the aftermath of a major banking crisis, a sharp fall in housing prices, and an overheated credit market fueled by rapid deregulation earlier in the decade. When oil prices collapsed in 1986, state revenues dropped sharply, exposing the economy's vulnerability to fluctuations in the petroleum market.

By the early 1990s, unemployment rose significantly, several banks required state rescue, and confidence in the Norwegian krone was under pressure. The currency crisis of 1992 emerged as another turning point: Norway abandoned its fixed exchange rate policy and allowed the krone to float freely. This marked the beginning of a new economic era, characterized by greater stability, more disciplined fiscal management, and the eventual rise of the Government Petroleum Fund—what the world now knows as the Norwegian Oil Fund.

The fund expanded quickly after its first deposit, and by the end of 1999 its capital stood at an impressive NOK 220.9 billion. In 2009, and again in 2013, the fund's value once again rose sharply.

However, in 2017, the Ministry of Finance decided to lower the expected real return on the fund's capital to 3 percent, reflecting a reassessment of future global financial conditions. As a result, the annual use of oil money has since come closer to the expected real return of the fund, while also relying on AI to achieve a new sense of stability.

As Nicolai Tangen, the CEO of the Oil Fund, has emphasized is known to be a driving force when it comes to utilizing AI in Norway as he once said, *"Oljefondet bruker kunstig intelligens til å forvalte, estimere og evaluere,"* the fund utilizes AI to manage investments worth 20 trillion NOK (1,9 trillion USD) as per 25 January 2025. In other words, the fund uses AI to manage, estimate, and evaluate a portfolio so massive it makes Scrooge McDuck's money bin look like a jar of loose change. This statement highlights the fund's reliance on advanced technology to steer wealth in complex markets and optimize strategies, so we get the maximum profit. However, while AI offers unparalleled opportunities to enhance decision-making, it also introduces new vulnerabilities, particularly in a financial ecosystem that is rapidly evolving.

To grasp the challenge facing Norges Bank Investment Management, one must first appreciate the asymmetry of its structure. Tangen stared at a problem that kept him up at night. His team of six hundred and seventy people managed more money than seems possible to comprehend—one point eight trillion dollars - scattered across nearly nine thousand companies around the world. He recognized that this wasn't an equation to be solved by algorithms alone but required humans who could influence behavior. His attempt to make artificial intelligence co-exist with his staff revealed a fundamental truth about organizational psychology which many leaders have experienced firsthand; when adoption is a choice, and not an edict - resistance often comes from the very people the innovation was designed to help the most.

The Magnificent Seven Dependency

"Magnificent seven" was a Western movie from the 1960s, directed by John Sturges, and depicted a group of seven gunmen. In the world of finance, the term has been re-framed to reference a group of seven of the highest performing and influential stocks in the technology, and include Apple, Microsoft, Google parent Alphabet, Amazon.com, Nvidia, Meta and Tesla.

Our fund holds stakes in nearly 9,000 companies worldwide, yet our fortunes are increasingly tied to these "Magnificent Seven" tech firms, which represent a significant concentration of our wealth. In fact, 55% of the fund's profits comes from US markets, and in 2024, Norway's Government Pension Fund Global (often called the Norwegian Oil Fund) financed one-fifth of the state budget. This was possible due the value of the Oil Fund has increased much more than expected.

This concentration became painfully clear in January 2025 when news of DeepSeek, a Chinese AI tool, sent tech stocks plummeting. Projections suggested that in a worst-case scenario, our fund could lose 40% of its value, approximately 8,000 billion kroner.

The issue

AI technology saturates the very fabric of the fund's investment strategies, something Tangen has readily admitted. Algorithms price complex assets, predict the ebb and flow of capital, and try to glimpse the future in the swirling tea leaves of the market. But this reliance on smart machines also creates opportunities. Imagine a chess grandmaster being dependent on the computer assistant integral tool. Even with the tool's assistance, a fraction of a mistake means a fine-tuned strategy goes out of the window. Similarly, data poisoning occurs when an attacker carefully introduces false or malicious data into a model's training set so that the AI "learns" the wrong patterns. That subtly feeds into the fund's AI to compromise decisions, leading to colossal losses. This scenario is possible because many AI systems, especially those trained on web-sourced or unpacked data—can be nudged off course if even small changes go undetected.

The fund's investment in almost 9,000 companies worldwide adds another layer of risk. While the golden rule of investing is to diversify, Norway's treasure chest is weighted heavily toward the "Magnificent 7", which enjoys a total estimated value of $5 trillion USD. It reminds one of the "creative destruction" of Joseph Schumpeter. Innovation, the lifeblood of capitalism, inevitably disrupts the status quo and concentrates power in the hands of the few who successfully ride the waves of change. Today's tech behemoths – the superstars of the market, may ultimately turn out to be tomorrow's forgotten relics. Any one of a variety of factors, such as an unforeseen disruptive technology, regulatory crackdown, or shift in public tastes, could send these stocks diving - taking the oil fund spiraling along with them. The near panic triggered by DeepSeek serves a reminder that in this digital age, fortunes can shift without warning.

Another episode that affected Norway's wealth occurred in March 2025, upon the announcement of the trade dispute between the U.S. and "the rest of the world". The value of the Norway's oil fund sank to 18.830 billion NOK on 22nd March 2025. Then there was a direct impact after the Trump administration set in motion tax reforms during America's so called "liberation day." Those reforms consequently jeopardized the outlook for oil prices on the heels of steep losses incurred during the previous week. I sense something worse might happen if a sane-minded leader fails to take the helm and steer the U.S. in the right direction.

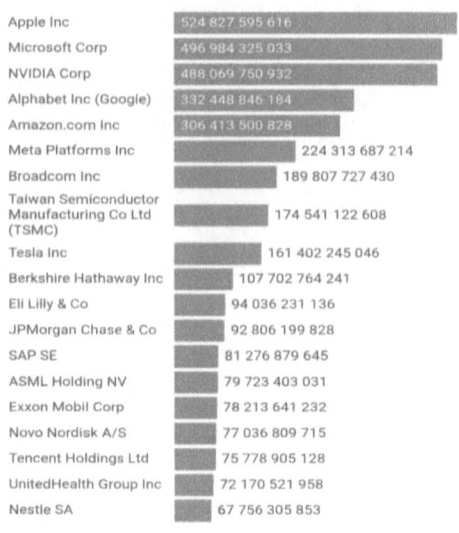

The Fragile Reality of Diversification

The Norwegian oil fund has benefitted significantly from heavy investment in the Magnificent Seven companies. By holding onto these big winners in the same way a typical index fund would, the oil fund has taken advantage of the same trend that allowed many passive funds to outperform active ones in both the US and Global markets.

Keynes warned long ago about the inherent instability of capitalism, its roller-coaster ride of booms and busts, and the perils of unchecked market power. The example of the oil fund's concentrated bet on a few dominant tech companies is a good example: monstrous giants wielding enormous influence in the economic, political, and social realm. Their decisions affect entire industries, alter the course of elections, and even change the way we think. Keynes might have pointed out that such concentration of capital and influence introduces its own form of systemic risk: the fund's fate becomes increasingly vulnerable to the fluctuations and fortunes of a single, powerful sector.

There's also the constant, lurking presence of cyber war, which serves as a dagger pointing at the heart of Norwegian wealth. A data breach that hacks into Norway's investment secrets would constitute a true national emergency. Imagine a hostile nation or shadowy group of hackers gaining access to the fund's strategic playbook. They could manipulate markets and make money hand over fist, crippling Norway's financial standing in the process. This is not only about money, but about national security, and Norway's place in the world.

Technological Sovereignty

While reflecting upon approaches like the Trump administration's 'America First' policy, other nations locked in competition might begin to prioritize their own immediate advantages through decisions that consequently endanger the global community. But this essentially a problem of collective action involving the pursuit of national self-interest that can lead to detrimental outcomes for the world at large.

This raises a critical concern: what happens when those creators are driven by ideologies that prioritize personal gain or unchecked power? Imagine an AI system reflecting the worldview of a leader who disregards human rights or sees technology solely as a tool for control. Such a system could be used to amplify existing inequalities, automate discrimination, or even enable mass surveillance. The potential for misuse is immense, particularly when those in power lack ethical constraints. This is not just a hypothetical scenario; history is replete with examples of technology being wielded for oppression under the direction of ruthless leaders. AI, with its unprecedented potential to analyze, predict, and influence human behavior, could become an even more potent tool in the wrong hands.

Evidence of this fragmentation includes Europe's efforts to establish greater digital sovereignty by building its own network infrastructure. Historically, dominant global powers understood the geopolitical importance of controlling new technologies, such as industrial advancements, and actively sought to leverage them. Conversely, China's late adoption of modern industrial technology was seen as a key factor in its late 20th century decline from superpower status, which lead to defeats rooted in a technological gap. Having learned from this experience, China now appears determined to never again lose a technological race.

Projects like Stargate (The U.S. launched the $500B Stargate Project with OpenAI, Microsoft, Oracle and Nvidia to build 20 AI data centers nationwide. Backed by SoftBank and MGX involved in this project), reportedly launched with the noble aim of curing cancer through AI, reflect this duality. However, such ambitions often face significant hurdles, from exorbitant costs to internal misalignment within the organizations spearheading them. Whether Stargate will succeed or even endure remains uncertain. Meanwhile, tech giants like Microsoft, Apple, Amazon, and Meta, which dominate AI development, operate in an environment that lacks clear governance, raising questions about who holds the ultimate responsibility for how this technology is used and to what end.

This evolving dynamic recalls Joseph Schumpeter's theory of "creative destruction," where innovation disrupts systems, often leads to a concentration of power among dominant actors. Keynes's warnings about capitalism's tendency toward monopolization also resonate, as unchecked technological and economic shifts risk exacerbating inequality and diminishing competition. This is further illustrated by policies of leaders like Trump. His emphasis on deregulation, corporate tax cuts, and economic nationalism fostered an environment which encouraged market consolidation and reinforced elite power structures. Whether intentional or not, this aligns with Keynes's and Schumpeter's cautionary views on capitalism's inherent risks.

AI the Fund Manager

For the last 5–10 years, organizations have prioritized data science and how we would mine this information into actionable knowledge in order to increase our intelligence and reporting. Managers currently sift new investment prospects and use them as they look across their portfolio to make sense of the information they capture. However, end-to-end analysis enables AI to recognize patterns and relationships that human or conventional models may not see, giving fund managers more in-depth insights and forecasting power. This gives the manager the ability to search for new products and solutions that would be worthy of investment. With continuous technological advancements, especially in machine learning and natural language processing, robo-advisors have gradually evolved from basic asset allocation tools into more sophisticated and detailed wealth management systems. Today, robo-advisors not only provide basic asset allocation advice but are also able to dynamically adjust strategies based on market fluctuations, macroeconomic indicators, and the user's risk tolerance. NLP can extract key information from large amounts of market news, social media data, and financial reports, helping the system understand market sentiment and investor psychology

"Algorithmic asset manager" activity currently accounts for roughly 65-80 percent of all the total trading volume in the world. Managers are using data to inform how they report updates to their investors. Additionally, by incorporating the concept of "HITLP" (Human-In-The-Loop), AI can help with risk management by highlighting the most profitable investments and moves. An astute manager should be able to understand the dynamics of their investment portfolio in order to make sound decisions for their clients or shareholders.

Complex algorithms decide which bond, market, and segment we should be investing our trillion kroner. Human fund managers typically guess market trends correctly, only about 25% of the time. Even the best managers have roughly a 50% chance of predicting if a stock will go up or down. But new AI tools can improve these predictions.

With better AI, managers can decide more precisely when to buy or sell. They might also lower fees because their decisions add extra value.

What concerns me is that if all of the fund managers generally use the same tools, only those using *accurate* AI tools will benefit. Additionally, they would need to reduce their fees to account for the increased value their AI tools will generate. Lastly, there is a high chance that we would consequently crash the economy using derivatives, which are bets on future events in the market. The issue here is that a derivative is normally linked to many other more obscure derivatives. Because the world is connected through the internet, a single event in one country can trigger changes in markets around the globe.

AI-powered mutual funds frequently show superior stock selection capability and outperform their human-managed peers. The question we should ask is, why use AI at all? The answer is simple; it isn't about following a trend - it's about survival. In an industry defined by relentless innovation and cut-throat competition, staying ahead means harnessing every advantage. According to Deloitte, the use of AI-driven investment tools is set to surge by roughly 80 percent between 2027 and 2028, as more firms entrust algorithmic systems with portfolio decisions.

Most of us have forgotten that any AI or machine built with code was initially programmed by a human being, and ultimately reflects the qualities and ethics of the person deciding the boundaries of the code, or the person responsible for programming the AI itself. If the code is ruthless and cold, like the recently elected U.S. president, this could set off a concerning trend where multinational tech giants adopt similar approaches in the development of AI. AI systems don't emerge in a vacuum; they are forged in the crucible of human values. Every line of code and every data point used to train these systems carries the imprint of its creators. Therefore, although funds that used AI as a non-systemic element of their investment strategy have proven over time to grow substantially in value, this does not imply that human wealth or fund managers will soon be obsolete. In fact, their profession is instead likely to be reshaped into a more strategic form of advisory work that requires them to become better – and more efficient – at using and understanding AI.

What if AI is Wrong?

The success of the oil fund is a point of pride for Norway, but it is also a reminder of the vulnerabilities inherent in a highly interconnected global system. Schumpeter, Keynes, and Drucker would all caution that in an age of rapid technological change, those who control innovation must be vigilant.

We cannot ignore the risks associated with the fund's dependence on AI, the impact of foreign technology, and the uncertainty stemming from geopolitical stability. Norway must take proactive steps to protect its resources, ensuring that the fund's future remains secure in an increasingly unpredictable world. Someone with bad intentions only needs to be active on the internet for a few minutes in order to spook the market into frenzy. Even if investors collectively believe there's a 99 percent chance the news or activity being fake, it can still trigger the algorithm to sell. AI will produce many more news in the near future, which could send the market into a selling frenzy, while a separate AI could see it as a buying opportunity to make millions.

The pressure will always be on fund management teams to make better predictions, make no mistake, AI will continue to support those efforts far better than any human is capable of doing.

When it comes to how wealth management firms value the notion of human – AI intimacy, it's clear they remain skeptical. However, it would appear the trend is certainly gaining traction, especially in other industries (consider online companionship companies like Replika AI and Character AI), where consumers are spending an increasing amount of building AI-human relationships.

From Algorithms to Accountability

The choice of LLM and argument that as mentioned earlier that each llm has its pro and cons and, thus In selecting an AI language model for its operations, Norges Bank Investment Management (NBIM)—which manages Norway's $1.8 trillion sovereign wealth fund—conducted rigorous evaluations across multiple platforms before choosing Anthropic's Claude. The decision wasn't arbitrary or based on hype, but rooted in practical performance metrics that mattered for high-stakes financial analysis. Claude Sonnet 4.5 consistently outperformed competitors in complex reasoning tasks, particularly in risk assessment and the analysis of sophisticated financial instruments where nuanced judgment is paramount. Critically, Claude demonstrated a crucial safety feature that resonated with NBIM's fiduciary responsibilities: when uncertain, it signals doubt rather than generating plausible-sounding but inaccurate information—a tendency known as "hallucination" that plagues many AI systems. For an institution managing public funds on behalf of Norwegian citizens, this honest acknowledgment of limitations proved as valuable as the model's capabilities. The choice also reflected alignment on broader principles, with Anthropic's commitment to responsible AI development matching NBIM's transparency requirements as a public entity. The results validated their selection: NBIM reported annual time savings of 213,000 hours and 20% productivity gains across their 670-person workforce, demonstrating that careful LLM selection based on institutional needs and values—rather than popularity or marketing—delivers measurable returns. Still, humans still seem to trust each other more than the machine, and studies (including the one reported by Gertjan Verdickt in the Financial Times on 17 September 2024) show a significant number people often distrust or reject recommendations coming from an algorithm—especially after seeing it make even small mistakes. Even if an AI model, such as Claude can make very accurate predictions or recommendations, investors won't act on its advice unless they believe it's reliable and that it is truly acting in their best interest. It's important to keep in mind that when our collective wealth is at stake, we must invest with common sense, and ensure any AI-decisions are implemented with proper oversight. In human wealth management advisor has a legal and ethical obligation (a fiduciary duty) to put their client's interests ahead of their own. Similarly, an AI should be held to the same standard in the sense that it should be able to demonstrate it will observe the same rules and ethical considerations that a human advisor would—and that its algorithm will act in a manner that safeguards and promotes the interest of any investor, institution, or country. In short, the race is on - "Good AI" versus "Bad AI"; human wisdom versus algorithmic efficiency - the desire to profit, versus the need to protect.

I don't know who will win this race. But I do know if we lose, it won't be because we lack wealth or technology. On the contrary, it will likely be because we forgot the lesson those simple farmers and fishermen knew in their bones—that it doesn't matter what you have, but rather whether you can keep it. The question now is whether anyone in power is paying attention, or whether they're too mesmerized by the algorithms' potential to see the proverbial cliff ahead without falling off. I already know the answer after witnessing how Norwegians previously handled these delicate situations time and time again.

Chapter 14
Project Leaders

Project management, as a profession, has existed for over 4,500 years. The Giza Pyramid, the Parthenon, Stonehenge, and the Taj Mahal were not divine miracles, but were constructed in an organized manner by people who led massive teams. They were, in every sense of the term – project managers.

The Project Management Institute defines a project as *"a temporary group activity designed to produce a unique product, service or result"* and its definition of project management is the *"application of knowledge, skills, tools and techniques to project activities to meet the project requirements."* Prior to the advent of AI, a project managers role were charged with overseeing projects through their traditional cycles: initiation, planning, execution, and closure.

Personally, I thrive during times of uncertainty, and in my experience, project management essentially amounts to a game of controlled chaos.

The Issue

Half of all human led public IT projects run into some kind of problem or issue, and I have seen how human error can cost both time and money.

- **NAV**: Allocated 872 million NOK to upgrade a 40-year-old system; initially set to complete by October 2020, it now targets early 2027—with no improvement in processing times.
- **Akson**: A national health IT initiative scrapped after spending 240 million NOK on planning, despite an initial estimated cost of 20 billion NOK.
- **Higher Education Sector**: 21 universities and colleges spent over 166 million NOK on a new IT system, the project was terminated mid-2024 after multiple delays.

These examples illustrate how even large, well-funded projects can face significant challenges. From my experience, success in public IT projects depends on thorough planning, realistic timelines, and the ability to adapt to unforeseen obstacles.

Planning Fallacy

The Romans built aqueducts that took twice as long as promised. The Sydney Opera House was supposed to cost 7 million dollars and took 102 million. Humans are bad at planning. Not sometimes. Always. Due to the fact that predicting into the future is very difficult (almost impossible) is something many out there are not capable of doing. And it's also partial due to once we have a plan, it gives us a false hope and fits into our pre-exiting belief, and thus we will ignore any contrary evidence telling us otherwise.

A significant reason behind such challenges, where projects run over budget and beyond deadlines, is a common cognitive bias known as the planning fallacy. This often occurs when policymakers or business owners assess the risks of a project. They tend to become overly optimistic, underestimating risks, probabilities, and potential setbacks. Norway, bless it, has made something of an art form of this. Which is strange, because Norwegians are generally sensible people. But there's a particular brand of Nordic cheerfulness — a kind of "it'll sort itself out" energy — that seems to survive contact with even the most alarming budget projections. Whether it's cultural, or simply what happens when a country is wealthy enough that nothing truly catastrophic ever follows from being wrong, is a fair question. Either way, the optimism persists, the projects balloon, and everyone acts surprised. Consider for example the development of a new drinking water reservoir in Oslo, recent road projects, ongoing historical building renovations, hospital expansions, or even IT initiatives. Time and time again, these projects run over budget and beyond deadlines. The core issue is simple: people tend to underestimate how long something will take—even when they've done it before. Social pressure to secure political or financial approval pushes planners to present overly optimistic forecasts.

Still, the same mistakes keep happening, and when confronted, project managers typically ask for forgiveness, and then ask for more resources to complete what should have been finished by the original deadline. Because Norway has so much wealth, it seems like the wasting another 150 to 500 million kroner barely raises an eyebrow.

Perhaps this is because politicians and bureaucrats, unlike private investors, are not personally on the hook for any financial risk that leads to massive losses. This lack of accountability makes it easier to carelessly spend "ownerless" funds carelessly and inefficiently.

The real culprit for why we human always fail to estimate is optimism — specifically, the delusional kind. We often operate under the assumption that past performance predicts future outcomes. Because we've successfully managed previous projects (or at least survived them), we optimistically believe the next one will also be manageable. This tendency to draw conclusions from past performance can blind us to potential pitfalls and the unique challenges of each new undertaking. It's the intellectual equal of landing a plane once and deciding you're basically a pilot.

Social pressure to secure political or financial approval pushes planners to present overly optimistic forecasts, further reinforcing this inductive bias. So, if this has always been the case, how can we expect to see any changes in the future?

The Future

Building on our discussion of innovation, Business Model Innovation (BMI) helps companies stay adaptable by re-configuring their offerings and structures so they can subsequently adopt new technologies and take advantage of the benefits of AI. This includes considering where value is added to the business through the introduction of new technologies, and taking into consideration the trade-offs that may need to be made. There are three core elements related to BMI that can influence how any firm can change their fundamental business model:

(1) the offering, which refers to the products, processes, and services that the firm offers;

(2) the experience, which encompasses customer interfaces and engagement; and

(3) the configuration, which refers to how the firm is organized or structured to create, deliver, and capture value.

There are various AI tools that make foreseeing risks, bottlenecks, and team communication much better and more efficient. I personally have saved a lot of time writing reports over the years using the right tool, and I am still amazed to think that in 5 more years 80 percent of all of my tasks will be run by agentic AI. In fact, AI assisted project management is already here, quietly reshaping the way we plan, track, and execute projects, and continues to augment or automate tasks within these phases - fundamentally changing the role of human project management.

The role shift from managers to project leaders

Paul Boudreau emphasizes in his book "*The Self-Driving project*", the importance of embracing AI and taking charge of its evolution. The term "project manager" feels increasingly outdated, like a horse-drawn carriage strolling down the road in the age of electric vehicles. What we're becoming - what we *must* become, are project *leaders*. This isn't just a matter of semantics; but a fundamental shift in our role in the workplace. Will we manage to embrace the opportunity to become visionaries, strategists, and architects of human collaboration?

When I became a project manager many years ago, it was essentially about predicting all of the various outcomes and risks, and then trying to re-align them with the expectations of a stressful and distracted project owner – all while keeping the team motivated. Now, after much practice, the utilization of agile methods and AI effectively serves as an extra pair of hands, ready to assist my team with the mundane tasks and offer solutions - before a risk can evolve into a real problem. Lately, my role has transitioned from "manager" to strategic leader. Taking into consideration the roles of other similar knowledge workers, project leaders are tasked with developing a unique blend of skill sets which can be utilized in concert with AI's capabilities. These new skills include critical thinking, and AI literacy (understanding the basics of AI – including its capabilities and limitations), and a high level of emotional intelligence. AI doesn't have the ability to understand or convey emotions, despite what the internet would have you believe. . That's why emotional intelligence is one of the many, if not the most important elements of our past experiences, future expectations, knowledge, desires, and beliefs.

The positive outcome using AI

When we talk about AI based project management, which includes generative AI such as ChatGPT, Microsoft Copilot, Rovo, Jira (AI-Powered teamwork tool), Confluence, Google Gemini, or Smartsheet (AI-driven automation streamlines task assignments and status updates), intuitive interfaces make it easy to track project progress without requiring extensive setup. GenAI's ability to generate novel outputs in six key formats—text, image, audio, video, code, and 3D specialized models—have changed the overall concept of what it will mean to be a project leader now – and in the future.

Project managers who use AI-driven tools report they delivered 61% of their projects on time versus 47% of those who did not use AI. Many projects include a degree of uncertainty and involve constant change. So, it stands to reason that having an improved agentic AI that is better at prediction can actually increase the success of the project by around 10–15%. It may not seem like much, but it's still something considering how prone we are to failing at our projects.

In many of my own projects there are choices to be made. AI algorithms can easily figure out which projects will bring the most value to your company based on a thorough analysis of your project data. Machine learning detects patterns and makes predictions that a project manager can't do manually. And often prioritizing is very difficult for us humans, especially since we often really don't know what we want and how we should measure it.

We all try to make the best predictions we can in every task we do. Still, in the world of project management, it is clear many people continue to repeat the same mistakes. These mistakes are due to cognitive biases that impair judgment, leading to repeated mistakes in project management. These biases can be categorized into how they affect beliefs, decision-making, and behavior, our social interactions, prejudices, and lastly, those which create false memories.

In this field, salaries in Norway reflect both experience and expertise. For someone with a minimum of three years of experience, the average salary typically starts around 700,000 NOK. For those with more advanced skills and a proven track record, compensation can exceed 1,1 million NOK. Given the fact that machine learning algorithms either automate or help perform most of our tasks, we can expect an optimal distribution of resources, time savings, and a reduction in human error—

which can increase the project's chances of staying on schedule. In many of my projects, I've found that stakeholders and the project steering committee didn't allocate enough time for proper planning. This would sometimes lead to frustration, especially when my team and I suggested having shorter, more focused meetings to work through the details. On the other hand, I've also been involved in projects where there seemed to be endless planning, but no real execution to follow through on those plans.

As I mentioned earlier, it's the management roles that will be impacted by AI after 2030. For instance, many are familiar with Copilot, which is today integrated into PowerPoint. Another amazing tool, Prezent, is an AI-powered presentation software that can help you create stunning presentations in minutes. It uses AI to automatically generate slides, format text, and add images and videos. Before ChatGPT or Copilot, I used and still use Grammarly to correct much of my writing, despite having a great editor on my team. My use of LLMs is not only practical, but research confirms GPT shows a high level of consistency, reliability, and consistency across diverse scenarios, which is crucial if project leaders are to be encouraged to use GPTs.

By leveraging historical data and real time information, AI can identify risks at an early stage—such as cost overruns, resource shortages, or delivery delays. AI can also suggest measures to minimize or manage these risks, and has often helped me stay proactive and offered guidance in implementing necessary actions before issues arise. The best part—AI also reduces the risk of human error and bias in decision-making, which is often an issue where one has to argue about goals, what is within scope or not, all in an effort to avoid letting our emotions cloud our judgment. Additionally, AI can ensure there are more objective and precise outcomes by providing suggestions infused with a better, more accurate fact-based analysis.

You may be wondering what tasks are left for a human to perform - and why would a company still bother paying me a top-notch salary if most of my tasks are done by AI? I estimate that 10% of the tasks in project management are dedicated to critical tasks that ensure the smooth execution and success of the project, which is now much more simplified due to AI. However, the remaining 90% of the role is about communicating and motivating, which are elements of project management in which AI simply does not excel. Projects still require *human based* emotional intelligence, strategic thinking, and the ability to navigate complex human dynamics.

I recently found myself leading a complex implementation project for a Norwegian client. The project was divided into three streams, each interdependent, with multiple consultants involved—many of whom were simultaneously assigned to two or more projects of their own. This raised an immediate concern: was anyone overbooked?

Experience taught me that the company's projects had an 80% to 100% likelihood of exceeding their estimated timelines. With that in mind, I knew we needed a solid impact assessment. What would happen if the project slipped behind schedule?

Additionally, although the project had many third-party integrators involved, issue could still arise if someone in that team became sick, or if there was a delivery delay for data being used to convert Or worse, what if someone on my project team decided to leave? These are very complex questions, and by using AI to put a risk management plan in place, I effectively had the answer to many of these questions – along the answers to many other questions that I never would have thought to ask.

I was able to focus more on communicating with the stakeholder and my team, rather than completing each individual task – all because I had the assistance of AI. Ultimately, AI gave me more time to prioritize the more human-centric approach of being a leader.

As project managers, knowing what questions to ask and which frameworks to use is no longer just a valuable skill, it's becoming a critical necessity. In light of AI's ongoing rapid evolution, particularly agentic AI, this will be even more crucial in the coming years. It's estimated that 33% of enterprise software applications will incorporate agentic AI by 2028, a massive leap from less than 1% in 2024AI to autonomously make 15% of an employee's daily work decisions. This percentage will only increase as better tools and more accurate data becomes available.

The Risk

After years of working as a project manager, one develops an intuition for the roughly 130 risks that might affect any project. The most common risks are scope creep (change), resources, schedule delay, integration defects, estimates, money, and technological dependencies. Every organization deals with risk in their own way. It's important to remember that bias is hardwired into our thinking and impossible to eliminate, which explains why many projects fail, especially when we don't adequately account for the increased complexity or challenges that come with the arrival of new technologies. Based on my own experience, the scope of a project always changes, and a significant portion of the work is routinely misunderstood while estimations are being formulated. Additionally, we often make poor estimates due to the granularity of the work because tasks are typically described in an overly complicated fashion, while also lacking sufficient detail. As humans, we also tend to underestimate complexity, largely because we overestimate both people and technology, make biased assumptions, and have a poor understanding of the role of probability and incomplete or disinformation.

I've found that using ChatGPT has tremendously improved the accuracy of my risk assessment, but again – this is all dependent on my reliance on credible and local data.

I feed any identified risks into ChatGPT or any other GenAI with the instruction to make a Pareto matrix, which generates a list of the biggest risk in any project. GenAI is also extremely effective in predicting "Black Swan" risks, which has proven to be nearly impossible for humans because we tend to underestimate the occurrence of unpredictable and impactful events. I then calculate a risk complexity index which helps me decide the project risk, assigning a value to each component of the project.

I use Tom Kendrick 2015 formula:

Index =(Technology + Architecture +System) x Scale.

Each factor (T+A+S) ranges from 1-5, while the scale factor depends on team size:

- 0.8 for teams up to 12 people
- 2.4 for 13-40 people

- 4.3 for 41-100 people
- 6.6 for over 100 people

The index generates a result from 0-99. Low equals an index below 20, medium is 20-40, and high is 40 or higher. Still, while AI is very good at understanding what might be needed, and able to predict potential risks based on historical data, it also lacks intuition. So, instead of becoming one of those project managers who end up guessing less than 40 percent of the risks that might occur, I often end up catching upwards of 70-80 percent thanks to AI tools like Claude.

The soft skills

Winkler emphasizes a democratic leadership style, where project managers encourage team participation in decision-making, fostering open discussions and collaboration. While this approach offers several advantages, it may not always be suitable—particularly when the project team consists primarily of recent graduates with limited experience. In such cases, relying solely on democratic leadership may hinder progress, and adopting a more autocratic style becomes essential to providing clear direction, streamlining decision-making, and maintaining project momentum.

Numerous studies have shown that 92% of project team members believe that soft skills are needed in their team's work, 60% believe soft skills impact project management, and 83% hold the view that soft skills are relevant to project team performance. Another study states that soft skills are responsible for 78% of the success factor of any project. This is why companies continue to pay top-tier salaries for project leaders. The answer lies in emotional intelligence, strategic foresight, and human-centered leadership.

Years ago, I worked alongside a highly certified project manager with impressive credentials. However, she struggled to manage emotions under pressure, leading to conflict and communication breakdowns. Unfortunately, her inability to handle interpersonal challenges overshadowed her technical expertise. I guess if AI had been available to automate her routine tasks, she might have been able to focus on developing her soft leadership skills. This opens the door to a set of essential questions every project leader should ask if they want to head up any AI project. These questions are derived from the framework of Graham–Englund model, which prompts critical questions:

- What should we do?
- What can we do?
- What will we do?

- How will we do it?

Understanding the right questions to ask is no longer a bonus, it is a necessity. A project manager should also ask themselves why they want to start an AI project in the first place.

Team Disputes

Within project management, it is vital, both for professional and personal advancement, to manage interactions within the team and with the stakeholders. I recall one particular project where an email that seemed harmless had a negative tone that in hindsight was an initial warning sign of underlying discontent from my team. And back then I wished I had a tool to alert me sooner! With the evolution of AI, software such as Microsoft's PowerAutomate now scan the sentiment in emails—marking messages with extreme negative sentiments before they blow up into full-blown disputes. Although sentiment analysis is not completely foolproof at this point, its capacity to sort through language and forecast underlying attitudes is quite exceptional.

Only recently have scholars begun to articulate leadership models that address the unique demands of project environments. One such model, often referred to as horizontal leadership, emphasizes adaptability in times of crisis. A project manager can delegate leadership to whichever member of the team is best able to tackle a challenge and take on a mentoring role.

Another emerging concept, known as balanced leadership, reflects a more fluid understanding of authority in projects. This perspective recognizes that effective leadership may shift among various stakeholders—including project managers, team members, subteams, and even external partners—depending on the circumstances. Such a dynamic view of leadership acknowledges that the best person to lead at any given moment is often determined by the specific needs of the situation, rather than by a fixed hierarchy.

AI in team collaboration and Efficient Communication

Communication is vital in any team. So, it's amazing to realize how efficient my work has become when I use AI that can make great plans, RACI matrix, or collect feedback from team members.

The following is a practical example of this:

Team communication plan: "Create a team communication plan for [type of project]. Give details about communication modes, frequency, and key updates required for stakeholders and team members."

Meeting agenda preparation: "Create a comprehensive agenda for a project status meeting. Topics to cover are [progress reports, issues, risks]. Give estimated time for each topic."

Team roles and responsibilities: "Create a RACI roles and responsibilities matrix for the team responsible for [project name]. Utilize the inputs below: [list of team members and tasks]."

Feedback collection: "For this project [project type], create a survey to collect team members' feedback on the effectiveness of current communication practices. Include questions on clarity, frequency, and means utilized"

Project Kickoff presentation: "Create an outline for a project kickoff presentation for [project name]. Include sections for goals, timelines, team roles, and expectations."

Escalation procedure: "For the project [project type], prepare an escalation procedure to follow when handling problems during [specific project phase]. Specify communication channels, roles, and timelines."

AI is very good at giving suggestions, but an actual experienced project leader needs to decide which suggestion would work best. In this way, AI will be more of a "collaborative partner" rather than a substitute, much like how we currently use the internet in our everyday lives. It will become a "normal" tool that helps make our work more efficient. Project leaders need to know many things and there are white-collar roles that are excellent when it comes to legal advice or interpreting the law. Next, we will see how AI might impact lawyers.

Chapter 15
Lawyers

In ancient Rome, the *iuris consults*—respected legal experts who lacked official authority—served as the empire's first unofficial legal advisers, and profoundly shaped Roman law. They helped citizens understand complex regulations outside the formal judicial system, demonstrating that legal expertise existed long before professional recognition. The systematization of legal knowledge in the Middle Ages, pioneered by the *legis doctor*, laid crucial groundwork, and established law as an academic discipline which required specific training. Its core function, however, remained constant: interpreting rules and settling disputes through their application. It wasn't until the late 1200s, under the rule of England's King Edward I, that early iterations of modern lawyers, "barristers" and "solicitors," began to formally represent parties in disputes, solidifying the adversarial system many recognize today.

Today, the legal world buzzes with terms like "legaltech," "lawtech," and "regtech," reflecting the increasing integration of technology. While these terms highlight specific areas (like regulatory compliance tech for "regtech"), no single abbreviation has achieved the universal dominance of "fintech," indicating the varied and evolving nature of technology's role in law, as opposed to the world of finance. Here are few insightful statistics about the number of lawyers around the world. In 2024, there were over 10,000 lawyers in Norway, 1.3 million lawyers in the United States, more than 200,000 barristers and solicitors in England and Wales, more than 130,000 in Canada, more than 160,000 in Germany, and some 2 million in India.

The impact

I have already seen a dramatic increase in new legal jobs for people applying AI technologies. We are also witnessing a restructuring of the industry itself, creating new opportunities for people with a wider range of skills.

Evidence of AI's growing capability is clear. In 2024, OpenAI's GPT-4 model achieved a score of nearly 76% on the bar exam's multiple-choice section, outperforming the average human test-taker by more than 7%. This demonstrates AI's rapidly advancing ability to process and apply legal knowledge.

Despite these advancements, the legal profession, which relies heavily on document-intensive processes, often lags behind in technology adoption. Conversations with lawyers reveal that many firms still use outdated systems, even as practitioners continue to work grueling hours, often 40 to 60 per week or more on complex cases. This paradox—technological potential versus slow adoption amidst consistently long hours—easily sets the stage for an era of AI related disruption.

A comment from a lawyer friend captures a persistent sentiment: "*I do expect AI to be the death of the billable hour. I can see big companies slightly expanding their in-house teams...*" This reflects a common assumption that AI-driven efficiency will simply reduce the volume of manual tasks, thereby eroding the traditional time-based billing model. However, understanding the economic principles at play suggests a more nuanced outcome.

Jevons Paradox

Historically, legal expertise commands high fees, consistently 2,000 to 8,000 kroner per hour in Norway, based on someone's level of courtroom experience. Critical thinking and meticulous attention to detail are the most essential skills, but AI programs can now perform much of that work—slogging through mountains of case law, researching precedents, drafting arguments - all with breathtaking speed and accuracy. Nevertheless, the usefulness of these tools hinges completely on the ability of the human lawyer to generate correct prompts and critically evaluate the output of the AI.

Here we are faced with the so-called Jevons Paradox. The preeminent economist William Stanley Jevons had a profound observation regarding the consumption of coal during the Industrial Revolution. He noted that using a resource more efficiently does not automatically lead to a reduction in overall consumption levels. He argued that conversely, savings through such efficiencies will lead to a reduction in the effective cost of the resource. This cost reduction can in turn lead to new applications of the resource, and increase demand so much that it actually brings about an increase in overall consumption levels.

When we translate this fascinating paradox to the legal world, it would imply that the use of AI, which streamlines legal processes, would result in legal services being delivered at significantly lower cost or within a shorter timeframe for each and every task. But it does not necessarily mean that there will be less overall work being done in the legal field. In fact, it may well lead to an increase in the overall amount of legal work. This is because the demand for legal services will continue to rise steadily as a result of an expanding economy, especially in a world that is increasingly complex and regulated. This will in turn fuel a more pressing and growing demand for overall legal counsel. Consequently, there will be more demand for greater research, more complete and detailed contract analysis, as well as dealing with a higher volume of regulations. It also entails dealing with a higher number of documents, patents, and suits than ever before. Most importantly, trained attorneys will be required to dramatically increase their AI prompting skills.

Consider, for a moment, a scenario involving a lawyer who uses agentic AI which is capable of autonomously running complex, multistep tasks. Prior to the advent of agentic AI, a lawyer would typically take weeks or days to manually review millions of case documents. But with AI, the same tasks can be completed in a matter of hours. According to the Jevons Paradox, this added efficiency does not mean the lawyer is suddenly out of a job. It triggers the exact opposite. Because AI drastically lowers the effective cost and time required per task, demand actually expands. The lawyer can now take on a significantly higher volume of cases that previously would have drained their resources. More importantly, this newly realized capacity unlocks an entirely new market, allowing lawyers to offer in-depth reviews to clients who simply could not have afforded the luxury of such high-level service before.

As AI slashes the hours required to process a case, high-tier legal assistance suddenly cracks for a massive, previously priced-out market. This isn't just a triumph for *rettssikkerhet* (access to justice)—it is a highly lucrative business model. The billable hour is not dying; it is simply mutating. Law firms are trading a few whale-sized invoices for a massive school of moderately priced fish. Jevons may have been studying 19th-century coal, and could not foresee he was also writing operating manual for the 2030 legal market such as Thommessen and Wikborg Rein.

Harvey AI

Harvey AI is the kind of tool which makes even seasoned legal professionals sit up and take notice. Imagine a system that doesn't just spew out data, but actually *understands* the nuances of legal language. Harvey AI slots right into a firm's existing setup, and suddenly those tedious, time-consuming tasks are handled. You need a complex legal question deciphered? Harvey AI does it. Got a mountain of documents to summarize? Done. Drafting a contract or court submission? It's on it.

And it's not just about automation. I have seen plenty of software that can churn out basic paperwork. It uses sophisticated machine learning to analyze the specific situation, providing insights and recommendations that are actually relevant. But technology such as Harvey AI is indeed different.

Debater in court

Another idea is IBM Watson debater, which was first shown in 2019. Rather than replicating a full-fledged debating system, IBM focuses on applying argumentation and NLP to legal tech so AI is being used to analyze legal documents, identify arguments, and predict outcomes. The same technology is also being used for fact checking and misinformation in documents. Recalling my discussion with Peter Kirwan a guest of mine during one of my podcast episodes, we talked about how it was possible to implement your own persona into a virtual self.

LLMs and advanced knowledge management AI can already process, synthesize, and retrieve information from enormous datasets, potentially exceeding a human's recall capacity. Agentic AI is developing the ability to use tools and databases to access and apply this knowledge to specific problems. Integrating a person's specific knowledge base (like a lawyer's case history and legal reasoning patterns) with broader legal data is technically possible to a significant degree. Agentic AI is designed to reason, plan, and execute tasks autonomously, maybe having a digital persona AI, that could fight your cases seems very intriguing, although there are aspects to consider such as reflection and ethical judgment. The aspect related to being unbiased and focused on the case and the outcome seems highly likely, but I am finding it hard to understand if these digital personae would be capable of implement real-time strategy based on their surroundings.

Flow of accurate and relevant information

Imagine something like ROSS Intelligence, but tailored for our Norwegian legal work in the near future. It's a tool, built on AI, that would be more than a "simple" search engine for information; it'd be a legal partner accessing data from lovdata and the norske domstoler archives. Think of the accuracy, the ability to find those obscure but vital links between cases and updated laws or principles. It could mean the difference between a successful appeal and a missed opportunity.

Current uses of AI in law

Some law firms in Norway and internationally have been using tools such as CoCounsel to help lawyers draft a contract. To do this, AI is simply asked to draft a draft of, for example, a rental contract. In order to refine the result, it is necessary to provide the tool with as much context as possible, including the law that applies. The AI will be able to draft a contract and will be able to redo it if the result is not satisfactory. The solution is also able to add footnotes, this means you can ask it to insert numbered footnotes (for citations or comments) directly into your draft, and it will render them in-line or in the Word footnote panel. And, if the task is too complex to tackle as a whole, it is also possible to instruct the AI to draft certain clauses or gives the lawyer a list of clauses that should be in the type of contract they want to make.

Norwegian AI law firm pioneer

The Norwegian law firm Thommessen used AI as early as 2023, using the paid version of ChatGPT4. They used the tool to draft proposals for contract clauses and write summaries from meetings. And they uploaded a text before a hearing to get an opinion on whether the response is reasonable, or even request a legal assessment. Their expertise ensures that everything is clear, precise, and legally sound. There was one point that was underlined: hallucinations. The results were only 50–90% accurate. It is also important to say that they sanitized all of the information before adding it into ChatGPT, since OpenAI uses whatever data, you add to train their
AI tool.

Thommessen is now also heavily investing in Norwegian–Silicon Valley startup Arcline. Arcline, who are making what I am to believe a similar AI tool CoCounsel had since 2023 - although that are my own observation based on articles. The minds behind this "new" AI tool, has promised to reduce nearly 90% of a lawyers time related to administration work. Again my question is raised what are lawyers supposed to charge if AI is taking the heavy lifting? Much of this trend is similar to what I experienced with the accountant profession, and many in that profession do not exist, since its become very easy to do accounting work with the help of AI and better technological tools.

Heavy lifting in compliance

Since 2023, Ernest & Young has been quietly building its own language model, a serious piece of tech, reportedly a $1.4 billion investment that took 18 months to build. Think of it: a bespoke AI, designed for the kind of secure, high-stakes environment lawyers operate in.

And here's where it gets interesting. They didn't just build it and leave it to gather dust. They partnered with Microsoft's CELA, their legal and corporate affairs team, and dove headfirst into practical applications. Imagine a rapid-fire project, a real melting pot of techies, lawyers, and academics, all thrown into workshops and hackathons. They were tackling the big questions: data privacy, confidentiality, and how to actually make this tech useful for lawyers.

The result? A GenAI tool, powered by Microsoft's Azure AI, that plugs right into Ernst & Young's existing tax platform. It's not just some fancy chatbot; it's designed to do the heavy lifting of regulatory compliance. This includes summarizing complex rules, drafting guidance, even comparing policies and tracking changes—all the tedious, time-consuming stuff that eats up a lawyer's day. These AI research tools are far from perfect and hallucinate between 17% and 33% of the time, and this occurs more often if the output being produced have more than 300 words. Longer answers are more prone to hallucination simply because there are 'more falsifiable propositions' - more claims that could be wrong - and require extensive fact-checking. Identifying these misunderstandings will require close analysis of cited sources. And I see this vulnerability as problematic for AI adoption in a profession that requires accuracy, clarity, and trustworthiness.

The future of AI in law

Assuming that a large fraction of jobs already are and will continue to be completed through AI, the next question is where does that leave human endeavor? This is a particularly important question in the legal profession, where accuracy, judgment, and trust are paramount. And while AI is stunningly efficient at processing masses of data, predicting outcomes, and automating repetitive workflows, there are essential elements (empathy, ethical judgment, complex negotiation, etc.) that AI cannot credibly copy—at least for the time being.

Some of these roles still require the knowledge and expertise of a licensed lawyer, many require completely different skill sets, and others require a mix of legal and other skills. The newly added jobs engaged in the delivery of law fall into several broad categories including:

Jevons Paradox jobs. These are jobs being created by more efficient legal work. One might assume that technology would kill many of these jobs (like traditional associate roles). In fact, such jobs are highly likely to continue to expand, in large part because the more efficient delivery of legal services will create ever more demand for the work of lawyers.

Jobs driven by the increased use of legal data. These jobs include every kind of data analyst role—those who manage data and are able to extract meaningful and actionable insight from such data about legal transactions. These include court-generated data, patent and other intellectual property data, data from public financial records, billing and pricing invoices, and case management system data.

Legal knowledge engineering roles directly involved in automating legal work. This includes lawyers, and others, who teach machine learning models how to scrape data from contracts, court decisions, dockets, and other forms of legal data; lawyers who encode legal processes into expert systems and document automation systems; and other roles where lawyers are embedding legal knowledge into systems and processes to automate the performance of legal work.

Knowledge management roles. This includes roles involved in capturing and distributing an organization's knowledge and expertise in order to leverage it.

Legal product management jobs. Legal tech companies package legal services in products. Increasingly, this includes law firms and other organizations that embed their employees' expertise into customer-facing products. Products, including productized forms of legal services delivery, are better built with the expertise of product managers.

Innovation and strategy roles. As legal organizations have turned to technology and new business models to support their delivery of legal services, new jobs have emerged for people capable of driving and supporting innovation, providing change management, and staking out a strategic direction.

Training and customer success roles. Legal tech vendors, law firms, and in-house legal departments have all started to recognize the value of a customer-centric approach to service delivery. This has led to roles that ensure customers are getting the most out of legal offerings.

Across 2,500 years, the essence of legal advocacy has stayed surprisingly constant: interpreting complex rules, crafting persuasive arguments, and guiding clients through uncertainty. Whether you're a Roman *iuris consultus* or a 21st-century lawyer, your real superpower lies in human creativity, empathy, and ethical judgment—qualities no algorithm can fully replicate.

It's common for most lawyers to speculate about the extent to which AI is taking away from their roles by automating some tasks and shifting some of their work to technology or other types of legal services providers. A common response to that line of thinking is that AI allows lawyers to eliminate routine and lower-value tasks from their daily workflow, allowing them to focus more attention on the important stuff such as advising clients, understanding their challenges, finding new solutions, and providing higher-quality service.

And to be able to give the higher-quality services, lawyers are now forced to hone advocacy, analysis, interpretation and the soft skills—these are not just modern inventions, but part of a long and evolving tradition of helping societies understand their complexities and strive for a sense of justice, however imperfectly achieved. Even if lawyers eventually could be replaced by AI, the smart lawyers out there who are utilizing the tool to be most effective will most probably have a lower rate or more clients as they collaborate with the AI. A third scenario could be that people who understand the law or even law students, or those like myself who have studied it but no longer pursue it, might as well handle simpler cases ourselves after 2030.

This chapter concludes my thoughts and predictions on the future of the field of law. The next chapter will discuss the field of software engineering.

Chapter 16
Software Engineering

A late afternoon in Summer 2024, my former colleague Espen and I were sitting at a cafe. We were casually discussing the possible impact of AI on software engineers' job future, given that he was a software engineer. *"Espen, I am writing a book on AI and job polarization and was wondering how has AI changed your day-to-day work?"* I watched my former colleague's face, noticing the concern in his expression.

We were catching up over coffee, and what struck me was the nostalgia in his eyes—not for some bygone technology, but for the struggle itself. *"I used to find immense satisfaction in figuring out how to solve a problem,"* he admitted. *"The hours spent coding, the rabbit holes of debugging, and that feeling of 'enlightenment' when everything clicked. I felt truly useful then. Figuring out different methods, understanding the 'why' behind every line of code... there was a profound sense of accomplishment. Now, I type prompts and watch AI generate solutions instantly. It's efficient, sure. But something vital has been lost. "I've almost dismissed the importance of those critical questions,"* he confessed, looking straight at me. *"Questions like, 'What happens if I tweak this parameter?' or 'What if we approached this problem from an entirely different angle?'"*

As he was talking my mind tried to figure out where did software engineering really start?

The story of programming is one of human curiosity and the quest for efficiency—a chronicle of people learning to talk to machines.

During late the 1940s, computing was more about hand calculations and using mechanical devices. Pioneers like Ada Lovelace and Charles Babbage laid the conceptual groundwork for programming, though practical software did not yet exist. When digital computers appeared in the late 1940s, programmers wrote instructions directly in binary or assembly code. This process was laborious, error-prone, and needed intimate knowledge of the hardware.

Since most people find it easier to write instructions in English rather than using complex symbolic representations, COBOL (Common Business-Oriented language) was invented. Since it was first commercialized in 1968, COBOL has been the lifeblood of Enterprise IT, along with millions of businesses' processes each day, from healthcare to airlines to government systems. In 1959, mathematician Grace Murray Hopper believed that the computer language should be understood by common people without advanced mathematical training. Although these languages abstracted away some of the machine-level details, programmers were still manually writing every line of code.

But even with languages like COBOL, writing software was still a manual, line-by-line affair. It took real visionaries like Margaret Hamilton to elevate software development to the level of proper engineering. Hamilton, who led the team in 1964 that created the software for the Apollo moon missions, understood that software was just as crucial as the hardware. Lives depended on it. She fought to get software development the recognition it deserved, pushing for it to be seen as a serious profession, just like building bridges or any other engineering profession. This effort to gain respect for software was crucial, not just for the Apollo program's success, but for establishing software engineering as a vital profession for the future.

The 1980s marked a shift from writing code as a linear sequence of instructions to designing systems as collections of interacting components with the help of C++. Then in the 1990s the internet introduced languages like Java and JavaScript (both in 1995). Software projects grew much larger and more complicated.

The comic strip Dilbert, by Scott Adams, is famous for humorously portraying the frustrating situations that arise when engineers work with bosses who just don't understand technology. Dilbert's "pointy-haired boss" is a classic example.

He is clueless to how software is made, but he's too proud to admit it. This leads to all sorts of ridiculous and relatable office moments. This kind of clueless boss and frustrated engineer situation was a real problem in the software world. Maybe this is why in Agile was presented in 2001 as the fix—a way to make things work better between the tech experts and the managers? It was like saying, "Let's set up some clear rules everyone can agree on." The idea was simple: if both sides followed these rules, Agile promised that everyone —engineers and managers alike—would be happier and the software would be better. These approaches focus on developing software in small steps, working closely as a team, and quickly adapting to changes as they aim to deliver software of the highest quality. Automating software deployments and updates, further reducing manual programmer tasks emerged.

Throughout this evolution, software engineers were the problem solvers of the digital revolution. They designed applications, wrote code from scratch, and debugged programs manually. The work required deep knowledge of programming languages—Python, Java, C++—and an ability to translate business needs into functional software. Until now.

The change I am reflecting around has been subtle, yet not unknown. GitHub Copilot suggesting a few lines here. Tabnine auto completing a section of code and automating a test. Another great tool is JamGPT that reduces the developers debugging time by 80% with developer logs, instant replay, and AI assistance. But behind these seemingly modest assists lies a revolution that's fundamentally transforming what it means to be a software engineer.

These tools take over many of the repetitive tasks that once took programmers countless hours. Having seen these changes firsthand throughout my career, the question is no longer if software engineering will change, but how—and what this means for the next generation entering this career. The statistics are staggering. According to Sundar Pichai, AI was already writing over 25% of Google's production code by 2024. Dario Amodei of Anthropic predicted that 90% of coding work could be AI-driven within a year. Even if these estimates contain some Silicon Valley hyperbole, the direction is clear. The days of humans writing most code, testing, and building software are probably ending.

The Interpreter

I have spent the past eight years as a project manager focusing on integrating new systems and building software. Overpromising and under promising results have been problems since the 1940s. For instance, only about three out of five ERP projects succeeded. Industry analysts and research suggest that AI projects face a considerably higher risk of failure than traditional software projects. Some estimates indicate that a significant percentage, as high as 70–85%, may not achieve their intended goals within the first few years. Additionally, there are growing concerns within the tech industry regarding the potential impact of AI on employment. A survey of 550 software developers by Evans Data Corporation, a market research firm based in California, found that 30% of developers were concerned that their roles might be replaced by AI by 2040. This reflects broader anxieties about job displacement as AI technology becomes increasingly capable. To see why AI feels so transformative, let's revisit how our code actually becomes machine instructions.

Computers operate using a fundamental language called machine code, which consists of only two symbols: 0 and 1. This is similar in concept to Morse code, which used dots and dashes to represent letters for telegraph communication. Just as Morse code translates letters into a transmittable format, a computer program called a compiler translates instructions written in more human-friendly programming languages (like Python or Java) into machine code that the computer can understand. However, the translation from a programming language to machine code isn't always straightforward. The same instruction can be translated into different sequences of 0s and 1s depending on several factors. These include the specific programming language used, the skill of the programmer, and the efficiency of the compiler itself. A skilled programmer can write code that's easier for the compiler to optimize, and a good compiler will produce more efficient machine code. Essentially, the same computer command can have different, but functionally equivalent, machine code representations. The gap between human thinking and computer execution is what programmers have traditionally bridged through their expertise. The real skill in programming has never been merely knowing syntax or memorizing commands. It has always been the ability to think through a problem with mechanical precision, to anticipate every edge case, and to translate fuzzy human intentions into the unambiguous logical steps that a computer requires.

In today's professional landscape, programmers often distinguish themselves by the number of programming languages they've mastered—Java, C#, Python, JavaScript, and so on. These languages become badges of versatility, markers of experience. Yet this measure of competence reveals something important: if you truly understand the fundamental principles of programming—the logic, the structures, the patterns of thinking—you can learn virtually any programming language. The syntax changes, the conventions differ, but the underlying challenge remains constant. You are still translating human problems into computer-executable precision.

What remains unspoken in many discussions about AI-powered coding tools is that this fundamental translation challenge hasn't disappeared. The computer at the end of the chain still requires that same precise, deterministic code to function. This complexity underlines the importance of skilled software engineers who understand how to write efficient code and choose the right tools to ensure optimal performance. While developers concentrate more on the implementation, the engineers focus on the design and structure of systems before coding. An engineer applies engineering principles to software development. They think systemwide: designing architectures, ensuring scalability, and solving complex structural problems across the development lifecycle.

Can it be trusted?

Behavioral scientist Lindsay Kohler notes that the primary barrier to AI adoption isn't management resistance but practitioner skepticism. How can you trust code you didn't write and may not fully understand? The trustworthiness and reliability of AI recommendations are ongoing concerns. Even with explainable AI techniques, ensuring that developers can fully understand and validate the outputs of AI systems remains challenging. The other aspect I found was the constant issues related to bias in AI models or the risk of over-reliance on automation, have yet to be comprehensively addressed, potentially impacting both code quality and human skill development. People are asking if they can trust AI and if they can demonstrate trustworthiness to stakeholders. In the domain of coding, the concern is thus not about the management of the organization not accepting automatic programming, but it is about automatic programming not being accepted by developers, due to lack of trust.

In February 2024, Google's Gemini image generator produced images that didn't match historical facts. For example, when asked to create pictures of Nazi soldiers, it included Black individuals in uniform—even though Nazi policies were explicitly racist and excluded Black people.

Similarly, when prompted to generate an image of a pope, the AI produced a picture of a woman in papal robes, despite the fact that no woman has ever served as pope in the Catholic Church.

The belief that AI always gives the correct answer is a misconception. Sometimes, AI generates hallucinations that are nonsensical or completely detached from reality. It's tempting to think that, because AI is a machine, these errors can be easily fixed by simply adjusting the code. But this isn't always true. Whether a human or an AI writes the code, there will be mistakes, and some of those errors might not be discovered for years. One example is an "overflow," which occurs when a computer tries to store a number that's too large for its allocated memory space. This can lead to data corruption, program crashes, or even security vulnerabilities. Overflows are difficult to prevent and fix if the code is made by an AI system.

A fundamental reason for AI errors is that AI models don't "understand" the world in the way humans do. They learn by identifying patterns in vast amounts of training data. If the data contains biases (like an under representation of women in leadership roles), inaccuracies, or gaps, the AI will likely reproduce those flaws in its output. It lacks the common sense and real-world knowledge to evaluate whether its conclusions are reasonable. This is where the crucial role of software developers comes in.

They need the ability to critically analyze the source data used to train AI, identify potential biases, and understand the limitations of the AI model. They must ask questions like: "Where did this training data come from? Is it representative of the real world? Are there any groups that are over- or underrepresented? Could the data contain inaccuracies or outdated information?" This critical evaluation of the data, combined with an understanding of the AI's limitations, is essential for preventing and mitigating errors.

When Not To Use It

My discussion with Espen continued as we sipped our coffee, discussing this tectonic shift, the point my friend was trying to convey became clear. Perhaps, for many software engineers, the ease of AI hasn't just streamlined workflows; maybe it's inadvertently cultivated a kind of intellectual laziness. Or perhaps, more sadly, it's begun to erode that innate drive to explore, to question, to simply be curious.

As Espen was explaining, AI agents should be avoided when there are simple, predictable tasks as it's much easier to use regular automation scripts. However, if one requires agility (speed), then you are much better off with direct API calls. And last scenario for those who are working with software programming—don't use it if you have fixed workflows, since AI agents aren't typically good for fixed workflows because they introduce unpredictability. The better alternative is traditional programming.

All good Vibes?

The conversation turned to what some are calling "vibe programming," a term that Espen delivered with a mixture of skepticism and resignation. The idea traces back to Andrej Karpathy, whose credentials are difficult to dismiss—co-founder of OpenAI and former head of artificial intelligence at Tesla. In February 2025, Karpathy posted a 1000 character tweet on X starting as following *"There's a new kind of coding I call 'vibe coding', where you fully give in to the vibes, embrace exponentials, and forget that the code even exists."*

What Karpathy described represents a fundamental shift in how software gets created. It's not really about traditional coding skills anymore, Espen explained. The new standard centers on patience and what's being called "prompt engineering"—essentially, knowing how to communicate effectively with AI tools, how to instruct them properly, how to coax out the results you need. The actual mechanics of writing code, line by line, become almost secondary. People who appear to know how to code might be working in an entirely different way than their credentials suggest. It was here that Espen's frustration became palpable. He fixed me with an intense, serious look, the kind that suggested he'd been carrying this observation for some time and was relieved to finally voice it. "I still think most programmers today are dinosaurs using stone age tools," he said. The statement hung in the air, blunt and uncompromising. But Espen wasn't finished. What truly baffled him—what seemed to cause him genuine bewilderment—was the resistance he witnessed across the industry. Modern AI agents exist right now that can enable a single software engineer to produce twelve thousand lines of production-ready code in a single day. Twelve thousand lines. Not prototype code, not experimental code, but production code—the kind that actually ships to users.

And yet, Espen observed, intelligent software engineers—people he knew to be smart, capable professionals—simply weren't using these tools. They continued working the old way, manually writing every function, every loop, every conditional statement. Espen leaned back in his chair, frustration simmering just beneath the surface. "We're treating these AI agents like miracle workers," he said, "but no one's talking about the chaos they leave behind." He pointed out the security lapses that had already cost companies dearly—production databases wiped clean, critical data gone in seconds, and entire systems down for hours. Then came the wasted time: teams spending days trying to coax an agent into doing a simple task, only to have it erase its own code or stall mid-operation. "You can see the evidence everywhere," he added, "in endless Twitter and Reddit threads where users pour out their anger, not just over bugs, but over the sheer absurdity of losing time and progress to something that's supposed to make life easier." And on top of that came the bills—hundreds of dollars burned on experiments that yielded nothing but broken scripts and frustration. "Efficiency," Espen said with a dry laugh, "has never been so expensive."

His frustration stemmed from what he saw as an obvious truth that somehow remained controversial: this is the future, whether people accept it or not. The practitioners who embrace these AI-powered workflows will operate on a completely different scale than those who don't. The gap between early adopters and holdouts won't be incremental—it will be exponential. Yet many in the field seem unable or unwilling to grasp this reality, continuing to take pride in hand-crafting code the traditional way, as if the old skills will remain relevant indefinitely.

For someone like Espen, who has always been at the forefront of his craft, watching his peers cling to outdated methods while the industry transforms around them isn't just frustrating—it's mystifying. How could people who are supposed to be forward-thinking, who work in technology precisely because they understand progress and innovation, fail to see what's directly in front of them?

The T-shaped Visionaries

So, what do I suggest for the future software engineers? Espen paused as his eye brows were fixed outside the café window as he was looking at people going by. And looked gently at me with a smirk on his face.

Unfortunately, we are already at a point where a developer who runs their CV through ChatGPT and pushes out AI-generated junk is in a stronger position than someone like myself, who takes their time to understand complex problems and invest in real learning. What concerns me is that both clients and consulting firms are uncritically contributing to making this practice the new standard.

And I also see there is a trend that both an engineer and designer, these two roles have and are being covered by the same individuals today by 2030, professionals and GenZ will need to brush up their T-shaped skills, whether they are middle managers or software engineers. T-shaped skills are defined as the ability to combine deep expertise in a specific area with broad general skills, such as communication skills, leadership/management skills, collaborative skills, and problem-solving skills (soft skills). The engineers in greatest demand will be those who can work at higher levels of abstraction—defining architectures, evaluating trade-offs, and ensuring AI-generated solutions meet business needs. They'll need to know not just how to write code but when to trust AI and when to apply human judgment.

This contrasts with I-shaped skills, which denote deep specialization in only one narrow area, or X-shaped skills, a mix of diverse but potentially unrelated abilities.

Why are these T-shaped capabilities becoming paramount? Because AI is automating the I-shaped tasks that once consumed much of an engineer's time. Industry trends highlight this shift:

Gartner's reported that by 2027, 50% of software engineering organizations will utilize software engineering intelligence platforms to measure and increase developer productivity. This shift is a significant increase from 5% in 2024, showing a strong trend towards integrating intelligent platforms in software development. The algorithms identify various patterns within the code, format it, correct it, and even forecast other glitches, making the code cleaner and more efficient. They translate instructions in natural language into code and have become useful in developing tools to create executable code snippets. This results in a considerable decrease in the number of hours devoted to completing sets of codes and allows for an increase in development speed.

Feedback on advanced LLMs like Google's Gemini 2.5 suggests they are becoming increasingly capable coding assistants, translating natural language into code snippets and supporting dynamic, 'learnas-you-test' approaches that go beyond basic, repetitive test scripts. These tools undeniably increase development speed and efficiency.

As our discussion came to an end, Espen looking outside the window as he took the last sip from his cup. *I think we need to be better at asking the manager and people whom we are creating this software for, what the value is for them. And actively define it with them in the early stage. Because in this new era, coding isn't just for engineers anymore. It's becoming an accessible skill that anyone who knows prompt engineering and can think creative may learn, like reading and writing. Instead, employees must evolve into problem pioneers, masters of identifying and defining the right problems to solve and be able to think critically and be able to evaluate the data. The future software engineers might require a new approach, where the AI outputs are critically viewed with alignment of the business goals.* He pauses. *While AI excels at being precise, fast, and efficient with data, logic and patterns, it doesn't have the human drive to create or solve problems that truly matter. That unique passion is something that we all have within us, as long as we find our work meaningful and are able to make something meaningful. Then again what seems to be meaningful for a software engineer, might not be for the manager and there will always be a gap and misunderstanding along the way, as long as things are measured the wrong way and the meaning of work is not well defined and accepted by everyone.* It seemed that Espen understood that while AI provides huge advancements, sometimes eliminating the human bottlenecks is the core reason that always will slow down processes, and thus being able to understand, create, and organize code will allow programmers alike to be a driver, or a pilot, an empowered creator through programming.

Chapter 17
Real Estate Agent

Long before the title "realtor" or "real estate agents" existed, people traded land informally—through tribal agreements or simple verbal deals. As societies evolved, so did the need for more structured transactions.

In the 19th century, as cities expanded and industrialization surged, urban land became highly sought after. In the early periods of industrialization, property transactions were often handled informally, relying on personal networks, lawyers, or local notaries.

The Industrial Revolution, which started in the late 1700s, caused a significant shift in society. As you might remember from the earlier chapter related to knowledge worker and white-collar workers. People began to be classified into distinct economic categories: low-class, middle-class, blue-collar, white-collar, and high-class occupations. As industries grew, many individuals found themselves with more wealth and the means to purchase property. This period marked a democratization of land ownership, as more people, not just the elite, began to acquire land and homes.

To support this growing need for land and homeownership, banks started offering higher-risk loans, such as home mortgages, in the late 1800s and early 1900s. This allowed more people to buy property, but also introduced the potential for greater financial risk.

Since buying and selling properties was considered to have greater risks as there were huge amount affiliated to these transactions, real estate brokers started helping people buy and sell, marking the beginning of the modern real estate industry.

Since Norway's formation as an independent sovereign state in 1814, its small open economy has, like its neighboring countries, experienced significant economic growth. In Norway, a key milestone in the history of real estate was the founding of the Norwegian Association of Real Estate Agents (Norges Eiendomsmeglerforbund NEF) This marked the formal establishment of professional real estate practices in Norway and helped standardize real estate transactions in the country. Banks in Norway are now in the real estate game. Aktiv works with Eika Banken. EiendomsMegler1 is tied to

SpareBank1. DNB owns DNB Eiendom. This mix of banks and real estate aims to offer more services. But it also means fewer small, independent agents.

Real Estate agents of today

Today's real estate agents do much more than simply show homes. They analyze market trends, price properties accurately, and blend both digital tools and traditional marketing strategies to secure the best deals. Although many agents now work closely with technology, they are also expected to handle the legal paperwork and provide market insights that stem from years of experience.

For many buyers and sellers, trust remains the cornerstone of any transaction. Even as AI tools begin to assist with tasks like drafting property listings or creating virtual home tours, the human element—empathy, intuition, and personal connection—continues to be essential. For instance, an agent who understands not just the market, but also the sentimental value a home holds, can make all the difference during emotionally charged negotiations.

Pioneers in the real estate industry

At Nordvik Eiendomsmegling, the team set out to explore whether AI could ease the workload of writing property listings—a task that demands both precision and a touch of human insight. Technology Director, Robert Bue, and Innovation Leader, Bjørnar Førre Skogstø, intrigued by the potential of ChatGPT after hearing about its use by students for exam papers, decided to experiment with it in a real-world setting. They brought experienced agent, Trym Valved, on board to guide the project, ensuring that the AI's output would not stray too far from the authentic perspective of a seasoned real estate professional.

Their experiment began with feeding ChatGPT essential details about a three-room apartment on Tøyen in Oslo—information that any good listing should include, like the number of bedrooms, apartment size, floor, and location. They also employed another AI tool to analyze photos and generate basic object descriptions, which ChatGPT then used to craft engaging captions. The results were a mix of impressive and puzzling: at times, ChatGPT produced wonderfully articulate text that exceeded expectations, while at other times it ventured into creative fabrications. The team quickly realized that the quality of the AI's output hinged on the clarity and specificity of the instructions given.

Despite the promising aspects, the experiment underscored a key limitation. While AI can generate a polished description of existing facts, it struggles to capture the unique charm and latent potential of a home—a task where human intuition and local expertise play an irreplaceable role. Valved then refined the AI-generated content, adding legal details and nuanced insights that only someone with hands-on experience could provide.

Much like the application of AI in the field of law and software engineering, the journey wasn't about replacing real estate agents but about discovering how technology might relieve them of routine tasks, freeing up time to focus on the creative and personal aspects of property sales. Nordvik's foray into AI highlighted a future where innovation and human expertise work hand in hand, proving that while technology can be a powerful tool, the human touch remains essential in the art of selling homes.

Automated Property Valuation

Most people who want to sell their home are used to the traditional appraisal process—scheduling on-site visits that take anywhere from 1–2 hours, followed by report preparation and lender review. I've sold two proprieties in the past myself, and the estimates that resulted from these valuations from various real estate agents, were barely ever aligned and often made me more uncertain.

When I was going to value my current flat, I stumbled upon a very smart method, known as Validated Automated Property Valuation (APV). APV involves using advanced algorithms and machine learning algorithms to analyze a huge set of information, such as recent sales, market trends, property attributes, and neighborhood attributes to estimate the value of a home. This system is not only faster than the traditional appraisals but also provides a more objective and uniform value. As a result, I received a proper estimate without needing to take time for on-site visits. Banks use it in their systems such as Sparebank1 and there even exists an app named Hjemla, which uses the same to give the owners an estimate of their property. And if you provide it with more data, it uses that as well.

Despite all these advantages, AVMs lag behind in surprise market fluctuations and can't assess a property's physical condition or the worth of upgrades—factors that often have the greatest impact on value.

Virtual viewing

Many real estate agents offer not to charge to show the house when negotiating for a new customer. But as buyers become smarter, especially the younger generations, I believe AI can also play a key role in creating realistic virtual viewings of homes. As many of us are pressed with time, and as I argued that our busy lives and the fact that Gen Z and other young buyers prefer working on their own terms, this innovation holds special appeal. I vividly recall the height of the pandemic when traditional house visits were nearly impossible. That challenging period forced many of us to embrace new ways of experiencing spaces, even if it was just through a screen.

These virtual viewings proved to be a game changer according to Harvard Business School, 22% of houses use virtual tours, and sellers who use virtual tours experienced an increase of 1.1% in sales profit compared to those who did not.

They not only made the home search process more accessible but also offered a comforting sense of presence, allowing potential buyers to feel as though they were really walking through the property despite being miles away. More than that, by reducing the need for in-person meetings, this technology helped lower the risk of infection, blending safety with convenience in a way that truly resonated with our need for connection during challenging times. The Norwegian AI real-estate tool "Visning.ai" addresses this issue by allowing users to input a property's listing link from Finn.no. Within approximately 30 seconds, the AI analyzes the entire sales document and provides a concise summary of the property's key attributes, both positive and negative. For instance, it can highlight concerns such as "costs related to lease fees" or "potential issues with the electrical system," as well as advantages like "flexible floor plan" or "sunlit property."

Visning.ai is a good example on how AI can help the buyers in making better-informed decisions but also sets a precedent for the integration of AI in property transactions. The new AI tool refines complex property information into accessible summaries; this way the tool gives the buyers more control to make more informed decisions, potentially reducing the risk of unforeseen complications post-purchase. At the time of writing this chapter, the tool is planned to have more integrations in the future.

Visning.ai Future Enhancement

Imagine yourself in *"not that far distance"* future considering buying a new apartment. You are scanning the QR code with this Visning.AIpp as you enter but no one is there, just a calm female voice welcoming you by your name. *"Welcome, if you have any questions, you can reach me via your mobile app."* Your social media profile has been scanned, and your bank credit is pre-approved, confirming you as a qualified buyer. You walk around the house excitedly. The owner is getting all the feedback. At work, the owner glances at a dashboard displaying real-time updates:

- Visitor count: 4 today
- High-interest zones: kitchen & balcony
- Estimated offer range: 4.2 - 4.5 million NOK

As you leave the house after spending an hour, the voice asks again, *"Would you like a follow-up brochure and financing suggestions?"* No personal data is stored beyond what you agreed to. You tap "Yes"—only the data you consent to is stored—and instantly receive a digital brochure plus a tailored financing overview. While this scenario is fictional, it's entirely feasible given today's AI capabilities and our current tech ecosystem. By transforming dense property disclosures into clear, actionable summaries, Visning.ai already empowers buyers to make better-informed decisions. And with future add-ons—AR overlays, smart contracts, advanced market analytics—this vision might be a reality.

Emma

Working as a real estate agent involves adhering to numerous routines, rules, procedures, and regulations. To address this, DNB Eiendom developed a quality handbook that included industry-specific standards, laws, and quality requirements. However, agents often found it challenging to locate and interpret the information contained within it.

The result was the creation of the real estate assistant, 'Emma,' which has positioned DNB Eiendom to better experiment with and integrate generative AI into the company. The GPT-based chatbot assists real estate agents with internal routines and guidelines related to property viewings, follow-up, and sales. In a highly competitive industry, the efficiency generated by AI is crucial for gaining a competitive edge.

Human connection and emotions

The human element remains irreplaceable—especially in the Norwegian market, where trust, transparency, and personal relationships are at the heart of every transaction. While AI can analyze data, detect patterns, and generate insights far faster than any human, it cannot understand the emotional motivations behind buying a home—the hopes, anxieties, and dreams that define such a decision. Norwegian real estate, still characterized by high prices (averaging around NOK 4.95 million as of mid-2025, with Oslo nearing NOK 99,000 per square meter), relies heavily on emotional confidence and interpersonal credibility. In contrast, the U.S. housing market—where the median home price sits around USD 435,000 and mortgage rates exceed 6%—is seeing more widespread AI adoption as a cost-efficiency tool amid stagnation and affordability challenges. However, across both markets, the core argument remains: AI's reliability and consistency can strengthen trust by offering predictable performance and transparent reasoning, while humans bring empathy and context that no algorithm can replicate. Yet, these benefits come with real risks. Legally, improper use of AI in Norway can breach GDPR or housing regulations, such as when automated systems reject tenants or price listings without valid legal bases.

Organizationally, lack of oversight or AI governance can lead to untrained employees deploying tools unsafely, while ethically, biased data can produce discriminatory outcomes—filtering applicants or skewing access to resources. Ultimately, AI should be treated not as a replacement for human connection but as a disciplined partner in precision and efficiency. The future of real estate—both in Norway's trust-driven market and the U.S.'s data-driven one—will belong to agents who can merge human intuition with technological transparency, building trust that is both emotionally authentic and analytically sound. The drive for efficiency often stands in paradox to the need for human connection. Though AI can perform an immense amount of boring, repetitive tasks—like property searches or deal negotiations—humans resist this. In 2021, my wife and I sold our first apartment. It was the first home we had lived in for more than five years. We were not just selling space, at a great location; we were selling the memories of sitting in the balcony in the summer, our walks around the area, the friendly talks with our neighbors, and the comfort of returning to a place that always welcomed us after a long day. Could any algorithm truly resonate with these emotions created by those moments and use those to give us the value we expected in return?

This emotional weight is why trust becomes so critical as years later, I faced a similar decision when selling my ancestral property. I stood again to choose someone based on the trust equation to deliver on their promise at the same understood my emotions. I introduced the trust equation—how trust is measured through expertise, reliability, and emotional connection. I had consulted multiple real estate agents before making a decision for many who didn't seem to care, and few were unprepared. There was one real estate agent I finally ended up going for, someone who exhibited the qualities described in the trust equation: expertise and the ability to establish a genuine emotional connection. His articulate approach and insightful suggestions throughout the process built trust and confidence within me, and I felt safe. Despite the growing influence of AI in real estate, this human element remains crucial—buyers and sellers often rely on trust and intuition when making such significant financial decisions. And similar to what my real estate agent showed me, many will need to focus on their interpersonal skills, negotiation abilities, and local market expertise.

Bidding with AI

Walmart buyers helped train Pactum's chatbot by providing scenarios that the algorithm used to create negotiation scripts. The chatbot closed deals with 64% of the suppliers on an average of 11 days, and they saved a significant amount of money. Now think of that tech, but for real estate. If a buyer made a crazy offer, the AI could dig through, market trends, to give straightforward facts and figures and suggest a more reasonable price. No uncomfortable silence, no "let me talk to my manager" nonsense.

But here's the thing - Can a robot sense when somebody's about to walk? Can it sense when a buyer's getting cold feet, or a seller's bluffing? I am referring to AI's inability to fully replicate human emotional intelligence in high-stakes negotiations, or how its predictive algorithms might still be prone to biases or inaccuracies. During negotiations, amidst the chaos of unforeseen challenges, the human touch retains its value—expertise with experience; the social aspect mixed with empathy creates a connection that data alone can't replicate. My agent would crack a joke, or just listen, and somehow, he'd keep the deal on the table. That's the sort of thing AI can't duplicate, right? Maybe someday they'll create an AI that can read humans like a book, but until then, I'm still leaning toward a human, to do the job.

Standing in the empty living room in the house I had spent 15 years of my childhood, I just know, that I am glad I had Altin (my real estate agent) during the whole process, he did much more than an AI ever could have done – he understood that we were closing a chapter of my life. No algorithm could have held that moment with me, offered that knowing nod, or understood the emotions I had throughout the process. Because at the end of the day, I wasn't trusting him with a house—I was trusting him with a chapter of my life. That kind of understanding isn't a line of code—it's human.

This concludes our third and final part. The next part which you are about to read are more ideas, vision of mine. It begins with universal basic income as a viable option if, in the future, knowledge workers have less and less work to do and therefore cannot pay for a decent life due to technology. The final chapter outlines my vision of a Semi-AI driven democratic society, in which the traditional role of politicians is transformed.

Chapter 18
Universal Basic Income

As I stated at the very start of my book, some chapters are meant to stimulate you to figure out some matters on your own. This chapter and the one which follows invite you to do so; therefore, I have been decisive when it comes to the level of detail, such as specific payout amounts or administrative structures, as I found it beneficial. It hopefully prevents you from getting bogged down and instead encourages you to consider the *idea* and its implications more broadly.

Universal Basic Income (UBI) guarantees every citizen a constant, unconditional cash stipend, regardless of their employment. Its lineage stretches back to Thomas Paine's 1796 Agrarian Justice, and it is now advocated by tech luminaries like Elon Musk—who foresees automation making *"almost all jobs obsolete"*—and Sam Altman, who calls UBI an *"insurance"* policy against AI job displacement. A UBI funded by common resources can supplement incomes, guarantee basic needs, and liberate us all to focus on more worthwhile pursuits.

Thomas Paine—an English-born political activist and writer influenced by John Locke and Benjamin Franklin, and later a member of the French National Convention—offered one of UBI's first sustained defenses in his 1796 pamphlet *Agrarian Justice*. It was motivated by a strong perception of injustice: Paine could see that the institution of private land ownership had radically altered relations between human beings and nature. Before enclosure and the establishment of property rights, people could forage, hunt, till the soil, and live off their own labor on common land. The privatization of these commons, though perhaps indispensable for industrial progress, had deprived the majority of people of their natural birthright.

Paine did not object to private property per se but believed that it came with a responsibility. He wrote: *"Every owner owes the community a ground-rent for the land he holds."* This ground-rent, determined by taxation, would provide compensation to everyone upon adulthood and again in old age as a pension. His reasoning was simple: these payments were not charity but recompense for what had been taken. Thomas Spence took Paine's argument a step further, advocating for complete common ownership of land with rents providing not just lump payments but ongoing revenue for all citizens—a true UBI. His rationale was that since land was a natural resource, it could not justly be made private property without providing compensation to those who were excluded.

During the Industrial Revolution, 12–16 hours shifts weren't unusual. Factory workers, even kids, were stuck doing back-breaking manual labor for that long, often in awful conditions. Then along came Robert Owen, a Welsh man who owned a textile mill but also had some pretty radical ideas for the time. He thought there had to be a better way. His big idea was "8-hours labor, 8-hours recreation, 8-hours rest." And believe it or not, that simple idea became a slogan that changed the world. Owen's labour-leisure formula focused on fairness and productivity, anticipating later UBI debates: as productivity rises, society owes workers a share in the benefits.

In 1914, Henry Ford changed the standard six-day workweek to a five-day, and he paid the workers double for their working hours. Then, on May 1, 1926, he instituted a five-day (40-hour) week at no cut in pay, reasoning that leisure would spur car sales. The statement "Every man needs more than one day a week for rest and recreation" was made by Henry's son Edsel. He didn't change it out of kindness; Ford was a capitalist; he wanted his product to be sold and saw this as a way to boost consumer spending.

Twelve years later, the English economist John Maynard Keynes wrote in his essay, *"We are being afflicted with a new disease of which some readers may not yet have heard the name, but of which they will hear a great deal in the years to come—namely, technological unemployment. This means unemployment due to our discovery of means of economising the use of labour outrunning the pace at which we can find new uses for labour."* The more the "cyber economy" evolves with technology, data, and digital infrastructure, the greater the contribution of AI in high-productivity jobs will be. In some fields, it will work hand in glove with human beings; in others, fully automated tasks might require less human intervention.

When Keynes first published his essay, I doubt he had AI in mind, although Keynes's warning about 'technological unemployment' speaks directly to modern AI, as machines outpace our ability to redeploy labour, a universal dividend may be the only way to bridge the gap.

On 24th of July, Sam Altman introduced *Worldcoin* as a new cryptocurrency that offers a new and unique method for identification, where others have argued that this in principle, this biometric-backed identity layer could serve as the foundation for universal basic-income (UBI)–style distributions to support individuals displaced by AI.

With Paine's centuries-old vision in mind, I sit here wondering how UBI might unfold in the Nordics—where we already assume short workweeks and generous social safety nets as a baseline. What do we do when automation begins to take even our high-skill, knowledge-worker jobs? This chapter addresses whether such a program is both feasible and necessary as we enter a period of ever greater productivity and even less work done by knowledge workers.

Redefining Productivity

"We have told it to do so. We have told it that technology is destroying jobs, but only because people are a cost. We have told it that people should be eliminated from the system. There are a set of choices, and we have actually built incentives into our economy to encourage those choices."

—*Tim O'Reilly*

Tim O'Reilly, an Irish American author, publisher and the founder of O'Reilly Media, reminds us that automation's job-displacing power isn't destiny—it's the outcome of economic incentives that treat labor as an expense to be minimized. In today's world, knowledge-worker productivity is often reduced to simple metrics: hours billed, tasks closed, or code commits pushed. And as increasingly many of our tasks are being handled by AI. But as Peter Drucker argued, *true* productivity only exists when our efforts yield **meaningful** outcomes—value that can be measured by its quality and impact.

As increasingly routine and even creative work is performed by AI, we need to ask ourselves: what's so unique about human work?

Cal Newport's Deep Work offers us a solid foundation:

Quality Work = Time Invested × How Concentrated You Are

Research shows that knowledge workers lose more than 50% of intensive work time to interruptions, meetings, and trying to find information. It's important to distinguish between *quality* and *meaningfulness*. Quality refers to the excellence of our output—how well we execute a task—whereas meaningfulness captures its impact and value—why the work matters. Only when both unite do we achieve truly productive results.

If machines can provide both on a large scale, it's clear that human dignity and security must not be predicated on old measures of work. That's why a universal basic income for everyone is more necessary now than at any time in the past.

According to economic theory, having more people working — even at lower productivity, which would be the case when AI is taking over more of the tasks from certain knowledge workers, could be better for economic stability, social cohesion, and consumer demand, because it spreads income more broadly.

Being meaningful

Some critics argue that introducing UBI may bring welfare dependency. In other words, people will gradually lose their motivation to work and thus live entirely on government-subsidized welfare. Such a stable life may also lead to the neglect of important issues such as the aging of the population, the disabled, and minority groups. I find this hard to believe, as most of us require something that gives us hope, and purpose and even if UBI was to be a substitute, I believe many would still do some work or find something more creative to do, if many are like me. Our DNA makes us to be social beings and are inquisitive minds pushes us to find ways to excel, so even if we got UBI on top of the money we already have, I don't see many of us slacking around.

But beneath all our worries and daily struggles, there's one shared problem: stress. And we already know that stress, especially when we're constantly worried about not having enough, can actually change how our brains work. Giving people cash offers the flexibility to deal with whatever causes them the most stress, which can really free up their minds.

Humans have over the many historic event since the Industrial Revolution our ability to plan for the future has never been accurate and in the process we made mistakes. While we now look with awe at the precision and efficiency of AI, we often in the past have overlooked the crucial role that human error plays in innovation and adaptation. Our capacity for mistakes, for learning from those mistakes, for approaching problems from unexpected angles, is a fundamental driver of progress. Machines, for all their processing power, lack this inherent capacity for creative, often messy, human ingenuity. This very human tendency to err might be our enduring advantage, a constant source of new ideas and solutions in a world increasingly dominated by flawless, but perhaps less adaptable, AI. Of course, this advantage holds only until machines themselves learn to 'fail forward'—to resonate, to err, and then to adapt in ways that surpass our own creative abilities—which I don't believe society would eagerly accept.

According to recent reports, productivity in Norway, as measured by value-added per hour worked, has slowed due to factors like reduced global trade and lower business dynamism. Fast internet isn't enough if workers are not able to harness the full potential of AI to reverse or overcome this productivity slump.

The internet and AI should be complementary—one enabling the other. Without adequate training and systems in place to fully capitalize on AI, the value of being connected to the digital world risks being left unrealized, preventing both individuals and businesses from reaching their full potential in the cyber economy.

As we look toward 2030, the key question isn't whether AI will change the nature of work—it's how organizations and their leaders will shape that change. The next generation—Generation Z—already sees AI as a partner, one that can amplify human potential and drive innovation. The question is: will we embrace AI as a tool for empowerment, or will it become a force that redefines work in ways we aren't prepared for?

Knowledge workers, who currently spend a significant portion of their time gathering and synthesizing information, may find these tasks partially or fully automated by GenAI tools are both eliminating certain skills (like manual tasks) and at some extent creating few new demands (like managing automated systems)—a shift often called re-skilling. But is losing a skill always a bad thing? Not necessarily. as strange as this UBI suggestion might sound, it gives us the chance to experience "well-being." Simply understood, the best way to increase happiness is to control how you use your time and consider doing activities that you enjoy. That's when you achieve "wellbeing."

And it's the definition of "well-being" that might drive more progress, as workplace needs constantly evolve. Rather than assuming an inevitable transition to universal income and leisure, we must critically examine how AI transforms industries, redefines the value of human labor, and as O'Reilly said it we are the ones who decide, and I believe Norway with its "work life balance" structure has great chance to test this concept out.

Taxing the Machines

Since 1985 up to 2024, Norway and other Scandinavian countries have maintained consistently higher taxation levels compared to most OECD countries. According to the Norwegian Tax Administration, Norway's total tax burden has ranged between 38% and 44% of GDP, while the OECD average has typically been between 32% and 35% of GDP.

For businesses operating in Norway, the taxation structure includes:

- When a company gets profit from their business, they pay an income tax rate of approximately 22%.
- Employer's social security contributions of approximately 14.1%, it's worth noting that Norway uses a geographically differentiated system with lower rates in certain regions (ranging from 0%).
- Mandatory employer pension contributions of at least 2% of employee income
- Company owners who are Norwegian residents must pay an annual wealth tax on

their net assets, including the value of their business ownership. The rate is typically around 0.95-1.1% on net wealth exceeding certain thresholds.
- Companies also collect and remit Value Added Tax (VAT), which is 15% and 12% for knowledge workers' services.

The arrival of "informational capitalism," characterized by the influence of data and AI impacting many roles, has led tax lawyers to consider how it influences state treasuries and the possibilities of tax avoidance by major corporations, particularly those in the AI industry. At the same time, concerns over how AI automation is fueling social disturbance are leading scholars and policymakers to consider imposing a "robot tax" aimed at slowing the job displacement wrought by machines. Robot tax would mean that if machines replace human workers, they should contribute to tax revenue in a way that offsets losses from traditional labor-based taxation. Currently, our tax systems heavily rely on labor income through payroll and income taxes. When businesses replace employees with automated systems. Based on this, business owners who focus on productivity and use AI or machinery overall to produce anything of value, might find it reasonable that these non-living entities might be taxed for the value it produces. The shift would be to something non-human, but creates value. I believe such an idea would be great and viable, seeing it would support this idea.

A significant cost tied directly to employing a knowledge worker. Reducing this would lower the cost of employing humans. Similar to social security, this is a direct cost of employment. The wealth tax is on the *owner's* net assets, not directly on the worker's productivity or the cost of employing them (unless the worker is also the owner). While part of the overall tax landscape, it's less connected to the immediate taxation of work/productivity itself. While VAT is relevant to the overall economy, it's less central to the specific about taxing productivity vs. supporting workers/funding UBI. I won't speculate how much this percentage would be; all I know it could be smart if one shifted the taxation towards the machines instead if this vision is ever going to become a reality.

Norway, have a unique asset. The Government Pension Fund Global (referred to in chapter 11). This enormous sovereign wealth fund gives us options few other countries possess. It could provide the financial muscle to initiate UBI, perhaps reducing the immediate need for drastic tax hikes on ordinary citizens while we develop long-term strategies. Of course, a sustainable scheme would likely still depend on smart taxation – probably involving higher contributions from top earners and adjusted corporate rates, perhaps drawing inspiration from Keynesian ideas about progressive tax structures that didn't necessarily kill the incentive to work. For me, UBI isn't just about patching holes in income; it's about giving people real opportunities – the chance to retrain, to shift into emerging industries, or contribute in other ways, without the constant fear of becoming a minimum wage earner barely able to cover their basic needs.

In addition to traditional tax revenues and our huge pension fund, our recent discoveries of substantial mineral deposits-including rare earth elements and seabed minerals-may provide a new foundation for national wealth. While extraction is not expected to begin until 2029, these resources could eventually play a critical role in funding UBI. The reason being Europe has long relied on countries like China, Morocco, and Russia to meet its phosphate needs, often dealing with unstable supply chains and geopolitical tensions due to the current geopolitical situation. As the phosphate found in Norway is located within the continent, the logistical challenges of obtaining the material are far less complicated, making it a potentially reliable source for Europe's growing demand for green technologies. or supplementing state revenues as the economy transitions away from oil and gas.

These days, the majority of countries with rapid economic growth, such as the United States, India, and even Norway, are facing a widening wealth gap. The current traditional social welfare systems in these countries do not allow for a comprehensive measure of wealth disparity, and as a result, they hardly seem to improve the livelihoods of low-income earners.

Given this future projection, I don't see why we can't aim to empower citizens to make choices unconstrained by the challenges of poverty and since the compulsion to work long hours seems to be less relevant after 2030.

As described, the meaning of productivity should be less about ticking off tasks and more about ensuring that our efforts lead to progress—whether for an organization, a community, or our personal growth. If we let the machines handle productivity, we as knowledge workers should be better at thinking, imagining, discover and enjoy life. The effect of AI or technology in general has always been either it may increase employment by reducing the price of an activity, and thereby increase the demand of the products, requiring less human capital when we use technology, which again means fewer humans are required to produce an output of value. As AI upends most of the knowledge workers, UBI isn't just a century-old idea—it could be the safety net that powers the next era of innovation.

I'm hopeful that someone can change my view on this because I certainly don't want this to happen. I would like the majority of people to keep their jobs, but I currently don't see a future where one of three things don't happen:

1. UBI is mandated.
2. Laws are passed that require companies to have X% of human workers.
3. A combination of the two.

I believe we have sufficient capital in Norway, and giving people money will help them spend, which boosts the economy. Furthermore, if we would allow people to re-skill or study while providing them with work, it would also increase production, which also boosts the economy. As previously mentioned, many of the jobs will be obsolete and there will be some new jobs created by AI. If we make our work programs more flexible, it will also allow more people to be employed after 2030. Unconditional programs tend to increase employment more than conditional programs. Social programs are important tools for managing the economy.

There are some challenges that experts have argued on the reality of implementing UBI, one being securing sufficient financial support. Many advocates argue that the government would need to obtain sufficient disposable funds through higher corporate income taxes. This means that the ultra-rich would need to be taxed more heavily.

However, this creates a potential issue—higher taxes could drive these individuals to flee the country, a trend that has already been observed in some regions since 2024. And since no politician has managed to crack this dilemma, which is one of the reasons why no country is currently carrying out a real policy of unconditional universal basic income.

Beyond the financial hurdle, there's also a more psychological barrier; the other major concern is us humans. According to Professor Wanja Wolff from the University of Hamburg, whose research was published in August 2024, boredom serves as "a powerful motivator that prompts us to seek more rewarding behavioral alternatives" and we need to feel useful and have some sort of motivation, otherwise we would feel empty and apathetic because we would feel that every action led to boredom. When I'm idle for days without anything engaging to do, I feel worthless. Researchers say that I'm under-utilizing my mental and physical resources. I believe most people feel the same way. We thrive on being productive, creative, and engaged.

Yet by 2030, many highly qualified individuals may find themselves out of work, not through any personal failing, but because they underestimated the capabilities of the innovations we've created. This obsolescence is not their fault. It will be hard for many to cope; we need goals to strive for, and it's in our nature to be useful and find meaning.

Therefore, one plausible solution for knowledge workers is to work alongside AI—perhaps for reduced pay—while receiving government support funded by new taxes in lieu of a universal basic income.

But we might need to rethink a new government structure in the near future, if UBI is to progress further beyond just a vision. Perhaps the challenge isn't just finding the right policies but lies deeper – within the structure of governance itself. The next chapter discusses the idea of a semi-driven AI democracy. Where the laws and policies are decided by expert groups and voted for by the citizens. In this model, there would be no political parties, potentially reducing political sluggishness. While politicians' ideals and intentions may be good, they do not always align with the long-term needs of the population. As I end this chapter, a reflection comes to mind, with the mind as brilliant as human being, we can create anything, we can also use it to good or something sinister and none of us think ahead of time, as most we think about "here and now".

Chapter 19 Where do we Go from here?

I started writing this book in my study while my wife gave me space to disappear into my thoughts. nine months and 1,500 hours later, I'm ending it with a question for you: When you look at your work tomorrow morning, will you see a career or a countdown?

The answer will determine whether you read this book as a warning or a guide.

My friend Espen sees his coding work vanishing into prompts. My real estate agent Altin still believes human connection can't be algorithmic. The Norwegian government just used AI to write strategy based on facts that never existed. We're all guessing which side of history we'll land on. The only certainty is that standing still is not an option.

Peter Drucker first identified "knowledge workers" as those who "work primarily with information or develop and use knowledge in the workplace." Standing here in 2025, I see how profoundly this concept has transformed our lives. We've all become knowledge workers now—processing, analyzing, and creating the information that surrounds us.

While looking at the various inventions, I was amazed at how our shared ingenuity has built upon the last innovation, layer by layer. From the first alphabet to the computer and later the internet, none which came from nothing but were aspired by something before. Each emerged from millions of minds laboring across time and space, usually unaware of each other but connected by shared human curiosity.

This is what gives me hope. We are unique—shaped by our different cultures, histories, and personal journeys—but it is these differences that enrich our collective wisdom. The most elegant solutions are the ones that emerge when differing visions come together for the greater good.

AI was first conceptualized 75 years ago, and since then slowly it's been reshaping our jobs and the very meaning of work. I am struck by how swiftly our world has transformed. Societies are built on shared values—ideas like money, nations, and human rights. Though intangible, they guide our collective journey based on information. Now, as AI begins to reshape these very foundations of work, we must reflect: what should our goals be like a collective society?

So, how do we know what our goals are if we don't even know what they should be, as Norway lags behind other small, open and digitally advanced economies when it comes to AI adoption drivers? Based on the most recent World Economic Forum Future Report (2025), there are certain skills you'll want to master by 2030, and they include the basics as well as some new ones. As the photo below illustrates, such skills as AI and Big Data, being computer-literate, being curious, constantly learning, thinking creatively, and analytical thinking are just a few of the skills you need to work on.

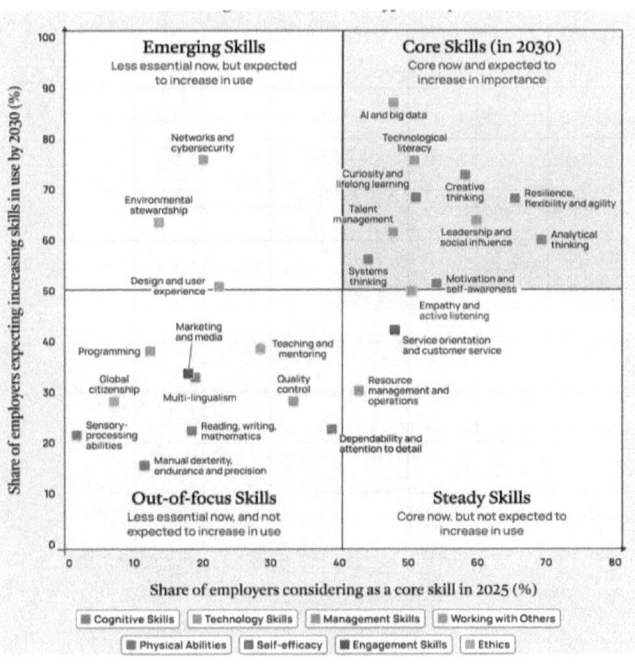

Throughout the history of technological philosophy, scholars have challenged the notion of technology as a morally neutral instrument. This intellectual tradition encompasses Karl Marx's analysis of technological relations to labor and society, Ernst Kapp's philosophical examination of technology as human projection, and Hannah Arendt's investigations into the relationship between technology and the human condition. Historian Melvin Kranzberg crystallized this perspective in his widely influential "Kranzberg's Laws," where he stated: "Technology is neither good nor bad; nor is it neutral." the statement captures a paradox which means technology doesn't have moral intent, but it also always has consequences shaped by design, context, and use. It's a warning not to think of tech as just a neutral tool, but to consider the broader social, economic, and ethical implications.

By the early twenty-first century, algorithmic systems had become powerful forces shaping social structures and regulating both individual and institutional behavior. These systems influenced fundamental life outcomes—employment decisions, credit approvals, housing access—through computational processes that could embed and amplify existing societal biases related to race, gender, and other demographic factors. Algorithms also shaped cultural consumption patterns, determining what music people heard, which books came to their attention, and potentially influencing political engagement. Critics noted that these systems exploited comprehensive data about human experience and behavior. As algorithmic governance became increasingly pervasive in modern society, individuals faced a dilemma: while avoiding these systems often required both technological literacy and deliberate action, in many contexts—such as financial transactions or housing applications—algorithmic assessment had become effectively mandatory, making such avoidance practically impossible.

As humans, our journey has always been about blending diverse skills and rethinking what's possible as creative beings. We constantly strive to invent more and expand, driven by what John Maynard Keynes rightly identified as endless human ambition. When we are warm enough, we don't stop—we ask how we can be warmer, more comfortable, or even admired for our warmth. Many ideas and hours have been poured into writing this book precisely to explore where we stand today as knowledge workers and where this inherent ambition, amplified by new tools, might be leading us.

Algorithms alone won't lead us forward; real value is created through their collaboration with knowledge workers. But what happens if AI becomes a knowledge worker itself, not merely a tool for knowledge workers? What if the generation, analysis, and application of knowledge become primarily the domain of algorithms? This isn't a hypothetical future; it's a rapidly approaching reality. In this context, the core of Peter Drucker's concept—the human element, the capacity for judgment, empathy, and ethical reasoning—becomes even more critical, not less. These indispensable human attributes will be crucial every time we engage with work or emerging technology like AI.

Reflecting on the global AI race—China, the USA, and beyond—I see that safety often comes at the cost of growth. Norway has had some inventions in maritime, oil, weapons, fishing and energy, but as I noted earlier our wealth from "black gold" has made us cautious and we should utilize it much better in the future. Norway's oil and hydropower weren't just lucky finds; they became powerful because we chose to innovate with them. AI is the same. It's not just the technology; it's how we use it to make our businesses and lives better. It's about a new kind of learning, where we and machines teach each other. The biggest benefits won't come from just selling AI technology to other countries. Instead, they'll come from how AI changes and improves the businesses and industries we already have. It's about how AI helps us do things smarter and more efficiently, leading to overall economic growth.

AI teams and leadership must reflect a range of expertise. Beyond AI specialists, we need domain experts who understand industry challenges, as well as "all-rounders" who can bridge technology and strategy. A diverse team is better equipped to identify biases, assess real-world impacts, and ask the tough questions that technical experts might overlook don't be lazy, and use the supercomputer between your ears.

For generations, our collective society has invented, but at the same time, work is an important part of our identity and gives many of us purpose. As we progress into a future where AI performs tasks once uniquely human, the nature and meaning of work are shifting. I do not know exactly how work will evolve in the near future, but what is clear is that our strength lies in our human capacity—our ability to be knowledge workers who ask the right questions, connect dots, and create value beyond algorithms.

With these lessons in mind, I'm reminded of Yogi Berra's warning, *'If you don't know where you are going, you'll end up someplace else.'* There is some truth to Berra warning and what I've shared is my informed perspective on what might come—not a guarantee. After all, no one truly knows what the future holds. All I can suggest is that we need to decide: will you take a positive shift towards 2030? Or will you passively watch from the shadows, assuming everything will be fine?

Afterword by Eirik Norman Hansen

After reading Victor Singh's Code Collar 2030, it's easy to feel both excitement and concern. The author's analytical and nuanced view of artificial intelligence (AI) and the future of knowledge work is compelling – and serves as an important corrective in a time marked by hype, overconfidence, and rapid technological change. He highlights vulnerabilities that we, as a society, must take seriously: our sometimes-sluggish ability to adapt, our growing dependence on a handful of global tech platforms, and the urgent need for ethical frameworks and responsible governance. These are not abstract warnings, but tangible challenges we face today and will increasingly confront tomorrow.

Victor's reflections are thoughtful, informed, and needed. And they are particularly valuable because they are not rooted in fearmongering, but in a sincere desire to spark awareness and dialogue. His call for vigilance and deeper understanding is a message that should be widely heard.

At the same time, I want to contribute a slightly more optimistic voice. Because AI, despite its risks, also brings with it a wave of opportunity unlike anything we've seen before. We are standing on the edge of a massive shift – not just in what we do, but in how we do it. Used wisely, AI can enhance our capabilities, free us from tedious tasks, help us solve problems faster, and even unlock new forms of creativity.

However, we must never forget one foundational truth: AI is a tool. It is an "it," not a "he," "she," or "they." It can be powerful, but it does not possess agency, intention, or empathy. It has no moral compass, no emotional intelligence, and no human experience. That remains in our domain. That is our responsibility.

And that responsibility is great. Because while AI can do many things, we humans still excel at the most important ones: critical thinking, creativity, deep reasoning, nuanced decision-making, emotional intelligence, and ethical judgment. These unique human capacities should not be underestimated or sidelined. In fact, they will become even more essential as we move into an AI-enhanced future.

We should approach this future with curiosity, not just caution. We need to lift our gaze and look at the bigger picture – to understand not only what AI can do today, but what kind of society we want to create with it tomorrow. Yes, we must be realistic about the fact that humans are fallible, as Victor rightly points out. But we must also recognize our power to choose how we use this technology. Like the internet or social media, AI can be used for good or for harm. That choice is ours.

One point that deserves emphasis is this: a job is not a monolith. It is a collection of tasks. As AI automates certain elements, it doesn't necessarily eliminate entire professions. Instead, it reshapes them. Some tasks will disappear, new ones will emerge, and many will shift in nature. This means we must be agile in how we think about work, skills, and career development. We need to stop asking "Will this job disappear?" and instead ask "Which parts of this role can be augmented? Which parts remain uniquely human? And how do we prepare that blend?"

The way we work is changing, and it will continue to do so. But change does not equal loss. It equals transformation. It opens doors. And those doors lead to new kinds of jobs, new kinds of collaboration, and entirely new opportunities.

To seize those opportunities responsibly, one thing becomes absolutely clear: we need competence. A population that understands AI, not just in technical terms but in practical, ethical, and societal dimensions. That means integrating AI literacy into education systems from an early age. But it also means continuous learning for adults, leaders, policymakers, and for everyone navigating the evolving landscape of modern life and work.

We must ensure that this powerful technology doesn't become the exclusive domain of a few, but something that empowers the many. We must democratize understanding, access, and application. That is the only way to ensure AI serves us all.

Victor is right to raise the questions he does. And I believe he would agree that the answers are not written in code – they are written by us. Our choices, our values, our capacity to learn and adapt. The future of work is not something we should fear or romanticize – it is something we must shape. With intention. With ethics. With vision.

We have never had more possibilities than we do right now. But we have also never faced more profound challenges. That makes our responsibility clear: we must steward this transition wisely, in a way that is responsible, inclusive, and sustainable. Not just for our own benefit, but for generations to come- we owe them that.

Eirik Norman Hansen
Entrepreneur / Futurist / Keynote speaker / Author

Acknowledgement

I would like to express my deepest gratitude to my wife, Jagroop, for her patience, encouragement, and loving support throughout this project. Her positivity and belief in me gave me the push I needed to complete this book, and her willingness to back this project emotionally —made writing this book relaxing and fun.

To my sweet and creative niece Arya, and my witty and sharp-witted nephew Rohan, who is clever and passionate about games.

My sincere thanks also go to AI engineer Simon Vestvik Edland, Maxim Salnikov from Microsoft, Siri W. Bogen, Peter Kirwan from MeBot AI, Eirik Norman Hansen, and Prof. Dr. Moutaz Haddara at University of Kristiana for their insightful feedback during the writing process.

To my dear friends Eric, Jan Kristian, Henrik, Florian, Khurram, Tom Erik, Øyvind and Nicolas— thank you for your friendship, inspiration, and constant encouragement. And to you who is currently about to read this book. My hope is that the insights within these chapters serve you as much as the process of discovering them has served me.

Notes

1. MastersInAI.org, "AI's Impact on Major Industries," accessed January 18, 2025, https://www.mastersinai.org/industries/.

2. Antoni Slodkowski, "AI Is Cutting White-Collar Jobs," *Global Finance Magazine*, January 24, 2024, accessed May 3, 2025, https://gfmag.com/technology/artificial-intelligence-cutting-white-collar-jobs/.

3. Investopedia Staff, "Blue Collar vs. White Collar: Different Social Classes," *Investopedia*, last modified December 15, 2015, accessed May 3, 2025, https://www.investopedia.com/articles/wealth-management/120215/blue-collar-vs-white-collar-different-social-classes.asp.

4. Jacques Revel, "White-Collar Workers, History of," in *International Encyclopedia of the Social & Behavioral Sciences*, edited by Neil J. Smelser and Paul B. Baltes (Oxford: Pergamon, 2001), 1, accessed May 3, 2025, https://www.sciencedirect.com/science/article/abs/pii/B9780080970868620238?via%3Dihub.

5. Adam Davidson, "Is the Blue-Collar Shirt Still Blue Collar?," *The New York Times*, September 6, 2015, accessed May 3, 2025, https://www.nytimes.com/2015/09/06/magazine/is-the-blue-collar-shirt-still-blue-collar.html.

6. T.B. Lee, "Why the Deep Learning Boom Caught Almost Everyone by Surprise," *UnderstandingAI* (Substack), November 5, 2024, retrieved January 30, 2025, from https://www.understandingai.org/p/why-the-deep-learning-boom-caught.

7. Q.ai, "Google Invests in Anthropic for $2 Billion as AI Race Heats Up," *Forbes*, October 31, 2023, retrieved January 30, 2025, from

https://www.forbes.com/sites/qai/2023/10/31/google-invests-in-anthropic-for-2-billion-as-ai-race-heats-up/.

8. BBC News, "Neuralink: Can Musk's Brain Technology Change the World?," 2023, retrieved January 30, 2025, from https://www.bbc.com/news/health-68169082.

9. CNET Staff, "Ballie, Samsung's AI Home Robot You May Actually Care About," *CNET*, January 8, 2024, retrieved January 30, 2025, from https://www.cnet.com/home/smart-home/samsung-ballie-ai-you-may-actuallycare-about/.

10. Rivery, "Data Statistics 2025: How Much Data Is There in the World?," Rivery Blog, 2025, retrieved January 30, 2025, from https://rivery.io/blog/big-data-statistics-how-much-data-is-there-in-the-world/.

11. SOAX Research, "How Much Data Is Generated Every Day?," SOAX, 2025, retrieved January 30, 2025, from https://soax.com/research/data-generated-per-day.

12. Tech Business News, "402.74 Million Terrabytes of Data Is Created Every Day," 2025, retrieved January 30, 2025, from https://www.techbusinessnews.com.au/blog/402-74-million-terrabytes-of-data-is-created-every-day/.

13. A.M. Turing, "Computing Machinery and Intelligence," *Mind* 59, no. 236 (1950): 433–460, retrieved January 30, 2025, from https://courses.cs.umbc.edu/471/papers/turing.pdf.

14. ResearchGate, "Arthur Samuel: Pioneer in Machine Learning," n.d., retrieved January 30, 2025, from https://www.researchgate.net/publication/224103556_Arthur_Samuel_Pioneer_in_Machine_Learning.

15. K. Briggs and S. Kodnani, "The Potentially Large Effects of Artificial Intelligence on Economic Growth," Global Economics Analyst, March 2023, retrieved January 30, 2025, from https://www.key4biz.it/wp-content/uploads/2023/03/Global-

Economics-Analyst_-The-Potentially-Large-Effects-of-Artificial-Intelligence-on-Economic-Growth-Briggs_Kodnani.pdf.

16. Ray Kurzweil, *The Singularity Is Near: When Humans Transcend Biology* (Viking, 2005).

17. Nick Bostrom, *Superintelligence: Paths, Dangers, Strategies* (Oxford University Press, 2014).

18. Sam Altman, interview with *Fortune*, March 2024, on AI courtesy costs.

19. Gisle Hannemyr, *Hva er Internett* (Oslo: Universitetsforlaget, 2005), 9.

20. Peter F. Drucker, *Landmarks of Tomorrow* (New York: Harper & Row, 1959).

21. Peter F. Drucker, *The Effective Executive* (New York: Harper & Row, 1966).

22. Tom Standage, *The Victorian Internet: The Remarkable Story of the Telegraph and the Nineteenth Century's On-Line Pioneers* (New York: Walker & Co., 1998).

23. Steven Roger Fischer, *A History of Writing* (London, England: Reaktion Books, 2001).

24. D. Schmandt-Besserat, *How Writing Came About* (Austin, Texas: University of Texas Press, 1996).

25. B. B. Powell, *Writing: Theory and History of the Technology of Civilization* (London: Wiley Blackwell, 2009).

26. Ethan Siegel, "Ask Ethan: How Do We Know the Universe Is 13.8 Billion Years Old?," *Big Think*, October 22, 2021, https://bigthink.com/starts-with-abang/universe-13-8-billion-years.

27. World History Encyclopedia, "Writing," accessed May 3, 2025, https://www.worldhistory.org/writing/.

28. Ray Kurzweil, *The Singularity is Nearer - When We Merge with AI* (2024).

29. L. Stavrianos, *Lifelines from Our Past: A New World History* (Routledge, London, 1997), 79.
30. E. P. Thompson, "The Making of the English Working Class," 1963.
31. Frank Barkley Copley, *Frederick W. Taylor, Father of Scientific Management*, vol. 1 (2022).
32. Frederick W. Taylor, "The Principles of Scientific Management," 1911.
33. N. Jaimovich and H.E. Siu, "Job Polarization and Jobless Recoveries," *Review of Economics and Statistics* 102, no. 1 (2020): 129–47.
34. Erik Brynjolfsson and Andrew McAfee, *The Second Machine Age* (2014).
35. Thomas H. Davenport and Rajeev Ronanki, "Artificial Intelligence for the Real World," *Harvard Business Review* (2018).
36. Nancy M. Carter et al., "The Hidden Costs of Distributed Work," *McKinsey Quarterly* (2022).
37. D. H. Bassiouni and C. Hackley, "Generation Z' Children's Adaptation to Digital Consumer Culture: A Critical Literature Review," *Journal of Customer Behaviour* 13, no. 2 (2014): 113–133.
38. John Maynard Keynes, "Economic Possibilities for Our Grandchildren" (1930), http://www.econ.yale.edu/smith/econ116a/keynes1.pdf.
39. M. Servoz, "Ai: The Future of Work? Work of the Future!," European Commission, 2019, https://ec.europa.eu/digital-single-market/en/news/future-work-work-futur.
40. Yuval Noah Harari, *Homo Deus* (2015). (Referred to for the term "Useless class").
41. Joseph A. Schumpeter, *Capitalism, Socialism, And Democracy* (2008).

42. F. Dell'Acqua et al., "Navigating the Jagged Technological Frontier: Field Experimental Evidence of the Effects of AI on Knowledge Worker Productivity and Quality," Harvard Business School Technology & Operations Mgt Working Paper No. 24-013, 2023.
43. World Economic Forum, *The Future of Jobs Report 2025* (Geneva: World Economic Forum, January 2025), https://reports.weforum.org/docs/WEF_Future_of_Jobs_Report_2025.pdf.
44. Peter F. Drucker, *Management: Tasks, Responsibilities, Practices* (New York: Harper & Row, 1973), 68.
45. J. Smith, A. Lee, and P. Gupta, "Impact of AI Tools on Management Consulting Tasks," *Journal of Business Research* 56, no. 4 (2023): 412–29.
46. Bertrand Russell, *The History of Western Philosophy* (London: George Allen & Unwin, 1945), 233.
47. SAP SE, "Introducing the AI Coach: Elevating Human–Machine Collaboration," SAP News Center, February 2024, https://news.sap.com.
48. Spanish Ministry of Finance, "Proyecto FRAUDE: Data-Driven Tax Fraud Detection," Government of Spain, 2023, https://www.minhafp.gob.es.
49. Norwegian Tax Administration (Skatteetaten), "Use of Machine Learning to Combat Tax Fraud," internal white paper, 2024.
50. Henry Mintzberg, *Mintzberg on Management. Inside Our Strange World of Organizations* (New York: Free Press, 1989).
51. S. Tong et al., "The Janus Face of Artificial Intelligence Feedback: Deployment versus Disclosure Effects on Employee Performance," *Strategic Management Journal* 42, no. 9 (2021): 1600–1631, https://doi.org/10.1002/smj.3322.

52. G. Bhardwaj, S. V. Singh, and V. Kumar, "An Empirical Study of Artificial Intelligence and Its Impact on Human Resource Functions," in *2020 International Conference on Computation, Automation and Knowledge Management (ICCAKM)*, https://doi.org/10.1109/iccakm46823.2020.9051544.

53. Tanja Schwarzmüller et al., "How Does the Digital Transformation Affect Organizations? Key Themes of Change in Work Design and Leadership," *Management Review* 29, no. 2 (2018): 114–138.

54. Brian H. Spitzberg, "The Composition of Competence: Communication Skills," in *Communication Competence*, edited by Annegret F. Hannawa and Brian H. Spitzberg (Berlin: De Gruyter Mouton, 2015), 237–269.

55. J. Anderson, *Cognitive Psychology and Its Implications* (San Francisco: Freeman, 1980).

56. G. Stavrum, "Nicolai Tangen:–Kunstig intelligens kan overta for journalister og advokater," *Nettavisen*, September 7, 2023, retrieved January 30, 2025, from https://www.nettavisen.no/nicolai-tangen/oljefondet/norges-bank-investmentmanagement/nicolai-tangen-kunstig-intelligens-kan-overta-for-journalister-ogadvokater/s/5-95-1315633.

57. *Finansforbundet*, "Pushet Oljefondet på kunstig intelligens," September 25, 2024, retrieved January 30, 2025, from https://www.finansforbundet.no/folk-og-fag/forbundsnytt/pushet-oljefondet-pa-kunstig-intelligens/.

58. Norges Bank Investment Management, "Ansvarlig kunstig intelligens," NBIM, 2023, retrieved January 30, 2025, from https://www.nbim.no/no/nyheter-oginnsikt/vare-synspunkt/2023/responsible-artificial-intelligence/.

59. M.B. Jørgenrud, "Oljefondet: KI-algoritmer for økt avkastning og cybersikkerhet," *Digi.no*, November 26, 2024, retrieved January 30, 2025, from https://www.digi.no/artikler/oljefondet-ki-algoritmer-for-okt-avkastning-og-cybersikkerhet/552613.
60. Norges Bank Investment Management, "Fondets verdi," 2025, retrieved January 30, 2025, from https://www.nbim.no/no/investeringene/fondetsverdi/.
61. NTB and Redaksjonen, "Teknodrevet rekord for oljefondet– men KI-krasj kan gi enorme tap," *Digi.no Nyhetsstudio*, January 29, 2025, retrieved January 30, 2025, from https://www.digi.no/nyhetsstudio/teknodrevet-rekord-for-oljefondet-menki-krasj-kan-gi-enorme-tap/68916?showFeed=1.
62. NTB, "1 av 5 oljefond-kroner kan ryke ved en AI-kollaps," *Kode24*, January 29, 2025, retrieved January 30, 2025, from https://www.kode24.no/artikkel/1-av-5-oljefond-kroner-kan-ryke-ved-en-ai-kollaps/82596682.
63. AJBell, "Why Are So Many Active Fund Managers Underperforming?," n.d., retrieved January 30, 2025, from https://www.ajbell.co.uk/articles/investmentarticles/284690/why-are-so-many-active-fund-managers-underperforming.
64. S&P Dow Jones Indices, "SPIVA US Scorecard: Year-End 2019," 2020, retrieved January 30, 2025, from https://www.spglobal.com/spdji/en/documents/spiva/spiva-us-year-end-2019.pdf.
65. S. Dhawan, "Magnificent 7 Earnings Under the Microscope as Big Tech Deals with Tariffs, AI Bets, and Market Pressure," *The Financial Express*, April 30, 2025, retrieved January 30, 2025, from https://www.financialexpress.com/business/investing-abroad-magnificent-7-earnings-under-the-microscope-as-big-tech-dealswith-tariffs-ai-bets-and-market-pressure-3826695/.

66. BestPractice.AI, "JPMorgan's New AI Program for Automatically Executing Equity Trades in Real-Time Out-Performed Current Manual and Automated Methods in Trial," https://www.bestpractice.ai/ai-case-study-best-practice/jpmorgan%27s_new_ai_program_for_automatically_executing_eq-uity_trades_in_real-time_out-performed_current_manual_and_automated_methods_in_trial.
67. Gartner, "Gartner Says 80 Percent of Today's Project Management Tasks Will Be Automated by 2030," press release, March 20, 2019, https://www.gartner.com/en/newsroom/press-releases/2019-03-20-gartner-says-80-percent-of-today-s-project-management.
68. Project Management Institute, "AI Innovators: Cracking the Code to Project Performance," *Pulse of the Profession*, accessed May 4, 2025, https://www.pmi.org/-/media/pmi/documents/public/pdf/learning/thoughtleadership/pulse/ai-innovators-cracking-the-code-project-performance.pdf?rev=acf03326778f4e64925e70c1149f37ea&sc_lang_temp=en.
69. Northeastern University, "What Is Jevons Paradox? And Why It May—or May Not—Predict AI's Future," February 7, 2025, from https://news.northeastern.edu/2025/02/07/jevons-paradox-ai-future/.
70. Bennett, Max. *A Brief History of Intelligence*.
71. Fodor, Jerry A. 1987. *Psychosemantics: The Problem of Meaning in the Philosophy of Mind*.
72. Gopnik, Alison, and Henry M. Wellman. 1994. "The Theory Theory." In *Domain Specificity in Cognition and Culture*, edited by Louise Hirschfeld and Susan Gelman, 257–293.
73. Greene, Robert. *The 48 Laws of Power*.
74. Anderson, John. 1980. *Cognitive Psychology and Its Implications*.

75. Ikromov, E. 2024. "Scientific and Theoretical Basis of Increasing the Efficiency of Service Enterprises." *Modern Science and Research* 3 (2): 103–109.
76. B. Alcott, "Jevons' Paradox," *Ecological Economics* 54, no. 1 (2005): 9–21, https://www.sciencedirect.
77. ResearchGate, "Theory of Mind," n.d., retrieved May 2, 2025, from https://www.researchgate.net/publication/324271983_Theory_of_Mind.
78. LinkedIn Marketing Solutions, "The Rise of AI-Generated Content on LinkedIn," LinkedIn Blog, December 2024.
79. Content at Scale, "AI Content Report: 189% Surge in Likely AI-Produced Posts, Q1 2024," March 2024.
80. Statista, "Share of AI-Generated Articles on Fortune 500 Company Blogs, 2024."
81. Studentbarometer, "AI in Education 2024: Usage and Training Survey," Studentbarometer Report, 2024.
82. John Doe, "False Positives in AI Detection: When Human Writing Gets Flagged," *MIT Technology Review*, April 2025.
83. OpenAI API Documentation, "GPT-4 Tokenizer."
84. Robert Cialdini, *Influence: The Psychology of Persuasion* (1984).
85. Hershey Friedman, "Cognitive Biases and Their Influence on Critical Thinking and Scientific Reasoning: A Practical Guide for Students and Teachers," *SSRN Electronic Journal*, 2023, doi:10.2139/ssrn.2958800.
86. J. A. Goldstein et al., "How Persuasive Is AI-Generated Propaganda?," *PNAS Nexus* 3, no. 2 (2024): pgae034. https://doi.org/10.1093/pnasnexus/pgae034.
87. T. H. Costello, G. Pennycook, and D. G. Rand, "Durably Reducing Conspiracy Beliefs through Dialogues with AI," *Science* 385, no.

6714 (2024): eadq1814. https://doi.org/10.1126/science.adq1814.

88. S. Afroogh et al., "Trust in AI: Progress, Challenges, and Future Directions," *Humanit Soc Sci Commun* 11, no. 1568 (2024). https://doi.org/10.1057/s41599-024-04044-8.

89. Christian Montag, Benjamin Becker, and Benjamin J. Li, "On Trust in Humans and Trust in Artificial Intelligence: A Study with Samples from Singapore and Germany Extending Recent Research," *Computers in Human Behavior: Artificial Humans* 2, no. 2 (2024): 100070. https://doi.org/10.1016/j.chbah.2024.100070.

90. Song, Binyang, Qihao Zhu, and Jianxi Luo. "Human-AI Collaboration by Design." In *International Design Conference – Design 2024*. Cambridge: Cambridge University Press, 2024. [Page range]. https://www.cambridge.org/core/services/aop-cambridge-core/content/view/45BC30ADFF2FE3B204D4A29DD67F6353/S2732527X2400227Xa.pdf

91. Tshilidzi Marwala, "The Algorithmic Problem in Artificial Intelligence Governance," *United Nations University*, January 23, 2025, https://unu.edu/article/algorithmic-problem-artificial-intelligence-governance

92. Democracy and AI." *Ash Center for Democratic Governance and Innovation*. Accessed [month day, year]. https://ash.harvard.edu/issues/democracy-and-ai/

93. Abbeel, Pieter. "Apprenticeship Learning and Reinforcement Learning with Application to Robotic Control." PhD diss., Stanford University, 2008.

94. Abbeel, Pieter, and Andrew Y. Ng. "Apprenticeship Learning via Inverse Reinforcement Learning." In *Proceedings of the 21st International Conference on Machine Learning*. ACM, 2004.

95. Acemoglu, Daron, and Pascual Restrepo. "The Race between Man and Machine: Implications of Technology for Growth,

Factor Shares, and Employment." *American Economic Review* 108, no. 6 (2018): 1488–1542.

96. Afroogh, S., A. Akbari, E. Malone, et al. "Trust in AI: Progress, Challenges, and Future Directions." *Humanities and Social Sciences Communications* 11, no. 1568 (2024). https://doi.org/10.1057/s41599-024-04044-8.

97. AJBell. "Why Are So Many Active Fund Managers Underperforming?." Accessed January 30, 2025. https://www.ajbell.co.uk/articles/investmentarticles/284690/why-are-so-many-active-fund-managers-underperforming.

98. Alcott, B. "Jevons' Paradox." *Ecological Economics* 54, no. 1 (2005): 9–21.

99. Altman, Sam. Interview by *Fortune*. March 2024.

100. Anderson, John. *Cognitive Psychology and Its Implications*. San Francisco: Freeman, 1980.

101. Bassiouni, D. H., and C. Hackley. "Generation Z' Children's Adaptation to Digital Consumer Culture: A Critical Literature Review." *Journal of Customer Behaviour* 13, no. 2 (2014): 113–133.

102. BBC News. "Neuralink: Can Musk's Brain Technology Change the World?." February 1, 2024. Accessed January 30, 2025. https://www.bbc.com/news/health-68169082.

103. Bennett, Max. *A Brief History of Intelligence*. New York: William Morrow, 2023.

104. BestPractice.AI. "JPMorgan's New AI Program for Automatically Executing Equity Trades in Real-Time Out-Performed Current Manual and Automated Methods in Trial." Accessed January 30, 2025.

105. Bhardwaj, G., S. V. Singh, and V. Kumar. "An Empirical Study of Artificial Intelligence and Its Impact on Human Resource Functions." In *2020 International Conference on Computation,*

Automation and Knowledge Management (ICCAKM). https://doi.org/10.1109/iccakm46823.2020.9051544.

106. Bostrom, Nick. *Superintelligence: Paths, Dangers, Strategies*. Oxford: Oxford University Press, 2014.

107. Briggs, K., and S. Kodnani. "The Potentially Large Effects of Artificial Intelligence on Economic Growth." *Global Economics Analyst*, March 2023. Accessed January 30, 2025.

108. Brynjolfsson, Erik, and Andrew McAfee. *The Second Machine Age: Work, Progress, and Prosperity in a Time of Brilliant Technologies*. New York: W. W. Norton & Company, 2014.

109. Campbell, Murray, A. Joseph Hoane Jr., and Feng-hsiung Hsu. "Deep Blue." *Artificial Intelligence* 134, nos. 1–2 (2002): 57–83.

110. Carter, Nancy M., et al. "The Hidden Costs of Distributed Work." *McKinsey Quarterly*, 2022.

111. Cialdini, Robert. *Influence: The Psychology of Persuasion*. New York: William Morrow, 1984.

112. CNET Staff. "Ballie, Samsung's AI Home Robot You May Actually Care About." *CNET*, January 8, 2024. Accessed January 30, 2025.

113. Content at Scale. "AI Content Report: 189% Surge in Likely AI-Produced Posts, Q1 2024." March 2024.

114. Copley, Frank Barkley. *Frederick W. Taylor, Father of Scientific Management*. Vol. 1. New York: Routledge, 2022.

115. Costello, T. H., G. Pennycook, and D. G. Rand. "Durably Reducing Conspiracy Beliefs through Dialogues with AI." *Science* 385, no. 6714 (2024): eadq1814. https://doi.org/10.1126/science.adq1814.

116. Davenport, Thomas H., and Rajeev Ronanki. "Artificial Intelligence for the Real World." *Harvard Business Review* 96, no. 1 (2018): 108–16.

117. Davidson, Adam. "Is the Blue-Collar Shirt Still Blue Collar?." *The New York Times*, September 6, 2015. Accessed May 3, 2025.

118. Dell'Acqua, F., E. McFowland, E. R. Mollick, et al. "Navigating the Jagged Technological Frontier: Field Experimental Evidence of the Effects of AI on Knowledge Worker Productivity and Quality." Harvard Business School Technology & Operations Mgt. Working Paper No. 24-013, September 2023.

119. Dhawan, S. "Magnificent 7 Earnings Under the Microscope as Big Tech Deals with Tariffs, AI Bets, and Market Pressure." *The Financial Express*, April 30, 2025. Accessed January 30, 2025.

120. Doe, John. "False Positives in AI Detection: When Human Writing Gets Flagged." *MIT Technology Review*, April 2025.

121. Drucker, Peter F. *The Effective Executive*. New York: Harper & Row, 1966. ———. *Landmarks of Tomorrow*. New York: Harper & Row, 1959. ———. *Management: Tasks, Responsibilities, Practices*. New York: Harper & Row, 1973.

122. Finansforbundet. "Pushet Oljefondet på kunstig intelligens." September 25, 2024. Accessed January 30, 2025.

123. Fischer, Steven Roger. *A History of Writing*. London: Reaktion Books, 2001.

124. Fodor, Jerry A. *Psychosemantics: The Problem of Meaning in the Philosophy of Mind*. Cambridge, MA: MIT Press, 1987.

125. Friedman, Hershey. "Cognitive Biases and Their Influence on Critical Thinking and Scientific Reasoning: A Practical Guide for Students and Teachers." *SSRN Electronic Journal*, 2023. doi:10.2139/ssrn.2958800.

126. Gartner. "Gartner Says 80 Percent of Today's Project Management Tasks Will Be Automated by 2030." Press release, March 20, 2019.

127. Goldstein, J. A., J. Chao, S. Grossman, A. Stamos, and M. Tomz. "How Persuasive Is AI-Generated Propaganda?." *PNAS Nexus* 3, no. 2 (2024): pgae034.

128. Gopnik, Alison, and Henry M. Wellman. "The Theory Theory." In *Domain Specificity in Cognition and Culture*, edited by Louise Hirschfeld and Susan Gelman, 257–293. New York: Cambridge University Press, 1994.
129. Greene, Robert. *The 48 Laws of Power*. New York: Viking, 1998.
130. Hannemyr, Gisle. *Hva er Internett*. Oslo: Universitetsforlaget, 2005.
131. Ikromov, E. "Scientific and Theoretical Basis of Increasing the Efficiency of Service Enterprises." *Modern Science and Research* 3, no. 2 (2024): 103–109.
132. Investopedia Staff. "Blue Collar vs. White Collar: Different Social Classes." *Investopedia*. Last modified December 15, 2015. Accessed May 3, 2025.
133. Jaimovich, N., and H. E. Siu. "Job Polarization and Jobless Recoveries." *Review of Economics and Statistics* 102, no. 1 (2020): 129–47.
134. Keynes, John Maynard. "Economic Possibilities for Our Grandchildren." 1930. Accessed January 30, 2025. http://www.econ.yale.edu/smith/econ116a/keynes1.pdf.
135. Kurzweil, Ray. *The Singularity Is Near: When Humans Transcend Biology*. New York: Viking, 2005. ———. *The Singularity is Nearer: When We Merge with AI*. New York: Viking, 2024.
136. Lee, T. B. "Why the Deep Learning Boom Caught Almost Everyone by Surprise." *UnderstandingAI* (Substack), November 5, 2024. Accessed January 30, 2025.
137. LinkedIn Marketing Solutions. "The Rise of AI-Generated Content on LinkedIn." *LinkedIn Blog*, December 2024.
138. Marwala, Tshilidzi. "The Algorithmic Problem in Artificial Intelligence Governance." *United Nations University*, January 23, 2025.

139. MastersInAI.org. "AI's Impact on Major Industries." Accessed January 18, 2025.
140. Mintzberg, Henry. *Mintzberg on Management: Inside Our Strange World of Organizations*. New York: Free Press, 1989.
141. Montag, Christian, Benjamin Becker, and Benjamin J. Li. "On Trust in Humans and Trust in Artificial Intelligence: A Study with Samples from Singapore and Germany Extending Recent Research." *Computers in Human Behavior: Artificial Humans* 2, no. 2 (2024): 100070.
142. Nettavisen. "Statsbudsjettet: Norsk økonomi mot et vendepunkt – eksplosjon i offentlige utgifter." October 2024. Accessed January 30, 2025.
143. Norges Bank Investment Management. "Ansvarlig kunstig intelligens." NBIM, 2023. Accessed January 30, 2025. https://www.nbim.no/no/nyheter-oginnsikt/vare-synspunkt/2023/responsible-artificial-intelligence/. ———.
144. "Fondets verdi." 2025. Accessed January 30, 2025. https://www.nbim.no/no/investeringene/fondetsverdi/.
145. Northeastern University. "What Is Jevons Paradox? And Why It May—or May Not—Predict AI's Future." February 7, 2025. https://news.northeastern.edu/2025/02/07/jevons-paradox-ai-future/.
146. OsloMet – Oslo Metropolitan University. "An Out-of-Control Race: Why We Fear Artificial Intelligence." Accessed January 30, 2025. https://www.oslomet.no/en/research/featured-research/an-out-of-control-race-why-we-fear-artificial-intelligence.
147. Powell, B. B. *Writing: Theory and History of the Technology of Civilization*. London: Wiley Blackwell, 2009.

148. Project Management Institute. "AI Innovators: Cracking the Code to Project Performance." *Pulse of the Profession*. Accessed May 4, 2025.

149. Q.ai. "Google Invests in Anthropic for $2 Billion as AI Race Heats Up." *Forbes*, October 31, 2023. Accessed January 30, 2025.

150. Revel, Jacques. "White-Collar Workers, History of." In *International Encyclopedia of the Social & Behavioral Sciences*, edited by Neil J. Smelser and Paul B. Baltes. Oxford: Pergamon, 2001.

151. Rivery. "Data Statistics 2025: How Much Data Is There in the World?." *Rivery Blog*, 2025. Accessed January 30, 2025.

152. Russell, Bertrand. *The History of Western Philosophy*. London: George Allen & Unwin, 1945.

153. S&P Dow Jones Indices. "SPIVA US Scorecard: Year-End 2019." 2020. Accessed January 30, 2025.

154. SAP SE. "Introducing the AI Coach: Elevating Human–Machine Collaboration." *SAP News Center*, February 2024. https://news.sap.com.

155. Schmandt-Besserat, D. *How Writing Came About*. Austin: University of Texas Press, 1996.

156. Schumpeter, Joseph A. *Capitalism, Socialism, and Democracy*. New York: Harper & Brothers, 1942.

157. Schwarzmüller, Tanja, Prisca Brosi, Denis Duman, and Isabell M. Welpe. "How Does the Digital Transformation Affect Organizations? Key Themes of Change in Work Design and Leadership." *Management Review* 29, no. 2 (2018): 114–138.

158. Servoz, M. "AI: The Future of Work? Work of the Future!." *European Commission*, 2019. https://ec.europa.eu/digital-single-market/en/news/future-work-work-futur.

159. Siegel, Ethan. "Ask Ethan: How Do We Know the Universe Is 13.8 Billion Years Old?." *Big Think*, October 22, 2021.

160. Slodkowski, Antoni. "AI Is Cutting White-Collar Jobs." *Global Finance Magazine*, January 24, 2024. Accessed May 3, 2025.
161. Smith, J., A. Lee, and P. Gupta. "Impact of AI Tools on Management Consulting Tasks." *Journal of Business Research* 56, no. 4 (2023): 412–29.
162. SOAX Research. "How Much Data Is Generated Every Day?." 2025. Accessed January 30, 2025.
163. Song, Binyang, Qihao Zhu, and Jianxi Luo. "Human-AI Collaboration by Design." In *International Design Conference – Design 2024*. Cambridge: Cambridge University Press, 2024.
164. Spanish Ministry of Finance. "Proyecto FRAUDE: Data-Driven Tax Fraud Detection." Government of Spain, 2023. https://www.minhafp.gob.es.
165. Spitzberg, Brian H. "The Composition of Competence: Communication Skills." In *Communication Competence*, edited by Annegret F. Hannawa and Brian H. Spitzberg. Berlin: De Gruyter Mouton, 2015.
166. SSB (Statistisk sentralbyrå). "Nasjonalregnskap." 2025. https://www.ssb.no/nasjonalregnskap-og-konjunkturer/nasjonalregnskap/statistikk/nasjonalregnskap.
167. Standage, Tom. *The Victorian Internet: The Remarkable Story of the Telegraph and the Nineteenth Century's On-Line Pioneers*. New York: Walker & Co., 1998.
168. Statista. "Share of AI-Generated Articles on Fortune 500 Company Blogs, 2024."
169. Stavrianos, L. *Lifelines from Our Past: A New World History*. London: Routledge, 1997.
170. Taylor, Frederick W. *The Principles of Scientific Management*. New York: Harper & Brothers, 1911.
171. Thompson, E. P. *The Making of the English Working Class*. London: Victor Gollancz, 1963.

172. Tong, S., N. Jia, X. Luo, and Z. Fang. "The Janus Face of Artificial Intelligence Feedback: Deployment versus Disclosure Effects on Employee Performance." *Strategic Management Journal* 42, no. 2021: 1600–1631. https://doi.org/10.1002/smj.3322.
173. Turing, A. M. "Computing Machinery and Intelligence." *Mind* 59, no. 236 (1950): 433–460. Accessed January 30, 2025.
174. Velldal, Erik. "Store skritt mot norsk svar på ChatGPT." *Titan.uio.no*, March 6, 2024. https://www.titan.uio.no/teknologi/2024/store-skritt-mot-norsk-svar-pa-chatgpt-.html.
175. World Economic Forum. *The Future of Jobs Report 2025*. Geneva: World Economic Forum, 2025. https://reports.weforum.org/docs/WEF_Future_of_Jobs_Report_2025.pdf.
176. World History Encyclopedia. "Writing." Accessed May 3, 2025. https://www.worldhistory.org/writing/.

www.ingramcontent.com/pod-product-compliance
Lightning Source LLC
LaVergne TN
LVHW091659070526
838199LV00050B/2209